EVERYTHING

AND

NOTHING

AT ONCE

EVERYTHING
AND
NOTHING
AT ONCE

A BLACK MAN'S REIMAGINED SOUNDTRACK
FOR THE FUTURE

JOÉL LEON

HENRY HOLT AND COMPANY

NEW YORK

Henry Holt and Company
Publishers since 1866
120 Broadway
New York, New York 10271
www.henryholt.com

Henry Holt® and Ⓗ® are registered trademarks of Macmillan Publishing
Group, LLC.

Part of "A Conversation on Afro-Normalism" was published on Ebony.com,
April 25, 2021; "Our Poetry Will Save the World" was included in the Our Human
Family anthology "Equal People" on Medium.com, May 15, 2020; a portion of
"The Eulogy of Charles Lorenzo" was published as "As a Black Man in America,
I Feel Death Looming Every Day" in the *New York Times*, December 5, 2021;
portions of "What Kind of Black Are You?" were published as "Don't Be a
Fuckboy—Don't, Just Don't . . ." in *Those People*, April 29, 2017.

Library of Congress Cataloging-in-Publication Data

Names: Daniels, Joel L., author.
Title: Everything and nothing at once : a Black man's reimagined
    soundtrack for the future / Joël Leon
Other titles: Black man's reimagined soundtrack for the future
Description: First edition | New York : Henry Holt and Company, 2024
Identifiers: LCCN 2023054873 | ISBN 9781250887108 (hardcover) |
    ISBN 9781250887115 (ebook)
Subjects: African American men—New York (State)—New York—Biography. |
    African Americans—New York—Biography. | African American celebrities—
    United States—History—21st century. | African American celebrities—United
    States—History—20th century. | Masculinity—United States. | United States—
    Race relations. | New York (N.Y.)—Biography.
Classification: LCC F128.57.D36 A3 2024 | DDC 974.700496/0730092 [B]—
    dc23/eng/20231220
LC record available at https://lccn.loc.gov/2023054873

Our books may be purchased in bulk for promotional, educational,
or business use. Please contact your local bookseller or the Macmillan
Corporate and Premium Sales Department at (800) 221–7945, extension 5442,
or by e-mail at MacmillanSpecialMarkets@macmillan.com.

First Edition 2024

Designed by Omar Chapa

All emojis designed by OpenMoji—the open-source emoji and
icon project. License: CC BY-SA 4.0

Printed in the United States of America

1   3   5   7   9   10   8   6   4   2

Dedicated to Linda T. and Charles Lorenzo—great trees bear miraculous fruit. Thank you for tending to my garden as best as you could. This book is my offering back to you. I love you.

I'm just like everybody else man
An average nigga with above-average potential
You know what I mean?

—DE LA SOUL, "THE GRIND DATE"
(FEAT. BÖNZ MALONE)

I have spent my entire writing life trying to make sure that the white gaze was not the dominant one in any of my books.

—TONI MORRISON

Tracklisting

EVERYTHING
AND
NOTHING
AT ONCE

What Kind of Black Are You?

All I've ever done, all I've known to do, is make a home out of language. I wrote my first book at fourteen years old. That book currently sits in a box in the closet of my old bedroom in my mother's apartment in the Bronx. The book started across two summers: the summer spent in Baton Rouge, Louisiana, with my cousins and the summer spent in Indianapolis with my sister, Tanja. I didn't know I had a sister until I was ten years old, her being the offspring of my father, who, unbeknownst to my brother and me, had a previous relationship before he met my mother. My cousin Leah gave me a collection of African American essays and poems written between the 1800s and the early 1970s, a foundation for my exploration into Blackness. My summer with my sister, my nephews, and my then brother-in-law Sean offered me three things: a newfound work ethic, the church . . . and puberty. Sean would have me trail him from salon to salon while he got his and my sister's business off the ground: a clothing boutique bringing the fashions of New York City to the Midwest. I spent days hauling plastic bags full of Enyce, Karl Kani, and Avirex gear. Think of Tyrese's character in the film *Baby Boy* but with a teenage sidekick to drive up the cuteness ratio. Outside of the grueling heat and sense of civic duty required to sell gear to Black women looking to style their kiddos and beaus, I was also doing a lot of reading and a lot of churchgoing. My Indianapolis summers also put me in a recording studio for the first time. Sean wanted to promote their clothing business, so he enlisted me and a couple of the younger church boys to essentially record rap jingles. They wrote theirs, I freestyled mine off the top of my head for the duration of the session. The summer prior to that, in Baton Rouge, had me go to my first party. A fight almost broke out between two rival neighborhoods. The security guard working the event plainly explained to the high-strung teens, "Y'all got all these girls in here and y'all wanna fight?!" Those summers began Bloodlines, my collection of essays, all handwritten, where I began exploring language. It was the first time, outside of the little poems I would write in grade school for homies trying to mack to the girls in our school and the sports column I wrote for our grade school newspaper, that I had started putting pen to paper to speak to the things I was still learning the language for. Every rap, every poem, and every essay since then has been reintroducing myself to myself for the first time. This endeavor is no different I suppose.

I am both greeting and grieving myself. There are endings and beginnings. As a Black father to two Black girls, there is rarely if ever a moment when I am not fully aware of what that means within the context of the world we are living in today. There is almost always something at stake, something to live for and fight for. And isn't that what manhood is supposed to be? If it is not hard or difficult then it must not be worth it. But I've decided for myself, for my girls, for my partner and family and friends and community, I want ease above all else. I want to make and leave room for a different way of being that doesn't subscribe to the notion that our pain, suffering, and trauma need to play a starring role in the stories of being. The greeting of myself is the reintroduction.

Lauryn Hill talks about having to reintroduce herself to her parents. Because there was a shift, a transformation. And while doing so, there is also a dying. For in the rebirth, there is also a conclusion, a burying of what needs to die to allow something new to live. It feels at times that collectively we are at the intersections of both. I've found it most helpful to meet the expansiveness of the moment by expanding right along with it. We are achieving so much and yet, in parallel, are losing so much in the process. This time we're in feels like a reflection point—an opportunity to sit with what was and has been, and the potential in what could be. In that potential, is love. Blackness is love, to me. To be loved is also very Black. And if we are looking at Blackness through that lens, then that love exists beyond a romantic sense of love and travels deeper into the vortex of humanity as a whole. Because to embody the fullness of Blackness and the spectrums of Black masculinity that exist within that framework, we get to reimagine what Blackness means with a new set of eyes and a new set of rules to play with.

I love being Black. Being Black is a birthright privilege, and a rite of passage, like learning how to parallel park or double Dutch. But just as much as I love being Black, I love being able to say I'm Black. The ability to speak, to use words, to use language, that ability to speak to a truth, to our ancestors—I'm in love with that, too. I am in love with language, with the languid and the lusty. With the length of a page and latitude of a levee

breakage. It is this love of words and their use that has moved me
to look at Blackness. Being Black is a noun and a verb. I learned
this by looking in mirrors, staring at my reflection, standing
naked, and seeing Black skin, Black body—my Blackness staring
back at me. I saw a thing, being. And leaving my family's two-
bedroom apartment on Creston Avenue in the Bronx, going outside showed me what Black was also *doing*. Doing Blackness as
a person living and breathing—dapping up elders, ducking into
bodegas for bacon, egg, and cheese sandwiches, reciting rap lyrics I learned from Video Music Box and snippets of the cassette
tapes my big brother D would cop near the D train on Fordham
Road in the Bronx.

Growing up, I learned that being Black is an all-
encompassing everything—it is both whirlwind and movement, progress and processed hair; it is fistfights and chicken
spots with "Fried Chicken" at the end of each title. It is liquor
in barbershops and boyfriends in hair salons; it is long acrylics
like Coko from the girl group SWV wore in her falsetto high
notes during *Showtime at the Apollo*. Her stiletto heels set the
benchmark for anything vocals-related in R&B videos during
my formative 1990s years. These videos and the Blackness in
them are what my younger self would watch and stare at, their
Blackness and the volume in them staring right back. I'd be
looking at all the caramel Black girls with the door knockers
on, clutching their earlobes to the ends of the earth, weave tips
reaching their waists. I say caramel because it was also here
where I learned that light-skinned was preferable; that color-
ism was a pseudonym for "acceptable." These are all constructs,
binaries meant to be broken and laid out on the living room
carpet for us all to bear witness to, a collective sigh of relief that

the baggage of titles and labels can be eschewed for a higher sense of being and self we often aren't afforded the luxury to have. Early on, I learned that masculinity for a Black man is a tapestry of images pulled together from the media portrayals of what you were "supposed" to have—the exotic, light-skinned, curly-haired girl in haute clothes modeling for cameras; the car with the roof missing, money flying out of the windows, gold chains attached to bodies like tattoos. To be Black, to be a Black man in the era I grew up in, was easily everything and nothing at once. And to exist in that, to have that live both in you and on you, like a tattoo that is at once foreign and also embedded in you with the ink forever drying, is a hard thing to grapple with.

The totality of that experience is also hard to put into words. Much of my journey and purpose has been in translating my Blackness and my experiences surrounding Blackness, not for white eyes or the white gaze, but for Black folks who have struggled with having the language to describe how they view the world. The words and ways of expression I lacked then now show up in the prosaic language I use to illustrate those times now. This language is now more visual than anything else, and as I've gotten older, the language I have learned to use to express my Blackness has shifted. Blackness has shifted.

It was me walking the streets of New York on sunshine-soaked summer days, me and the ragtag, assembled crew of hood boogers trapezing the block, looking for somebody else's parked car to perch on. In those days, we'd sit idle and watch our older brothers and friends passing a brown paper bag or a football around while the stories were rehashed—who fucked whom, who shot whom, who got slapped for what. We'd wait to be called in for a game, and some of us would have already had a pass of whatever was in the crinkled container that shielded the rest of the world from its contents. In those days, we did not punctuate words and did not use the right grammar in any of our sentences. In that era of Blackness, we were reckless and carefree enough to pee in the streets, pants hung low, eyes glued to the concrete. In that era, I wanted a gold chain, we all wanted a gold chain because your gold chain was your flex. So was your car. Your light-skinned girlfriend. Your piece. Your J's. I wanted wanted wanted, but couldn't afford, so therefore I couldn't have. All of these things attached to what I thought I was supposed to be as a Black man. That language was forcibly handed to me, a language I was told to own by others who had been told to do the same, without question. We learned this language because we were taught this language: this language of mistrust, of machismo by any means.

I thought I was close to what I believed was the right way to be Black, and had the right kind of language needed to survive. But then I'd watch *Martin* and see how fucked-up Martin was to Gina and how light she was and how dark Pam was but Pam was the butt of every joke. I'd laugh because they were telling us how to be Black men. No one tells us that our manhood is not about Black women or white supremacy or fire hoses, about lusting after white women or lean or Black & Milds; not about Mike Brown or Jim Brown or James Brown or O.J. running in the airport, or driving in the Bronco during the Knicks vs. Rockets final; not about loosies or "I can't breathe" or asking for your dead mama for nine minutes with a knee in your neck, or about knowing the math and supreme knowledge.

That's because no one taught us feelings. Nobody taught

Black boys how to feel things. No one around us knew how. No one told us feeling things mattered just as much as the things you wanted on your neck, in your wallet, in your pants. What I did learn from the culture, what I absorbed growing up, was that white would always be right; that Black women were side characters or nonexistent; that Black men were good for comic relief but not good enough for names in title cards at the beginning of any sitcom; that Black death was a laugh track; that if I just worked as hard as the white people on TV I could be successful on my terms. And maybe I didn't aspire to that success, but I could see it in my peripheral, knowing it was there. The same way I would watch TV and I'd see the hot white girl, never the hot Black girl. The Black girl was never labeled as "hot" or a catch. Sometimes, the Black girl wasn't even on-screen. And when she was, she wasn't the star, she wasn't painted as desirable. I learned it but didn't know I was learning it. None of us did. This was the language they gave us. The language we never asked for. I came up with my own. Here are my ten Be a Better Black Man Commandments:

I.

1. If you're a good guy, you don't gotta keep saying you're a good guy. In fact, just stop saying who and what you are and:

   A. Let others do that for you and—

   B. Just do the things that SHOW who you are. Normally, it's the dude puffing his chest out in the quest to be the all-mighty alpha who has the least valuable thing to add to the conversation.

      Also, just shut the fuck up more often. Period.

II.

1. If she turns you down, walk away, holmes. Like, really. Do some yoga, contemplate life, jog around the block, call ya moms . . .
2. Whatever.
3. But, whatever you do, leave her the fuck alone, bruh.

III.

1. Give up ya seat, fam. On the bus, on the train. Like, I get it. You had a hard day, too. You was at ya desk flirting with ya work wife, or you was standing up all day at the construction site working for The Man. I feel you. But, she had to go through shit you can't even fathom. Plus, just a nice fucking thing to do. It ain't that serious.
2. You can sit yo' ass down when you get home. I know you got a couch at the crib, shun.

IV.

1. Be honest. Like, I done had some very fuckboy moments. I've lied, I've cheated, made promises I ain't keep, ran from situations with no real explanation as to why.
2. All you got is ya word. Stand by it.
3. Stand behind it. If you are honest FROM THE JUMP, it just saves you a whole lotta trouble. Someone may still get hurt or even hate your existence, but hey, at least you can say you were up front. Intentions are everything. EVERYTHING. Be aware of yours. Be

honest with the people in your life. But most importantly, be yourself.

V.

1. Stop trying to police feelings, hair, body parts, clothing . . .
2. JUST STOP!
3. Yes, we live in a free society, with free will. Deal. People will do and/or say what they want, how they want, and when they wanna do it.
4. Yes, you can have an opinion. But said opinion does not have to be demeaning or offensive. She's breastfeeding in public? That bothers you? You saying anything gonna make her say, "You know what, lemme stop doing this natural thing with my natural body that ya natural ass mama did for you when you was a little-ass person?"
5. Nah. So stop.
6. She's twerking? Bet ya moms woulda twerked for MLK if he came down 138th and the Grand Concourse.
7. Check why YOU'RE offended, homie.

VI.

1. Stop catcalling. Just stop. There's mucho places to get ya holla' on: the club, library, college campus, class, bar, museum, party, coffee shop, concert, zoo, aquarium, a baseball game, at work, the dentist's office . . .

2. Just don't do it in the street.

3. And if you reeeeeally need to have the convo, don't
    grab her arm or pull her, champ. If she got ear-
    phones in, let her be.

4. And unless you are also reading The Framework for
    Dissecting White Male Privilege in the Twenty-First
    Century, let her be. Smile, and keep it moving.

5. I just made that title up. Cool title, though, huh?

VII.

1. Do not send unrequested dick pics. Do not send
    unrequested dick pics. Do not send unrequested
    dick pics. Do not send unrequested dick pics. Do
    not send unrequested dick pics. Do not send unre-
    quested dick pics. Do not send unrequested dick
    pics. Do not send unrequested dick pics. Do not send
    unrequested dick pics. Do not send unrequested dick
    pics. Do not send unrequested dick pics. Do not send
    unrequested dick pics. Do not send unrequested dick
    pics. Do not send unrequested dick pics. Do not send
    unrequested dick pics. Do not send unrequested dick
    pics. Do not send unrequested dick pics. Do not send
    unrequested dick pics. Do not send unrequested
    dick pics. Do not send unrequested dick pics. Do not
    send unrequested dick pics.

2. DO. NOT.

VIII.

1. Don't hit her. Don't rationalize hitting her. Don't
    make veiled comments about hitting her. If she's

pregnant don't threaten her with hitting her. If you ain't laying hands on her for a massage, a prayer, or some coital action, nah. No excuse . . .

2. None.

3. She tryna' put hands on you? Walk away, call the police, jump out a window, I dunno . . .

4. Just, nah.

IX.

1. Don't be a creep. Don't follow her home. Don't send creepy texts and DMs. Don't call her a thot or a bitch or a ho or a slut when she curve you. That's life, man. Dust ya self off. You will live.

X.

1. Be aware of your privilege as a man and don't use it to be a coward or a sucker by saying and doing things to take advantage. Be understanding, LISTEN to others. Just because you hurt doesn't mean you get to hurt another. I know we as men have been taught that's soft or whatever, but we gotta invest time for love and healing and compassion and understanding. That's real strength. You wanna lead with machismo and brute force? Cool. Just know you won't last very long. The journey we on ain't for the faint of heart. Leave a stamp on the world that matters. In every interaction, be humble and gentle and sincere. The wind can be gentle and firm. It's still the wind, though. So, be that.

No one teaches you how to talk about being a Black boy. No one gives you *that* language. You learn that on your own, like I did. I learned it from watching it: from my window, at train stations, at bus stops, and in front of bodegas. Then one day you grow up with your dick in one hand and if you're lucky enough maybe a diploma in the other, and the world tries to tell you how to be a Black man in America. We think we are connected to what it means to be a man because we are told to do manly things, and so some of us do them and some of us don't. Some of us do them well and some poorly. This doing and not doing is essentially the undoing of it all, because so much value is placed in the boxes and categories that we have been told are supposed to define manhood. The shoes that fit us at eight will not fit us at eighteen, yet arbitrary rules created largely by an oppressed society that once believed the earth was flat and that Black people weren't even considered to be human have our views of what it means to be Black and to be a man in a vise grip.

Much of how we view and talk about men and Black men and roles and our identities is wrapped in customary traditions. Traditions that are carried over and never questioned. Because to question them would mean challenging their validity. And challenging that means we would have to then challenge all the other systems that benefit from those traditions and ideas. Men, especially Black men, are seen as providers. There is a distinct need for us to be producers of work, to do work, to make work happen. We are to protect, expected to, and if there is lack in any way where protection does not seem possible, we are considered weak and disposable. There is an unspoken, expected weight we are meant to bear. And we are to carry that weight without sweat, without grimace; without complaint or worry. We are beautiful Black machines, are robots void of feeling. Chivalry is a part of that time-honored tradition—the notion that there are things that must be done in order to prove that we are indeed men and are showing up as men.

And if those things are not being done, without question, what kind of Black man are you? Slave to the patriarchy, to the patterns that live as fabric on us, no? Walk on the right side of the road. Put yourself in danger, in harm's way. Be the one to be hurt first. Protect at all costs, without the flinching that happens when the heat from the exhaust gets too close for comfort. Walk into the fray. Defend defend defend. Pay for everything. Take charge. Be a leader. I would often say my mother gave me all the language I needed and required to be a better human, to be a better man in whichever ways society had expected of me. But what I lacked were tools: functional, tangible ways to apply these ideas and terms in the real world. In the real world, whining my waist as an Afro-Caribbean man could be seen as effeminate. Having queer-identifying, gay male friends also made you gay and queer. Riding the train home from school, pants cuffed slightly, also opened me up to being called a faggot by grown men. There are traditions we uphold and there are still rules to follow. Walking home in Brooklyn one day, I overheard a young Black boy, no more than nine, sobbing to whom I perceived to be his mother. She lashed out at him, "Stop crying like a little bitch. You acting like a faggot right now." At that moment, I realized how hot and frustrated, and tired she must have been. Unable to see how masculinity has played out in her own life, perhaps in both past and present. That boy was expected to stand on the right side of the road, too. And be either heralded or chastised for it, either in public or private, for not adhering to and following the precedents laid out before him. As I walked by them, I had a separate conversation in my head, one that would propel me and the young boy into the future: Who would he become? What would he aspire to? Who would he harm? Himself? Others? None of my questions would sit in the space of "if" but "when." It is expected that someone so young and so available be swayed by what the whims of the world dictate safety looks like and would have those same whims lean into the outward-facing punishment of himself and others that comes from being chastised and punished by the same persons charged with creating parameters for how your safety is measured: your parents and guardians. In that moment of reflection, I also had to ask what would a masculine man do.

We so often say what we would do when the challenges of real-life humanity show up at our door. I often think that a real man would have confronted her, and challenged her use of the language. Would that have been safe for the boy? Would that have been safe for her? Masculinity also doesn't shy away from ego—it leans in wholeheartedly, chest out and bare. I think about that boy often. About the ways the world will wilt and deflower him to make him into a machine, to turn him into the robot cyborg metal that will be as shiny and as strong as the cars he is to be hit by in order to protect whoever is on the inside of the road. Tradition. How much of what we hold on to is about carrying over the energy of our ancestors? How much of our traditions are boxing us into ideas that no longer hold precedence? What does it look like to hold space for the past while also understanding that not everything in the past needs to play a part in how we think about the present and our collective futures?

Being Black, for me, has always been about everything and nothing at once, and the coded language in between. It is all of those things and none of those things. Blackness is not a monolith—it is as nuanced, as different, and as bold as our hairstyles, our fashion choices, and our vernacular. It is the space between a comma and a bar, a breath taken or breaths strangled out of us. Because of this, we are so much more than whatever may live between the lines, between the highs, the feigned hubris and machismo and flavor and style we so casually give to white consumerism, to money-making industries hell-bent on taking all that is ours and selling it back to the highest bidder. We talk different because our uncles did, and their brothers did and their fathers did and their aunties and barbers and cousins and cellmates and codefendants and classmates did, too. We teetered between block and boardroom with an enviable ease, with easels between our teeth, painting worlds with words and coded language meant for only us. Being Black for me has always meant being in the know when no one else knew but us, a stellar star of a secret, blending in and bleeding out and being closeted or being out and free, and our "about us" is always something enviable and new. And in between the contrasts and the constants of all those things there is some sort of Claymation manhood being bought, built, sold, and commodified. There are constructs that I have been forced to deconstruct and unlearn. Unlearning has forced me to reconsider and investigate what I may have deemed to be a solid definition of

Blackness. But Blackness is too fluid to be neatly defined, to be pigeonholed and labeled.

Whether you are Black, have a Black friend, or wish you could be Black without the work, à la Rachael Dolezal, there is probably some long-standing lens through which you have viewed Blackness. These are the conditions in which manhood is tested and fortified live or whatever Talib Kweli said. These are the spoken rules, the time-honored traditions passed around in red Hennessy-filled red cups shared at summery backyard barbecues. You hold doors, you fight off intruders, you pull out chairs, you pay the rent, you pay the bills; you're to remain silent because women love that but you're also to be loud when you need be because women love that, too; be nice with your hands in case of an emergency. Pump the gas, change the flat tire. Because if you cannot do these physical things, a man with more physicality, more bravado, will replace you. Because you are disposable at best if you are not meeting the bill.

Who am I if I am not a Black man? Can I be anything else other than that? And if I am more than the construct, if we are more than the sum of our inextricable parts, does that make the construct worth something meant to be identified with? Meaning, if all we are deemed to be are men who are only Black, that leaves no room for us to be anything else. I want us to take our identities, these identifiers that have become the signatures for how we à la carte our experiences as Black, living beings, hold them up to the light, and see if it still sticks. I want us to be more curious, a bit more intentional, a tad bit more loving, and a lot more introspective about Blackness, about the ways we talk about manhood, about growing up as a Black boy who will surely also become a Black man (that is of course if time, and the police, and renegade white, racist vigilantes permit). And reflect on how much space we can collectively hold for us not to be defined by what we think we know but rather by what we have yet to imagine. Can we be bolder in our thinking and in our rhetoric? Can we be sharper, hungrier for something that loves beyond the stereotypes of heteronormative behaviors, which would rather see us be slaves to predetermined versions of man, rather than an open, freer type of masculinity that can just be. I wanted to write a book that examined the spectrum of Black masculinity with language that didn't feel linear, or like a copy and paste. My journey as a Black man has been a long, arduous one, filled with many a mistake. I've been a misogynist, a narcissist, a cheater, a liar, and a manipulator; I've been sexually abused, scared, and suicidal. I've also been joyful, abundantly happy, overwhelmed with love, empathy, compassion, and spirit. Being Black is complex. Being a Black man is another intersection. But so often, Black manhood is talked about through the lens of Black men in relationship to Black women, to white women, to white supremacy, to sports and hip-hop. I aim to tear apart, to pick, to probe, and to ponder. In reality, I am writing this book for me—lower-middle-class, sometimes poor, sometimes too nerdy and too romantic and too lost and too soft and all the *too*s that make me.

The essays in this collection touch on everything from mental health and suicidal ideations, to parenting and fatherhood, to race. I'm not some PhD or a scholar with a master's degree. I wouldn't dare consider myself an intellectual. For better or worse, I am here showing up with the language I have. I am flawed. I have made mistakes. I've been unfaithful. I've lied and misled. I've fallen short of who I'd have liked to be on too many occasions to count. I will forever be a work in progress. We all are. I am not only pushing myself to be better. But I want to push all Black men to be better. I want all of society to just be better in general. But I think starting with the community closest to me is a good place for this work to live. By no means is this exhaustive; this is not remotely close to the totality of the Black masculine experience, not by a long stretch. This is merely an introspective look at Black masculinity from my personal experience, using personal narrative as a way in.

My hope is that this will encourage other cis-hetero able-bodied Black men to dig deeper, to engage with their own sense of entitlement, of shame, fear, and vulnerability, so we can be better accomplices and allies to all members of our community. We implore the white community to talk to themselves about themselves. I ask us to do the same. This body of work is my way of examining this moment and encouraging all of us to do the same with an open mind and an open heart. What does it mean to be a Black man, now? I'm not sure I have the right language for that. My goal is to try to find it.

And with that, hopefully, we'll discover ways to redefine what our Blackness gets to be. Because the New Black will play tennis and win awards and break cardboard stereotypes with their feet. She will throw on ballerina slippers and dance and frolic in her Blackness. She will have blue hair and be a gymnast, or an Afro cloud as high as Mars. The New Black will bring old Blacks in to teach dance to Black magical little girls in the house American slaves built. The New Black comes equipped with director's chair accessories, natural hair products, Forbes 30 Under 30 mentions, and viral hashtags. The New Black will write books about Blackness and teach us about reparations, will make songs about Jackson 5 nostrils, and dance with Black berets at big-ass football parties. New Blacks ask socialists what are they doing now, and ask progressives about the unlawful imprisonment of young Blacks. New Blacks aim to offend you at the sheer thought of the newness of their Blackness. The New Black comes with Ultralight Beams. The New Black will not ask questions or ask for a seat, or suggestions. The New Black dismantles old ideas and old ideals and deals with the old structure per Industry Rule # 4080, which applied to record company people, as per Q-Tip, but proves to be widely applicable in almost every other context possible when talking about anything America-related: People can be shady. Move accordingly.

But while sifting through this New Black consciousness, one may begin to ask, What kind of Black are you?

Are you a brown paper bag Black? Are you surveillance cameras abounding and mall security guard Black? Are you death by asphyxiation in a jail cell Black? Are you when you get on you gonna marry a white girl, or a Kardashian, Black? Are you a white Bronco Black? Perhaps you are a you don't sag your pants, where are your parents, shhh take these Quaaludes Black? You may be the "raise your hand in class" kind of Black, or "make fun of the Black kid who raised his hand in class" kind of Black. Perhaps you don't even identify as Black. You don't want to be tied or bogged down by labels. Maybe your father is Caribbean with a dash of Scottish and New Wave European, and your mother is German, Puerto Rican, South African, Guyanese, and 10 percent Australian. But, you got a record with Snoop? You in a Tyler Perry movie snapping your neck and smacking gum?

You in.

Join the club. Grab you a bag of Flamin' Hot Cheetos and grape drink and have a seat. Better stop at your local DMV and get your driver's license updated to read Blacker Than the Blackest Motherfucker because to some, the percentages of Blackness, whether those are 100 percent or three-fifths are not enough. Maybe you could be the kind of Black who ridicules another Black for their choice of who they love, especially if they aren't Black. Because there are unspoken guidelines to your Blackness; there are penalties and consequences for stepping outside of the regulations preset long ago by elders who were finding their way between busing and lynchings, pork fat grease, ham hocks, and cotton bale finger pricks. In their eyes, to defy these laws is to defy yourself, to defy your people. Yes, your people. You are kin, even if you have not chosen to be. You will speak, must speak, to the soul and spirit of all those who share the complexion of you, the complexities of you.

They will tell you how Black you are, or aren't. They will tell you this based on your pigment, which HBCU you chose, what sorority you pledged. You know who the Soledad brothers are? Liquid Swords or Iron Man? You play spades? Dominoes? Can you handle a grill? How's your Cupid Shuffle? Electric Slide? Give me a quote from *Boyz n the Hood*. How about *Menace II Society*? Know the first verse of LL's "Around the Way Girl"? Know how to fry a chicken? Ever been to or hosted a deep fry? Loose definitions of what your Blackness means to you are not as important as the rigid caste system set in place that requires others to define for you what your Blackness means to everyone else. It will also place a *z* in place of an *s* when spelling out the word *others* because the standard, the rules, they are no longer the same because we have decided to change them, rename them something that better fits our today. Lauryn Hill so eloquently asked: "Who made these rules, I say? Who built these schools, I say?"

Word, Ms. Hill. Conflated stereotyped versions of stereotypes. They are exaggerated versions of themselves, we are made to be exaggerations of us, caricatures of the characters portrayed on lenses and screens both big and small. The middle ground, the gray areas, are traced and lined in chalk.

Certain kinds of Black cannot be washed away, cannot be dimmed or chained or rinsed off, held down or tied up. You cannot hide away a certain kind of Black—the kind that does not wait passively but is insistent on having a voice heard about and around and above the screeching of police bullet banter. This kind of Black has Barbie dolls created in her likeness. This New Black sounds like trap, sounds like Paak, or Pac. This Black celebrates magic in little Black girls, creates hashtags to help find kidnapped girls, creates dances, votes and puts people in office, runs for the mayor of Baltimore, and takes photos that get featured on the cover of *Time*. This Black redefines feminism, dissects intersectional feminists, tears down patriarchy, and detangles the roots of misogyny. This updated version of Black buys record labels. This new streamlined version drops albums at midnight with no press release or promotion, and sells her album to a major cell phone carrier and goes platinum before the album hits the shelves.

That certain kind of Black is all tied up and mixed in with all the other certain types of intersections that we either hero or vilify, depending on the flavor of the month. I want us to be able to hold a mirror up to all these things, while holding ourselves accountable. And that accountability gets to be met with forgiveness. It is also nuanced and happens on a case-by-case basis. And we get to factor in the context in which we are evaluating people, their Blackness, their intersections, their interactions, their shortcomings and triumphs, and how all those get to live in conjunction with one another. Like some beautiful gumbo. And while we hold our fave Black celebs to the fire, we must also do so with our parents, with our uncles; with our aunts who perpetuate the mythology of the Black men who must only provide and protect and nothing else. We must ask how we're all complicit in upholding the belief system and structures that keep us all placated and bound to certain ways of being. We also get to ask, Who is benefitting? And we get to hold the mirror up to ourselves first and foremost. And the more we do that, the more we can also look at others and how they show up for themselves: Black mothers, sons, daughters, partners. We can see people as more than their affixed labels and even views, and hold more room for their expansiveness. We are more than our beginnings and endings. We are more than the things we are shedding.

With this understanding came other questions: What kind of Black would I be, could I be? What kind of Black did I wish to be, to become? What kind of Black lives in me? What kind of Black died in order for my Black to live? How far will I go to acknowledge my Blackness, to live up to its potential?

This body of work has my body and breath in it. I spent a lot of my years trying to be somebody I wasn't because I wanted to make everyone else around me happy. Being an extraordinary Black. A talented Black. A nice Black. I want this work to maybe cut somebody else's time in half. This book is my offering to us, and to the younger me who just wanted to be loved but didn't have the language to say how. Writing this book has been my salvation. I hope it can be the same for whoever is reading this.

This journey all began by me simply asking myself, What kind of Black are you? Holding a mirror to all the versions of me, sometimes forcefully, sometimes gently, but always with love.

Belly

My belly is the shape of a rounded tire. I am tired of looking at it. Even now when I look at it, I think of its history, its story, its trajectory. I am forty-one. Which means my belly is forty-one, too. It is hairy. It is smooth, unlike me—wrinkled, weary. My belly does not feel forty-one, whatever forty-one is supposed to feel like. No one prepares a Black man for aging. Mainly because we don't expect to age. My belly feels like it has a life of its own. And my belly is the kind of belly I have learned to hide, to fit in and sneak into spaces like some sort of concealed weapon into a nightclub, the kind of nightclub we used to go to in my twenties when we would drink Incredible Hulks until we forgot who we kissed where, and we would parking-lot pimp, spitting whatever calcified game we learned from the elders around the way or from movies where brothers were generally cooler and more paid than we were until it was time to clock into our retail jobs, my belly in the shadows of my collared shirt the entire time. And so I buy extra-large T-shirts and I can fit in them now. Not like how I used to wear them, which was to purposely not fit them, wearing them like I saw my older brother do and the other brothers who weren't my blood but felt like it. We wore big clothes because that was the fashion of the day—everything oversize—food, jeans, T-shirts, personalities. When I suck in my stomach when I am walking in the street trying to look naturally slimmer than I am, or when I am on the train against the train doors it's because I am also trying to hide the years of semipoor living sitting inside of it. It is small enough and big enough, I guess, for my partner to rub on and say she enjoys it. I do not. Because it is a reminder that exists when at times I can slip into more comfortable distractions. When I am holding my breath in to suck it up like a human vacuum, I can imagine I am a deep-sea diver digging for ancient artifacts instead of an embarrassed adult man ashamed of the weight gain that nobody seems to notice but me. In my leaner, younger years my belly was not a belly or barely even a pouch. It used to fit in sizes smaller than larges and extra larges. Medium-size graphic tees were my thing. Standing as tall as my five foot nine would allow, my back straight, there could have even been a slight semblance of a six-pack rearing its cute little head. But I moved back home with my mother and stepfather after my first daughter was born, after the engagement had broken off and I had cheated. Twice. Before Aunty KK died and I wore my Ben Sherman checkered shirt to work and she told me how good I looked in it. And I gave the shirt away because who wants the shirt your aunty loved that you wore the day she died? And I was broke. And depressed. And about to have my first child. And still performing in the Lower East Side with the hopes that some non-talented major record label A&R would see our energetic but not exactly fully rehearsed hip-hop/soul/other world sounds band and decide to sign us on the spot, help us record an album, and take us on tour. So I did what anyone would do under those same given circumstances . . . I drank a lot of juice.

High-fructose corn syrup journeys galore. My mom and stepdad would make the trip to Costco's every other week and get the jumbo-size juices: exotic fruit flavors I'd drink straight from the bottle if I was desperate enough. When I was a kid, I would pray and wish the water fountains in school would have buttons that would let you select the kind of juice you wanted to come out of them. I'd go into restaurants and imagine myself jumping over the counters and drinking from all the soda machines. Anytime I was forced to drink water, I'd just imagine I'd be swimming in a pool of one of my favorite juices—Kool-Aid Kiwi Lime. Anything Tropicana or Minute Maid. Welch's White Grape Juice. Hawaiian Punch Fruit Juicy Red, Yellow, Orange, Green, and Blue. I memorized the songs in the commercials by heart. I'd drink the juice straight out of the container it came in. Grabbing a cup and pouring it took too long. And it tasted different. It didn't feel as edgy, as delicious. Sometimes it would drip down my chin and onto my shirt, red 40 and yellow 6 coming together and making a mini color palette portrait on my shirt. I told myself I'd open my own restaurant just so I could drink all the juice and eat all the food.

At my moms', I ate a lot of Kennedy's fried chicken. My order was almost always the same: popcorn chicken, fries, cheese drenched in even more cheese and hot sauce. A soda, generally a ginger ale or a grape soda, orange soda if I was feeling feisty. Kennedy Fried was my version of comfort food. It still is on some nights. My brother and I were raised on it. Maybe there are different variations of Kennedy's in your hood. There are definitely

in mine—Crown, Lincoln. On Decatur Street, there's Krazy BBQ
Chicken. Kennedy's was and is a hood staple. Depending on
what city you lived in and what hood you were from, a _____
Fried Chicken was your gateway drug. The menus are always the
same. They are colorful, they are large, and they have plenty of
numbers for all of the different varieties of easily reheated, frozen foods they serve as their delicacies. When we were younger,
Dwain would get the cheeseburger and an order of fries. You'd
get a free soda and a hot roll. And I'd wait for him to share it.
When he started making more money sometimes he'd get me my
own. Our routines almost always centered around food. When
D would take me to get my haircut at Tony's we'd stop by the
Fried Chicken & Seafood spot on the Grand Concourse right off
the Fordham Road D train stop, and we'd get a chicken cutlet
sandwich on white bread, mayonnaise and ketchup on the bread,
with a side order of fries doused in even more ketchup. As an
adult father, struggling to make ends meet, struggling to make
anything meet at all, there were late nights, coming back from
putting Lilah to bed, being tired, being on a train and thinking of my bed and a comfort meal. Also, knowing everything
would be closed but Taco Bell and Popeyes. So, it would be me
and my Kennedy Fried. My new routine became rushing to
leave work, picking up Lilah from day care, getting her dinner ready, putting her to bed in her mama's room in the private
house she lived in by Eastchester Road, and coming back home
on the Bee-Line bus and walking back to Creston Avenue, going
back to the same bedroom I grew up in, sans a bunk bed. I would
sit on that bed and stuff my face and be happy and sad at the
same time, watching whatever new documentary I could stream
off the Chromebook that I got during a Best Buy sale. Settling in

with my popcorn chicken takeout was the closest thing to love-making I had the time or room for. My belly thanked me for it by growing.

I wouldn't call us poor growing up. I always had a birthday cake and candles. I got gifts. My Gameboy was a cherished possession. Dr. Mario and a random fighting game that wasn't on my wish list but it didn't matter. McDonald's and Roy Rogers were for special occasions. I loved Roy Rogers because it smelled like fast food when you walked in. The grease and salt mixing and loving on each other. You could taste it when you walked in. It was across the street from the Fordham library. I remember most things based on their location to food. While growing up, even with the knowing that we had less than many, there were kids who had even less. I saw them and knew them. But it was little things that served as a footnote that let me know our lot in life: the green lunch tickets in elementary school that let you know you got free lunch. Uncle Winston bringing us groceries when the fridge was empty. My father leaving food stamps in the apartment (and me subsequently hiding them under my underwear in the dresser in the bedroom D and I shared, ashamed because I knew what real dollars looked like and these weren't it) or me getting SSI checks that my mom would use for school clothes and supplies. Ms. Helen gave us the hand-me-downs her sons no longer wore. NY Giants hoodies, rugby polos, and long-sleeve tees. On certain Fridays, if my father wasn't drunk or hadn't spent his own SSI check at whichever bar he fell asleep at or around, he'd bring me pizza: extra cheese with sausage. I'd eat and watch *The Super Mario Bros. Super Show!* on Fox 5, greasy fingers, deconstructed paper napkins abounding, eyes glued to Captain Lou Albano doing his best Mario impersonation. I'd lick my fingers and wipe the oil off with the back of my hand. On Friday nights, while my mother slept on the couch, resting before she'd have to leave for the night shift at Jacobi Hospital, I'd toast bread and spread mayonnaise on top while watching Balki make a fool of himself and the English language on *Perfect Strangers* on ABC 7 during the TGIF lineup. I was always hungry: hungry for attention, hungry for love, and hungry for food. No matter how much I got of anything, I always wanted more, needed more. If there was anything I loved more than sugary juice (and masturbation), it was food. My appetite was voracious, insatiable. Mainly because there were nights I could not have what I wanted, and on those nights what I craved more than anything else was food.

Food was my balm, my salve. So, I'd eat. Anything. I would rummage through the cupboards and not knowing how to cook meant I would just need to make things work. I opened cans of corned beef. I ate Vienna Sausages. I ate frozen sausage links, fearful to touch the stove because I didn't want to start a fire. I was scared and naive, an innocence that kept me from doing anything too harmful or too dangerous. When my brother would leave the leftover french fries he got from Woolworth, where he worked the kitchen, or the boneless chicken and pork fried rice he got from the Chinese food spot from around the way and didn't finish and left in the fridge, I'd sneak in and take as many small bites as I could in hopes he'd never notice. My nickname used to be Mikey, like Mikey from the old-school Life cereal commercials: "Give it to Mikey. Mikey will eat anything." If anyone had food left on their plate they didn't want to finish, I'd be anticipating the question, hoping they'd direct it toward me: "You want the rest of this?" This meant my mother shopped in the husky section of the V.I.M. clothing store, us finding the pants that were just the right kind of baggy, the belts my mom bought cinching the waistline, the hand-me-downs Ms. Helen gave my mom being put to good use, helping to hide my breasts.

You hide it so well, they say. I hear it often enough I could tattoo it on my head, could recite it like a rap lyric or a poem I used to know that still triggers me, still sits faintly in my chest. Because I know I do. I hide many a thing well.

It is an art, framing photos a certain way, posing and appropriate angles and getting the right kind of shirt with the right kind of fit to make sure nothing seems out of place. I am a Capricorn—a stubborn, hardheaded, and practical survivalist who would die without his image and ego. I am mindful of this because, who am I without my adequately attractive looks? I ask myself this question often as I stare at gray hairs, as I feel the weight of older New York City knees. Arthur C. Johnson wrote, "We should not avoid thinking about the loss of our abilities. On the contrary, we should lean into this thought—contemplate it, consider it, meditate on it." So, when I look at my belly, I think of how everything is starting to shift and change and morph into an older version of myself that my body is moving into but my heart is not willing to accept. My belly tells me so. When it is quiet enough, when the rain has slowed and the biker boys have tucked in for the night, when the bodega lights have turned down and their awnings and gates have closed, I can hear my belly. It calls for the fruit snacks, for the chips, for the late-night salty and sweet cravings that will temper me until the next craving.

In our history, being big and labeled as such was at one time considered to be noble, of royalty. I am not big. But my potbelly may say otherwise. I keep thinking if I am less heavy in my belly and more Black in my substance, I will love myself more. I

have decided already that having a six-pack will make me better. Still, my Iron Gym collects dust, and so I move it downstairs
in front of our building in Bed-Stuy because I know somebody
else will find use for this, this thing that tells you it will help
you make your body look like the white man on the cover of
the box. I gobble down Bojangles during layovers in airports,
my greasy hands fumbling over my phone screen while I think
about my eldest daughter in Houston I am on the way to see.
I'll maybe daydream of new push-up moves I will try in the
morning. When I look in the mirror four weeks later, I will smile
at my sweat, smirking at the near-invisible muscles showing
themselves in the mirror. I look at my man boobs in disgust,
asking if it was all the months of soy milk. When Bria touches
my body or tells me she loves it, I hate her for it, because how can
you love me so much? How can you lie so well? How can you
love the thing I loathe with everything I have, this belly that I
loathe so much that I will do nothing to change it but complain
about it, because that requires no intention or dedication, just
a big mouth? When my shirt sizes changed from the mediums
I would wear with suspenders to the large that I'm finding comfort in, all of it just another way for me to hide, I am
reminded of how I used to poke my stomach with a cutting knife
in elementary school. I was tired, and if I somehow poked hard
enough, the husky section at V.I.M. would be an afterthought
and my belly would be a balloon, deflating itself. The knife was
one my mom would sharpen from time to time, the same one
she would use to cut meat loaf, to slice bread pudding and sandwiches. I would stab hard enough to feel the point of steel poke
my bare skin but never drawing blood. Maybe I thought it was a
hot-air balloon that would burst and let all the air out and float

away with everything else my belly was hiding. My disgust and angst and hurt and anger would all trickle out along with it. The pain was less concerning than the need to feel it. Another way to hide and separate myself from everything else happening around me. The crumbling Bronx blocks we played freeze tag and baseball on, my angry father and eventually locked-up brother and overprotective mother. A way out was a cold knife to the belly sometimes.

The pants I used to own that once fit a few months ago, now cut into my waist during flights, a constant reminder of how my skin is fighting me, too; I unbutton them to breathe, to give myself space, to let the blood back in. When I talk or walk too long, I run out of breath. My lungs are tired of me. I cut my sentences shorter, giving my fat time to catch up to my thoughts. It is an exercise of holding the stomach in the street, a constant mirrored drive-by, looking into store and car windows to see if my bulge is noticeable enough. My belly is now a barrier to entry—to my partner, to my mother, to my daughters. They rarely see the gut as much as they'd like to. I have become a stealth shirt changer, hiding and covering up and turning my back whenever my partner gets too close, turning my body away from any mirrors that might reflect the shame. Or I may change in the living room away from the mirror and away from her gaze. I am ashamed of my belly, but my belly is not ashamed of anyone or anything. Holidays and family gatherings are the constant indication that we generally as a Black community lack the ability to speak about things like weight gain or even weight loss. We opt into the teasing that is often the way we show love, slight jabs that point to an awareness that something has changed: a belly, a bigger face, longer or shorter hair. And the remedy to most of these things is to either limit or add food. Food is a viable and valuable resource in a world full of food deserts and lack, the food that is available is a thing used to soak up our rage, our loss, and our heartache.

The way privilege works is simple—the more aware you are of it, the more it stinks and shows itself outwardly to any and all who want to winningly participate in pointing it out to you. Examples include: I always had an athletic build, so my able-bodied self can shield weight. I do not "show" fat. The fat I carry is the humorous, dad bod kind, the one patriarchy makes seem okay: chugging beers, remote control in hand, in front of the grill, not afraid to hide it. My privilege shows again because I am a man, and belly fat on men is not evil or wrong, no, not like the anonymous body-shamers with numbers for names and American flags and sports cars for profile pics who live on Instagram, who have made it an art to call out and demean women's bodies. This belly and body get a pass. It's comical. They make pilots centered around it. Affable and lovable, the love handles and dad belly are symbolic for court jesters causing a riot on-screen. A fat Black man is not political in any way, primarily because the fat Black man is generally not leading the charge for the body to be political. And in the spectrum of fat Black men, I'm just considered out of shape.

My belly wholeheartedly disagrees. My belly has thought of numerous ways to kill itself and me in our sleep, drown us in a sea of Hostess and Little Debbie; tank us to drown in the ocean of Pepsi products and Dole pineapple juice. My belly protrudes, and it is cute and cuddly, warm and bearlike. But the more I come over to my mother's on holidays and she tells me I am getting fat I prove her right and eat more cake, gulp more high-fructose corn syrup juice, drink more soda. I indulge and shrug and laugh and my belly laughs with me, too, and jiggles, and on my way home I can ignore it again and act like it doesn't exist. Even writing this now, I am prepared for all of my new social media followers to send me their trainer's numbers; my new friends who are not my actual friends, but the ones who read my words and feel like they are because I have made them feel like they all have space in my head (to offer me ideas for meal plans, new teas, vegan diets, and lists of superfoods); and then there will be others who will poke and prod and joke, sending me directions to the nearest gym or posting GIFs in my DMs from Weight Watchers commercials.

My weight, even in my husky phase, was well hidden. I was built like my father, like a southern Daniels man—broad-shouldered, a beer belly with no beer or alcoholic rage to show for it. My father's side of the family is all heavy—all thighs, neck bones, big bellies. Even now, I am my father in all the ways I wish I weren't but still admire—the thicker-than-life mustache and beard, the chiseled jawline, the shoulders. There is a picture of my father standing with boots on and a shirt too tight. He's standing in the flower shop holding a flower pot, and I cannot remember if he works there, if he's buying flowers for my mother or some random woman he's dating, or if he just happened to be hold-ing a flower pot and someone thought it was a nice enough shot to make a memory out of. Whatever that moment was, I always think about how I look like him when I stand in the mirror and I'm naked in only my skin or almost nude in my underwear, and how my belly bends the waist, overlaps and hangs, dangles and rests against the fabric, instead of standing sleek and solid like the washboard abs I see on Instagram or on *GQ* and *Esquire* covers. When I think of the pictures of my father, like the one where he is in that flower shop, with the hanging belly over the waistline of his jeans like an eager mass, anticipating the shirt will stretch, I see him fully. I know my family history: diabetes, high blood pressure, heart attacks, high cholesterol. Our big mirror from IKEA highlights all of this: the rolls, the stretch marks, the cellulite and dimples. I've begun taking pictures, but the *befores* and *afters* are still not ready yet, even though I am still contemplating posting a body-posi flick for the gram, but I'm not as confident or as cool in my physical as I used to be, as I wish I could be—age and gravity are my masters. I am fragile like the shipping boxes, the glass half-broken inside and all the other things that should have been wrapped well, not. Me and my belly, toiling and tumbling to the next buffet or $1 slice.

So, when I compare myself to or contrast myself with others, and begin to imagine taking my shirt off at the beach and not being ashamed or embarrassed or sad or miserable, I laugh because that is not at all possible. Everyone takes pictures of their *before* and *afters* and I celebrate them while wondering why my *before* is taking too long. My belly is an accumulation of all the trauma yet to be cleansed, all my *befores* coming to haunt me in Magna Vision, screening live on pay-per-view. When I see my belly I am not seeing my belly but I am seeing the sheer magnitude of my failures as a Black man showing itself in all the ways that society has told me I have failed: even with a home, a loving and doting partner, two beautiful, healthy little Black girls, I am still the light-skinned Black kid from the Bronx with a fragile ass ego; the same kid who girls wouldn't date because I was too nice or didn't have money. The same kid who was called gay and f*ggot by older boys because of my boot-cut jeans and "soft" ways.

When I take my shirt off now, I think about how my belly has never really left me. I would ask myself how I got here, but would not wait for an answer. But I didn't want one or need one. The asking alone was the only incessant thing that I was being called to do. An answer would be too much, too much soon. And I don't have time or room for it . . . my belly is enough. I fantasize about the flat tummy, about all the videos I will take lifting my shirt up. The more confident me who will get to wear whatever he wants in public without having to hold anything in. Will I start wearing muscle shirts? Heading to Dyckman during summers with gold chains to the max, arms too big for my shirts? The *after* me will flex for no reason in the mirror other than to get a glimpse of the solid core I've built doing all the gym routines taught me. The *after* me is going to have a whole highlight on Instagram titled ABS, will have a whole Twitter thread about clean eating and workouts for dads who are tired of having dad bodies that get celebrated in sitcoms, are tolerated by lovers, but made fun of and discarded in group chats. I say all of this while recognizing all of this feels like some slow jerk off for patriarchy and male privilege and color privilege and all the other privileges that I've been afforded. I acknowledge the potential silliness that comes with hearing a man complain about something as trivial as belly fat, knowing that there are those who suffer from bulimia, those who are medically diagnosed as overweight and have been on the receiving end of painful and severe bullying. Part of the reason I never spoke about any of this is mainly because of that: the feeling that my feelings about what I have suffered pale in comparison to others, and therefore thinking I neither deserve nor do I have the right to complain about my marginalization, knowing that there are others on the fringes of society who may indeed have it unbelievably worse. I was never "fat" enough to be called fat. There were jabs in lunchrooms, being told I was getting "big" by my mom at Thanksgiving, having your family tap and jiggle your belly and say "look at that thing." Couple that with being a man, and you have a recipe for harmful but normalized language. Me being a Black man, no matter my complexion, meant there was very little room to be sensitive or to feel a certain type of way about anything that referred to body image. For the most part, boys didn't talk about each other's bodies in school. We spent far too much time commenting on, describing, and objectifying the bodies of the girls we shared classrooms, playgrounds, hallways, streets, and later bedsheets with. But I knew what I heard and saw: I know I saw grown and not-that-grown women who damn near lost their lives over a naked and sweaty D'Angelo in a video crooning about how it feels while thinking about his grandma's collard greens. I remember Will Smith running to catch bad guys in *Bad Boys*, him jumping over cars with his shirt wide open, knowing that's what box office numbers need. I remember LL Cool J never wearing a shirt anywhere, ever in the history of his career. Never. I know I saw DMX bark and yell in overalls and that masculine aggression, its rawness and realness, authentically savage and severely sexual, spitting itself into TV screens and knowing the girls around the way didn't care which name Earl Simmons called them in "What They Really Want" as long as he called them over. What I saw and what I was continually given glimpses of was the ideal Black male body. The Black male body is a fetish factory, becoming a thing to be beckoned by hungry eyes and hands.

I remember a former lover and potential partner asking me

if I planned on working out again. Her question was probing about not only my dedication toward fitness but what I also perceived to be the ideal body she wanted me to have, while also speaking to what she wasn't seeing: chiseled abs, toned arms and shoulders. It also spoke to what she was saying: a man with a belly. My belly screams "I AM LAZY AND DO NOT MAKE TIME FOR THE GYM" every time it pokes my shirt forward, too forward for it to be anything but the reflection of a man who does not care enough about himself to make his body look attractive.

I want the perks of a flat tummy. The freedom to try a shirt on in a store without going into a changing room because I don't care if anyone sees me. In fact, let them gawk, let them stare and wonder if I'm a good lay. The vanity in me begs for it, yearns for it. They won't know all the nights I ate ramen because I was broke, or the times I wanted to die instead of show up to school, or how I wore all my brother's clothes because I wanted to be as cool as him and didn't think I could be because who falls in love with the chubby kids but their mothers? Let them take a picture of me standing erect on a basketball court, full-on Blackness, and let them post it on their stories or their TikTok or whatever social media platform the Russians will have infiltrated by the time you read this. Let them rename their group chat "JOÉL'S ABS" and all it will be is photos of my abs that look like different food groups. Maybe they'll create the #JOÉLSABSCHALLENGE and everyone will be encouraged to take pictures of their own rock-hard and solid abs in order to cure cancer or police officers. Let them write think pieces about my new body: *People* magazine, Blavity for the brunch crowd, Bossip for the ratchet ones. People will photoshop my abs onto themselves. After they do, I will have already moved on: I will have found a new thing to torment myself over.

By the time you read this, my belly will have moved on, too. We both are too tired to argue, to fight over the last dibs of who owns what, who has a say over who I am, and who I choose to be. So, I'll let them go before they leave me first. That's what stubborn people do. My belly is a mere stratagem for the frail and slight version of myself I hide behind. I do it so well. My belly will have packed its bags, and I will be hawking workout gear and gadgets, and selling you plans on how it's really "mind over matter," and not capitalism weighing you down, holding us all up by the noose of self-deprecation, by the long bootstraps of perfectly built and aesthetically pleasing shapes and contours, these false ideals of positive body images, and count calories. I'll write a new self-help book about my struggles with weight as if my struggle is greater or more pronounced because of where I came from, and look where I came from! But none of this will matter: I will have found a new thing to make my misery, to drag myself into a coffin for. My belly is subterfuge. I honestly don't know who I am without it. We have become the best of roommates, each of us laughing at the other's discomfort. My manhood won't let me cry about it. The world will tell me I shouldn't cry about it. My belly is all the analogies you can think of to describe the dimly lit hallway of the male psyche. My belly deserves a round of applause, because it continues to save me, to see me in ways no other part of my body or any other body has seen or ever will. It is intimacy redefined. It is a rogue renegade defending my choices and my decisions and smiling proudly along the way. Because my belly sees all that I see. And I want to live in a world where we all can accept our bodies, our belly, our skinny and our fat, in the ways required in order to climb ourselves out of this hole of self-shame that keeps us closeted, scarred, scared, and detached from the world around us. A large part of why there is so much lack of acceptance is because we find it so hard to accept ourselves—the discord and nuance that exist between the conversations in our heads about our bodies and the language our bodies require to feel loved by the humans who house them. My belly, much like the gap that lives between my two front teeth, is something I still struggle to accept and love, but accept it and love it I must. That love is no constant, nor would I label it as consistent. But it's there, like my belly is. It has carried me home, through many a storm and hot meal, casual drinks, late-night parties, and past-midnight snacking. There is so much love in what our bodies can offer us.

Ask my belly.

Sensitive Thugs You All Need Hugs

Not every nigga knows how to fight. You learn this early on when you grow up in the hood. Throwing hands, or at least looking like you can, more often than not will save your life. And you're taught to never run from a fight, even if it's a fight you never started. Flame retardant to the fires of youth we hope to be, ducking and dodging anything that feels like something that can progress to some sort of inner-child violence lived outwardly amongst our peers. But what your hands can't and won't do for you, adrenaline and your feet will. I never had to find out if my hands worked. I was good at running. I was never the fastest, never the most athletic. But what I lacked in size and speed I made up for with determination. I was determined not to be a statistic. I was determined to "make it out." By any means necessary. And if that meant looking like and feeling like a sucker, then so be it. There was no one teaching me or telling me how to fight. At times, I was jealous of the kids who grew up having to survive in the ways I didn't. I never wandered into trouble. I generally avoided all forms of danger and mayhem. I was afraid of my mother, one. Two, I was afraid of what would befall me if

I couldn't stand on my own two feet like so many my age had to learn how to, the hard way. There was no one there to show me the ropes, per se. We were all little hood boogers on our own. Our older brothers were busy learning how to be men the hard way, too. Which didn't leave much room or time for them to lead us either. We learned by example, by watching. We were all each other's invaluable understudies—each of us watching and observing the other—a petri dish of learned behavior if there ever was one. But I needed no one to teach me flight, fight, or freeze. We didn't talk about Darwinism where I came from, but there has always been a cultural understanding as to when to make moves for survival. Track-and-field gym stars we are, Olympians of the concrete. But running for sport was never my speed. My knees and shins just weren't built for it. And the discipline wasn't there. Running, to me, was only called for where it felt like an absolute need, a hurried advance to get from one end of a thing to another, that thing decided by circumstance, not necessarily for exercise or exhilaration. Running up and down the court during a fast break, running across the street to beat the light, running blocks upon blocks to not get your ass beat by unknown assailants.

I never was good at doing the things they asked me to do. I was never in enough of the fine arts groups, none of the bigger rap groups. Felt less inclined to join the writers groups and poetry circles. Was too scared to venture out to do big boy things with my art that would require me to show parts of me that felt nontraditional, outside of what was most comfortable—me in my room with G.I. Joes, *Source* magazines, notebooks of raps, freestyles stammering about my brain. I could never spend enough time in any of the niche crowds, the right crowds, to be considered a part of them. Always four years too early, too late, not close enough to the right people, the right institutions. And so, when there is nothing else to do, you run. And it is a thing we are told Black men do best. I think of all the times I ran when something felt too hard. Never like my life depended on it, but fast enough, and for long enough, for folks to know better than to try and catch up. It was the kind of running that, watching from a distance, one could tell I didn't want to be caught or found. And if caught, who wants someone who doesn't want to be kept? We've all run from something. Some of us are better at this than others. Running would become my default, my standard. I would run from mathematics because I struggled with understanding equations and problems that had nothing to do with fanciful language and art. I ran from actually talking to girls I liked and wrote secret poems instead because I knew how shame tasted. Shame was broke, broken and bitter, chubby and unlovable. I played better with myself and imaginary friends because the rules were mine, and so was the ridicule. I could be and play all the roles I wanted for myself. I could be smooth, witty, and aggressive, and running would never be a part of any of those stories I would concoct in the privacy of my mother's bedroom while she slept on the living room sofa. But in the hood, we've all learned how to run.

It starts with someone yelling. Always the yelling, first. And, if you're in a group, a group of say, two or three people that includes yourself, and that group just happens to be Black kids in their formative eighth-grade years. Or any years for that matter. This is a learned thing, a thing you learn watching Black movies and listening to the retelling of Black stories, by OG niggas with broken fingers and missing teeth and malty breath from Olde English brew, they tell these stories randomly and repeat them, and you learn them, you learn them so well and you almost forget that you've had that story. The story may be different—my brother D got his chain taken underneath the train tracks. My man Rich got his chain and took the actual train. I always tucked my shit, plus my shit was low frills barely there silver type that nobody would want. My neck never turned green but I always checked—that kind of silver. But we learned quickly, so that when the time came, it was instinctual, like evolution, like genetics, like in our DNA, like giraffes growing their necks longer because, survival. And to be in survival mode, all the time, is how you survive in the streets. And sometimes you get caught slipping. Sometimes, if you're not fast enough, big enough, strong enough, scary-looking enough, you can get got.

So, when I'm walking on Fordham Road after school, Nautica sweatpants that aren't mine, Black leather jacket that was mine but wasn't before, Nautica T-shirt that wasn't mine, Timb boots that my mama bought, a Nautica cap that wasn't mine, the sorta-silver chain that was mine but wasn't before, and I am walking and it is slightly dark but not too dark so that you can still see Fordham Road and all the people shopping and buying things, all the cute girlies too old for me, or the cute girlies my age but I am too young for them; when I am walking and Cory and Christian are walking with me. On maybe a late spring day, waited on a bus and I waited with them, and while waiting we were approached by some dude saying I was talking to their man Carlito's girl, this "some dude" is a "some dude" I recognized from elementary school who was a little older than me, and was still a little older than me at the time that he approached me about Carlito's girl, and was still a little older the previous time he approached me and asked me where I got my Timbs from and what size they were, and if I lived close by, and me already knowing to lie about any information given, because those Timbs would not be on my feet if I stated anything other than a lie. So while waiting with the bus, and standing with "some dude" and some of his dudes, and Cory and Christian, and a mysterious blade comes from someone's pocket and that someone asks about my watch and tells me it's nice, and when Christian tries to leave and they pull him back from his bus, and also snatch his durag from his head, and leave Christian walking in a circle asking for his durag back, and when someone else asks for my bus pass and I give it to him, knowing bus passes cost money and I cannot tell my mother I was robbed for my bus pass because I hate asking my mother for money, because my mother has been working nights at Jacobi Hospital for almost twenty years at that time, and is always tired and always working and working hard. Knowing the last thing my mother needed was her Black son crying about his bus pass, her Black son (me) put on the performance of his life, crying, flail-ing arms, yelling to them and no one and everyone that, verbatim, "I don't need this shit (I really did not), man! My mother is fucking dying of cancer (she really was not)" and yelled this, over and over again, until one of the "some of his dudes" came back, and apologized, and gave me the bus pass back. And I waited until they were a safe distance away and yelled "FAGGOTS!" before Cory, Christian, and I ran full-speed in the opposite direction. This was at a time when calling someone a gay slur was as close to what we would consider the worst violation possible. Masculinity, especially when seen through the cis-hetero lens, is fragile in that way—fragile like a flower, or a decaying time bomb waiting to be pushed, played with, incited. This behavior is rampant in the hood—we shout words of hate, anger, despair, and longing for what lies beyond our reach. And the *F* word feels flagrant enough for us, us clinging to a gossamer of being, so light and delicate that the mere mention of being remotely attracted to the same sex is enough of an offense to get you brutally harmed.

The soundtrack to that moment would play back in my mind walking Fordham Road on a balmy day after school with Cory and Christian maybe a year later or so. We were walking around the block, window-shopping, girl-gawking, doing the normal things preteens do when they want to sit in the joy of being young without any real cares besides how cool they look. I know I posed at least five times in the mirror before I left the house in that outfit that I stole out of D's closet. But it was in those moments of us walking on Fordham that I heard Cory yell-whisper "Start running" and I asked "What? Why?" and Cory yelled again, louder for emphasis "NIGGA START RUNNING!" and so I didn't ask again, and instead I just followed their lead and ran, and I ran faster than I have ever run, in my entire life, even until this day. And, we ran, hard. Hard like our lives depended on it. Like we didn't know what was on the other side of a calculated beatdown or worse. We ran because running sometimes can save your life, even when you're not sure what you're running from. We ran past people and liquor stores and bodegas and parked cars and stoops and umbrellas; we were running against wind and the cold and I was running in Timbs and a leather coat. Timbs. Timberland construction boots. Not Asics, or New Balances, not Reeboks or Air Maxes. Timbs. And I kept pace, kept pace with basketball and track all-stars. And so, we ran. Then, we stopped. We needed our breaths, and we felt like we lost them. Nah. Christian yelled "They're back!" and so we ran again. And, we split up—Christian and I go one way, Cory goes another way. But, we run. We wind up at Christian's crib. And I know we ran at least thirty blocks or so, pure adrenaline. He offers me water, I take Sprite (hood nigga youth shit). And, I strip. Sweatpants? Off. Leather jacket? Off. Hat? Off. And, we wait minutes, moments, and I leave, stuffing all the items I took off my body into my not-so-large Jansport book bag. Standing in Christina's kitchen, next to the boxed Sprite cans, I was left with my T-shirt and the gym shorts I wore underneath it all, hoping that changing out of outside clothes would make me less identifiable to a potential Blood hunting for a light-skinned high schooler. It is at least forty degrees, at least. I walk to the train, before GPS and Google Maps, and I find it, and I wait for the above-ground 4 train near Christian's home, cold and, I hope, unnoticeable. And scared. Scared someone will find me, notice me, and see me and see through me at the same time.

All the times we was throwing fake gang signs in class, the times we'd mean mug for a picture in front of a camera, make the gun figure with our fingers, curse at the top of our lungs to Biggie and Hov and Nas, the times we'd drink Crooked Ides, the soft drink version of the malt liquor class St. Ides, and pretend to be a favorite rapper or gangster, all those times went out the window, baby and bathwater included, when some real shit went down. I got home, and my mama's phone rang, and it was my man David. He and I went back to elementary school. David and I had a faux fight near the staircase in second grade, and had to be escorted to the principal's office; "faux fight" because all we did was pull and grab each other and he fell and tried to swing and I tried to swing and we both missed, little hood nigga kiddie kind of shit. So, when David calls, I still pick up, I still answer.

David: Yo, I think I saw ya man, what's his name, Cory
or whatever, running and getting chased by
like, a gang of like forty Blood niggas down
my block? You good??

Me: What?! Get the fuck outta here! Did they catch
him? Do you know?!

David: Nah, I don't think so. He was ouuuuut! He was
booking!

Me: Shit! Yo, lemme call this nigga . . .

I called. Cory was home. Cory was safe. We're all safe. I was
still scared, still shook. Was it the same dude who had tried to
rob me of my bus pass at knifepoint and some of his dudes?
Did they remember me, remember the faces? Or, was it random,
some dudes who saw some kids they could rob, or jump, or
stab, or all of the aboves and etceteras? I remember the outfit
I wore because the gray Nautica sweatpants with the Nautica
blue and gold stripes on the side were D's, the white Nautica
T-shirt was D's, the navy blue Nautica baseball dad cap was
D's, the black leather jacket used to be D's but he gave it to me
because he had a flyer Guess leather jacket now, and the almost-
silver chain used to be D's, too, but he got a flyer, real gold chain
so he didn't need the other chain anymore. I remember feeling
myself, I remember thinking I looked superfly in my brother
D's gear, that I felt cool, I felt confident and unfuckwittable, that
I looked like I had just stepped out of one of my favorite rap

videos. I probably even had a toothpick in my mouth at the time, and walked with the serious b-boy bop; I may have even had one pant leg rolled up just like LL used to do in all his videos and at all of his shows. Did I draw that attention to us, did I bring that drama to us, was it my fault? I thought about all those things on the way back home. That's what trauma does to you when you are too young to properly sieve through the causation behind why people choose to do the things they do. I will never know the answer because I don't know who chased us or why. Being older, I now know so much defies reason, is left up to chance, mere happenstance will have you in the wrong place at the wrong time, getting your guard up, fixated on the stance you need to take to either take a punch or flee a scene in a moment's notice. I remember a gang of us waiting for the bus in middle school and two girls getting off the bus fighting and one girl giving the other a buck fifty right across her whole face. We saw blood. We oohed and aahed and I have no idea what happened to either. We talked about it, joked about it probably, went home and grabbed quarter waters and finished our homework, and did it all over again the next day. We were numb to it all because shit like that happened all the time. Somebody got shot or shot at, somebody got stabbed, somebody got jumped. Running from violence wasn't new to me. It was a response to the normalcy of the violence.

When I finally got home from Christian's, still tired and still slightly shaken by what had just transpired, D came home from work. I don't recall why I mentioned it or why I told him or what compelled me to share what happened with him. Not to say that my older brother didn't deserve to know that kind of information, but I'm not exactly sure what kind of reaction

I wanted or expected from him, you know? But, I told him. He wasn't pleased. At all. Threats to manhood, especially to Black manhood, are dangerous. Things like staring too long, the wrong kind of bump in a crowded street, scuffing someone's shoes by stepping on them, or, in this case, getting punked, are intolerable. D felt like I got punked. By changing out of my clothes to hide, I exhibited a fear far worse than the running that occurred—by D's rationale, I had allowed my fear of pain to make me do something less manly than expected. The hood is full of stories of snitches, of shook ones, folks caught in the crosshairs of block beefs and corner gunfire, because they ran, because they couldn't muster the courage to stand up to someone, to something. For what it was worth, I was scared as shit-scared of being robbed, scared of being cut and humiliated, scared of being harmed, and fearful of what that had the potential to do to my psyche, to my heart. D would argue at times that his need to stay close to home for college was due to my naivete, that my youthful innocence was subject to a certain kind of danger that I was none the privy to. I used to want to tell D that my window was enough for me to see and know that the Bronx was dangerous, that people died on Creston Avenue, and that, despite the whispers, I knew Miguel was stabbed in that hallway by Mexicans over something silly, and that the building and D had lost something innocent in his murder, and he was fearful of me losing that same innocence; that his staying was the sort of protection that I required that he had never received because we lacked a father who was equipped with the skills needed to protect young boys from the kinds of danger newspapers and media outlets reported about in the days of crack and gangs that seemed to dominate his upbringing, and also mine. There was an innocence lost in those times, in a way innocence is always lost when you are growing up Black and semipoor with other fatherless, poorer peoples, particularly Black boys, each strangling the other for air, each chasing blouses, churning the broke for bejeweled pendants, stroking each other's dicks for approval, hypothetically speaking. No amount of staying or leaving would have kept me alive. We think we have power here. We are told to believe in a white god who will somehow redeem us in heaven for the sins of our ways, all the while white supremacy and its forefather, capitalism, continue to guide our dilapidation with the stroke and swipe of a keyboard type. Even the control we think we have is at best a lukewarm understanding of what can be done to us by others who, too, are just as lost, just as hopeless as we can be. And even in that running, there was competition—I needed to get to wherever we were running to, first.

I tell this story often, oftentimes reminiscing either with glee or distraught, retelling all or some of the parts, partially to remind myself and those who do not know me well enough to know my nickname, or who only know me as me who I am and not me as I was, of authenticity as a patron of the hood. Me still wanting to show off the perils of living ghetto, like a badge of some sort, a subtle way to justify when and how I say "nigga" or get emotionally invested in street drug and rap battles. This younger me, still drawn to certain elements that paint pictures of a kind of hood that is attractive, that is alluring, a certain kind of dangerous Blackness that has become popular, and profitable. Every time I tell this story, it is almost the same: I am the hero, I am naive, I am in fear but I am safe; but it is also beautiful, and it is appealing to anyone who does not look like me, does not come from where I come from, and has not lived in the danger. I call this "hood adjacent," those who are not of the hood or ghetto, but desire to be in the story, to live in the skin, if even for a day, a moment, and feel like they, too, are a part of the story. It is here that I am most aware of what running looks like because the story always finds you. And you find yourself changing out of street clothes into basketball shorts, always running, from gangs or board meetings or spaces with too many white people, too much violence, and too much left behind. I wonder how much better we would have all fared if we had learned how to love each other more? What would our homes, our blocks, our schools, and our communities look like if we took the time to nurture our young Black boys rather than judge, demean, and ridicule them? What would it look like to not toughen our boys in preparation for the world we tell them will not love them, but encourage and support and love them like every breath and every smile was worthy of love? Like every crossroad deserved warmth. They teach us the world will only loathe our hair, our skin, our smiles, and our strength . . . but what does the world look like for us on the other side? We are made to be statues, void of feeling, big, Black robots with muscles and muscle cars and guns, gums flapping proudly to everyone, all of us mimicking movements we saw in rap videos or hustler circles all the while cupping our hands and the cold in them while fantasizing about white women or the Black women we hate proudly. They imagine us to be monsters or something close to it. The same reason I ran away from the Bloods who chased us on Fordham Road those many years ago is the same reason I cross the street whenever it's late and I'm walking behind a white woman, or I either steady my pace or speed up to walk past a Black woman to not be mistaken for a stalker, a rapist, or a predator—fear.

When I tell the story now, it has less power and range as I've aged. The story is boring now. I used to wear the story like a badge, a reminder that I came from a place that many in the circles I was now privy to enter, the seats I had earned the privilege to sit in, had never seen. But now many of us wear our trauma proudly. Our trauma has taught us how to live in a world that wants to frame us as anything but what we truly are: Black and free and beautiful. This story doesn't impress niggas who used to slap box for fun, got stole on by their pops, or did juvie before they graduated high school. Because when you grow up and come from a certain environment, the violence is ordained in you; we are matriculated into the trauma. You grow up and everyone around you is poor, is hungry, is desperate, is needy, and is ready. Ready to snatch, to rob, to steal, to run. We are also just as likely to love, to laugh, to cry, to vote, to protest.

On a Brooklyn late night, when it is almost winter and rain pellets the street, I scroll Instagram while listening to cars make their ways en route to their homes, their workplaces, their girlfriends, lovers, and exes. While scrolling, I see a post from my photographer friend, Gina, in which she shares these strikingly beautiful images of moss. Gina, when talking about moss, talks about how resilient it is—it can be buried under ice, snow, and some can survive underwater, she writes. I almost looked up *casurvive* until I realized it was a misspelling. If you are Black in America, and even more so if you are Black and grew up in and around poverty, were reared and raised by it, a next-door neighbor of sorts, you, too, are moss. You are deeply submerged in environments not deemed suitable for most of those who walk this world. And unbeknownst to those around you, those who have never walked or run in your shoes, or have had to dodge snowballs from older kids or had to navigate a bus ride that could turn into a stomping, or turn your headphones up to ignore the calls of faggot for no other reason besides you being you, you are surviving under remarkable circumstances even still. Even under the most humbling duress, the crippling pang of distress lurking around a corner or alleyway, we are still finding ways to grow. I ran that day after school because I instinctively knew the odds of my body and ego surviving what would have happened if they'd caught me were slim to none. And I was ready to run again if I had to. I'm still ready now.

All Gold Everything

Feat. Mr. T, Slick Rick, Michael Jordan

Gold all in my chain,
Gold all in my ring
Gold all in my watch
Don't believe me, just watch nigga nigga nigga

—TRINIDAD JAMES, "ALL GOLD EVERYTHING"

For you meet him with rich blessings; you set a crown of fine
gold upon his head.

—PSALM 21:3 ESV

Trinidad James's 2012 hit single "All Gold Everything" was a hit right out of the gate. The combination of the repetitive, emphatic chorus, the simplicity of the lyrics, and the trunk-rattling bass combined to create one of the catchier records of the year. What also stood out was Trinidad James himself: in the video, Trinidad epitomizes the emblematic, mirror image of not only the song lyrics but the physical manifestation of another gold rocking, eighties icon.

My brother D loved *The A-Team*. By default, I loved *The A-Team*, too. And what was not to love? A bunch of ragtag mercenaries from varying backgrounds, with various skill sets, hell-bent on getting the bag. I mean the A-Team and the Wu-Tang Clan are apples from the same tree. Another essay for another day. One of my favorite parts of watching *The A-Team* was seeing B.A. Barakus lay down the law. While "I pity the fool" would be the tagline most remembered and repeated by most, pulled from his appearance in the *Rocky III* saga, Mr. T, born Laurence Turead, was a larger-than-life presence all his own. From cartoons to commercials to professional wrestling appearances, Mr. T's attitude and haircut dominated. Before conversations surrounding representation became mainstays in mainstream media conversations, Mr. T's whole being was an oversize superhero while standing a mere five foot ten. Gravelly, booming voice, Chicago flavored, a Mack truck in full throttle. Mr. T held the balance of an aggressively stoic antihero, a Black robot on steroids crushing and pummeling anything in his way on-screen. His ability to command spaces lived in all the arenas he played in: savage neighborhood boxer turned villain, former special forces member turned soldier for hire, guest star in popular eighties sitcoms and varying commercial products. But that ability was mastered in the one place ubiquitous with Black superstardom: the nightclub.

It was as a bouncer that Mr. T's reputation grew and his name solidified. The moniker itself, Mr. T, is thought to have originated a few different ways—while the name seemingly was an abbreviated version of the surname bestowed by his minister father who left the family when Laurence was five years old, it also seems the name Mr. T as an identifier for a young Laurence Turead took on a more significant meaning when he held court for the movers and shakers of the world, looking to gain entrance to a place where money and status are indeed everything. The nightclub is a fortress, and bouncers essentially play the role of exterior kings for the latter part of evenings, dealing and dueling with passersby and potential velvet rope hoppers, all looking for a way to be seen, to feel something, anything other than whatever hype moment is eating their lives up. It's in this space Mr. T would be seen, his glaring mohawk eating attention. It's also here that Mr. T's signature trademark, beyond any one-liner or hairstyle, would essentially make a mark that would outlive any trope attached to him: gold chains.

Mr. T's early, earnest collection was connected back to the nightclub scene, the same scene where he would both pay and earn his dues. Any jewelry that was taken, whether by force or neglect, was left at the clubs Mr. T worked in. Those same chains would become souvenirs, medals of honor for a real-life former soldier, formerly at war with the Vietcong, now at war with stars and starlets trying desperately to enter coveted spaces he was being paid to guard. The gold chains adorning his neck also served as a warning shot, an act of defiance and bravery on his part, daring those who lost the items to come get them themselves, or forcing them to be taunted nightly by his cavalier approach to wearing gaudiness so nonchalantly on his body on any given night without fear or regard for anyone getting in his way. Maybe Mr. T was menacing before the gold chains, or maybe it was the gold chains' euphoric magnetism that gave him that grandiose feeling all-powerful. One chain makes you invincible. Two chains make you immortal—ask Tauheed Epps. Multiple chains? Godlike. All-knowing, all-seeing, all-showboating. But following the rise of hip-hop, the gold chains were worn as an honorary symbolic gesture to the dealers and pimps of our folklore, because they became an accessible commodity, a clear way to identify oneself as someone with power, influence, and a certain level of status. Mr. T was only emulating what our ancestors had shown us about the power of gold and our affinity for it. It was the brazen levels of coolness steaming off Mr. T's body that would lead Sly Stone to cast him in *Rocky III* as the harbinger of terror and pain Clubber Lang. Serving as the preamble to Ivan Drago, future Rocky nemesis and murderer of Apollo Creed, Clubber Lang was the bad guy everyone loved to hate. Unless you were a Black kid in America. Apollo Creed in both *Rocky* and *Rocky II* served as the richer, more polished version of the Black Republican American dream, playing the pre-Reagan-era role valiantly. But Clubber Lang? Clubber Lang was all nigga. Badass, bold, brash. No gold chains, no matter. His goal was to whoop on Balboa and inflict pain. What was supposed to be a brief appearance turned into a role with lines inspired, not by a fictional character, but by the heat Mr. T gave off by merely being himself: Black, and hungry.

I talk about Mr. T in the past tense not because he's no longer living but because he subsequently has done a one-eighty, a born-again Christian who has forgone his chains, maybe literally and metaphorically. Because as much as Mr. T was indeed himself, he also had become a caricature. Part of the reason Mr. T refused to make a cameo in the film reboot of *The A-Team* was, I suspect, that he knew, believed, and understood that the chain-wearing, mohawk character being portrayed on the screen was still him. To have someone else play Mr. T as B.A. Barakus would be another level of meta: Quinton "Rampage" Jackson, a former UFC star turned actor, playing Mr. T, playing B.A. Barakus. The artist formerly known as Mos Def, Yasiin Bey, once shared, "I began to fear that Mos Def was being treated as a product, not a person," speaking to the rap moniker he carried around as the undisputed champion of backpack rap, up until 1999. Similarly, Mr. T's namesake was also a product. Mr. T's pivot is important to note: despite the well-spoken version displayed off camera, he was always unequivocally Black. His name was created to force white people to respect him. His name may have been given to him by others, but the name Mr. T was honed, owned, and shaped by Laurence Turead—he added his flavor, his style, his voice to the persona that America grew to love and, at times, loathe. The gold was just an added formality, a character in and of itself. The gold chains, stacked, screamed kingly. They beckoned and called us to pay attention to both the man and the personality behind him. The choice was bold, no doubt inspired by the street culture Mr. T witnessed growing up: he was born and raised in the Robert Taylor Homes of Chicago, Illinois.

Residing within the collection of public housing known as the Black Belt of Chicago, the Robert Taylor Homes ironically were named after civil rights activist and Chicago Housing Authority (CHA) board member Robert Rochon Taylor. By the time Mr. T would hit fourteen, Chicago would be the home of one of the most notorious public housing units in America, and also known for being the city that would receive the Reverend Martin Luther King Jr. with rocks instead of hugs. The Robert Taylor Homes would house not only Mr. T but also other notable stars such as former NBA player Maurice "Mo" Cheeks, rapper and comedian Open Mike Eagle, and former MLB all-star Kirby Puckett. The

Homes would also house the Mickey Cobras (MCs), Gangster Disciples (GDs), and Black Disciples (BDs), some of the most well-known gangs in this country. It is no stretch of the imagination that Mr. T's use of multiple gold chains as a sign of respect and luxury was pulled just as much from the cover of Kurtis Blow's self-titled debut rap album—him bare-chested with several gold chains adorning his body—as from the Black hustlers and dealers in his housing projects on any given day. Self-professed millionaires wore jewels as expensive as a down payment, as a home, as a condo, as someone's life insurance, someone's car, or someone's funeral; each gold chain was a symbol of something more. The chains in gold were a possibility cemented in a metal. King David, Larry Hoover, Jeff Fort, Flukey Stokes—these are just a few of the Chicago drug trade legends Mr. T would have either known about or potentially rubbed shoulders with as a bouncer and, later, bodyguard, in the mid to late seventies. Mr. T's Blackness was loud, front and center, and undeniable. Before unapologetically Black became part of your lexicon, brothers like Mr. T were the living embodiment of it.

Chains are both oppressive and cyclical—they bind slave to master, connecting skin to metal and freedom to a hierarchy defined by systems. They also are a 360-degree representation of life, of birth and death, and the forces that interact in between. It is that circle, whether used as a means to keep communities in captivity (one could look at the slave patrols who ensured slaves would not leave their owners and remain in chains, that would eventually mature into the current-day police force that uses another form of chains, handcuffs, as an oppressive tool of captivity) or in wealth, that makes the cipher complete. The circle of life of bondage and existence is as close to God as heaven, as two hands humbled for prayer. The only thing that is as close to holiness is gold. Gold is the standard, and within Black communities, gold and the jewelry it is attached to create an accessible kind of luxury that feels tangible, and affordable. But that access also drives a need and a want. And want is correlated directly to the scarcity found in the homes, in the cities, in the schoolyard playgrounds with the rickety fences parted open for the young ones to poke their fingers through, watching like I did across barren streets at the corners full of the men moving their hands, moving weight whether it be their own from foot to foot to stay warm amid the winter rough of the hustling season, or the weight moved from interstate road trips, one car dashboard to another.

D got robbed for his chain under the train tracks in the Bronx in the nineties. He talked about the incident with his friends like he was talking about the flu, or the Mets winning a spring training game—expected and very matter-of-factly. We internalize trauma so skillfully. The weight of our chains keeps us in bondage. We tucked our chains when we walked on trains, especially if you weren't ready to defend your life for it. This was the New York where gold in your teeth, on your neck, ears, or wrists subjected you to a pat down or a beatdown. Brothers died for the weight of it all. And in the carrying of the chains around the neck, we continue the work of those that came before us— those whose chains were captivity to escape from; others holding chains as a means of something to aspire to the hustlers, the ballers. And sometimes, the ballers showed themselves outside of the streets. Sometimes, they were balling on the blacktop. And sometimes, they were inspired by Planet Rock.

Ballers like the great Pee Wee Kirkland were balling outside of the Rucker. And it was that other foot that lived outside of the margins that made gold not just part of our culture, but also our identities. "Legend in two games like I'm Pee Wee Kirkland" —Clipse, "Grindin."

The story goes Pee Wee turned down his NBA deal to keep dealing dope. Hustling is the fabric of the culture—our ancestors were traded on blocks and auctions, and ballers get traded and drafted on TV screens. Hustlers engage in the art of trading narcotics for dollars. The gold chain was the come-up piece. Pee Wee covers the front of *F.E.D.S.* magazine, a white suit, black tie, and a gold necklace gently hugging the neck collar. You either wore a gold chain or stick-up kids robbed you for one. The gold chain declared you official, and it spoke to a generation of have-nots that you, too, could gain acclaim with a Benz, a beeper, and a gold chain. Fat Cat, Supreme, Larry Davis, Ronnie Bumps, Rich Porter . . . the dookie gold chain was part of the allure of drug culture. Outside of being a fashion statement, it was also part of the come-up. Runners and lookouts, those who dealt drugs to addicts hand to hand, and the latter, who watched the streets to let dealers know when cops were approaching, couldn't afford gold chains. The bigger the name and persona of the person, the bigger and weightier the size of the chain. The dope boy aesthetic was simple: cop an outfit from Harlem legend and style icon Dapper Dan; rock a gold chain or necklace to go along with it. Hustlers and pimps would turn gold chains into art forms; would take chains of oppression and turn them into street art. In 1980, gold had risen to $850 per ounce. While prices would eventually come back down, Reaganomics along with the influx of crack in urban communities created room for the return of the luxury metal to hit the market just in time for a booming drug trade that would correspond with the creation of a new art form, taking the gold chain to new heights.

Kool Herc could trace his lineage back to Jamaica's clashes of sound systems, where deejays owned the party scene, battling each other over music and microphones. He would take that same energy and, along with his sister Cindy Campbell, put together the Bronx party that Kool Herc deejayed and Coke La Rock emceed, and would create the phenomenon known as hip-hop. While Herc wasn't rocking gold at the tender age of sixteen, the hustlers who would attend the parties would don thick chains, heavy chains, chains modeled after bicycle locks, can tops, and ropes. It was this that the Kurtis Blows of the world would emulate, rocking bare skin and multiple chains on his self-titled debut LP. Kurtis Blow would make way for a slew of rappers—the LL Cool Js, Ice Ts, and the Kool Moe Dees of the world. Big Daddy Kane, Kool G Rap, and Rakim were all known for gold rope chains that were reminiscent of drug dealers in days past. Slick Rick was the king of the gold chain, stacking multiple versions of different-size chains on top of each other and fully living out every young aspiring rapper or dope dealer's dream. But it would be the kings of rock (and gold accessories), Run-DMC, who would take the gold chain out of the glorified spaces of street lore and into mainstream Black culture and eventually, pop culture. The brothers from Hollis, Queens, established the gold chain as part of a brand, and some could argue created branding for the culture of hip-hop before its audiences were aware of its significance, or had the language to describe it. Gold ordained Biz Markie. Big Daddy Kane wore it like a championship belt. LL Cool J would make gold feel like sex, among other things. Rakim wore his gold like a crown. And while gold in hip-hop would make way for the Black power medallions in the late nineties worn by the likes of X Clan, Queen Latifah, Public Enemy, and De La Soul, it would see its return in the era of gangsta rap marked by former hustlers like Snoop and former hustlers turned street poets like Jay-Z. But before that, there would be one who would walk so others could run on the golden era road paved with the riches of those seeking someone to rule over all those with a forte for exquisite wordplay, an eye patch, a wit to match John Cleese, and a storytelling ability that hasn't been heard since. The Ruler.

Slick Rick was born Richard Martin Lloyd Walters in the southwest London district of Mitcham. In 1976, Richard and his Jamaican immigrant parents landed in the Bronx, three years after Kool Herc would put hands to vinyl on Sedgwick for his older sister Cindy's house party, which would change the landscape of Black music forever. Richard attended Fiorello H. LaGuardia High School of Music, Art, and the Performing Arts, the same high school I would graduate from over twenty years later. Majoring in art (I, expectedly, majored in drama), Richard would connect with another rap legend, Dana McCleese, better known as Dana Dane. A chance encounter with Doug E. Fresh of the Get Fresh Crew would lead to two of the biggest singles in hip-hop history: "La Di Da Di" and "The Show." However, the 1986 album *The Great Adventures of Slick Rick* cemented his legacy.

Slick Rick's chain was simple: a gold dookie chain. The chain was no different from what any other hustler, dealer, or baller would have been wearing back then in the Bronx: a borough chock-full of fire-torn buildings, desolated blocks affected by the drug trade, poverty, and urban renewal. When I think of the

1980s, I think of my oldest brother, Skee, whose chain fit his neckline like some sort of Egyptian prince meant for the block. It was simple, it was clean—not too gaudy, but nice enough to know that he spent some bread to cop it, and was probably holding on to something to protect, seeing as he never tucked it in. Because tucking your chain was for suckas. And Skee wasn't a sucka. But Skee did get caught up in the glitz and glamor of the drug trade. Skee was hustling hard and had the cherry-red Corvette. All his pictures are of him in some fly kind of leather, jewels all on his fingers, a pretty woman by his side, a smile as golden as the simple chain dangling around his neck. Skee was a genius—a born mathematician with a gift for singing and drawing. My brother D and I still talk about his illustrations of realer-than-life football players that hung on the brown metal closet in our room, the closet that held none of Skee's clothes. He kept his already worn gear on the top bunk bed in our shared room, keeping myself and D nestled in the bottom bunk up until my middle school years. Skee was never home. And if he was, it was because he was coming home late in the wee hours of the morning. Some nights it was a studio session. Some nights it was some sort of party: The Fever, Latin Quarters, Rooftop, The Roxy, The Castle, Limelight, Palladium. Other nights it was hustling. The door to my mother's two-bedroom apartment would open like church bells at mass at 2:00 or 3:00 A.M. Skee would enter smelling like Newports and joint ash, carrying a bag of White Castle fish sandwiches. I'd walk on his back when he asked me to, him sore from long days and nights. Cutting a dub of Al B. Sure!'s "Rescue Me" brought my brother some real critical acclaim in the music scene. Skee dropped out of Edison High School to pursue his full-time singing career while simultaneously keeping one foot in the streets.

A future label deal was pinned on the hopes of one-hit wonder Mikey Jarrett, who had a smash in 1992 with the song "Mack Daddy." Skee would be locked up not too long after. Instead of stepping on his back, I'd write him letters and poems while his parole kept getting denied, riding with my mother on long trips to whichever upstate facility he was stationed in during his ten-year bid for a very hefty drug charge. The golds Skee wore around his neck spoke not only royalty but also a nigga getting paid. Getting paid is Black man iconography. Gold chains were and are our status symbol. A reflection of all the excess we weren't privileged enough to obtain when we were stolen and brought to the Americas. The golds were a symbol of our labor. I benefited from this labor. We all have. I benefited from Skee's labor in the same ways many of us who used larger-than-life drug dealer stories—rappers, writers, scholars, journalists—to tell our personal stories, our community stories, did. Skee's life showed up in my raps, much in the way the sounds and colors of Blackness show up in Donald Glover's *Atlanta*: proximity. If you couldn't deal dope, wear the gold chains, or drive the Beamer, the least you could do was lean into the ancestry of hype pilfered through the stories, closets, and histories of the ones who laid down the framework. When Hov told Nas, "Nigga, you ain't live it, you witnessed it from ya moms' crib, scribbled in your notepad and created your life," I knew who he was talking to. He was talking to the lot of us who never got their hands dirty enough to talk brick-talk the likes of Kool G. Rap (another strong gold chain advocate) and, in later years, Roc Marciano, Pusha T, Benny the Butcher—a countless array of dealers turned rap lords.

In this way, the gold chains that my brother Skee wore felt like mine, too; they felt like symbols of prestige that I got to inherit simply by being his youngest brother, the one who got to give him massages by stepping on his back in our bedroom after he was done dealing drugs for the day. And all that energy of the Bronx: of hardship, of loss, of grief, and the chase for power while still ducking the Five, stickup kids with ratchets tucked in trench coats, that Slick Rick's wordplay and penchant for rocking an unscrupulous number of gold chains would raise his profile and legend. "Children's Story" is the blueprint for rap storytelling: a close-to-nonfiction attempt at depicting characters Slick Rick would rub elbows with at the nightclubs he performed at, the streets he would have been raised on in those formative years. Slick Rick's golds were larger than life. And like Mr. T, the stacking of the chains eluded subtlety: they were brazen, overt, and loud; much like the scenes and environments Black men who chose to wear gold chains would often be found in. Slick Rick's chains, much like the patch he wears over the eye he was blinded in as a child and the Clarks he wore on his feet as a remembrance of his Jamaican roots, are a part of his human and character arch. They are as much Slick Rick as the stories he told, as the raps he delivered. But the amount of gold does not the man make.

Still, were we so wrong in wanting them? King Tutankhamen was buried in his ropes and robes of gold to bring him closer to God. There are over four hundred mentions of the word *gold* in the King James version of the Bible. For the sake of comparison, the word is mentioned thirteen times in the Qur'an. Gold is indeed the Christian, American way. Many scholars believe Nubia is derived from the ancient Egyptian meaning "gold." The hieroglyphic meaning "gold" was a broad collar, potentially the first instance of a gold chain set in stone as language, as art. The yellow metal stone was used for daily life, funerals, weapons, to keep away evil spirits, for good luck in death, and in honor of the flesh of the Sun Ra, worn by the noble elite and commoners. Gold medals. Gold trophies. The Akans of Southern Ghana were known for it. Henry VIII showed favor with it. The Signare women of Senegal were adorned in it. My brother D was robbed for it, snatched from his neck at gunpoint—a constant reminder of the threat Black men face that has become as common as breathing, to the point where the trauma that stems from the event becomes a topic of conversation, a turn of phrase pointing to the ever-so-common "that's just the way it is." The gold chain has spoken to not just the aspirations of the communities that support the crafts of those who wear them, but also to the vision of the ancestors from yesteryear. In each era, there would be someone who epitomized the gold chain as a means to indicate to others their value, worth, and levels of success. In some instances, it is less about success and more about the showmanship of it all. There is something inherently Black about the gold chain on a Black body while doing extraordinary things in that body. It may be why Michael Jordan dunked in it. Dr. J. and Wilt the Stilt rocked the gold metal on the basketball court to varying degrees. However, it was Darryl "Chocolate Thunder" Dawkins who made gold chains on the court illegal in the NBA, with the league banning wearing chains during gameplay following the 1980 finals. So much of the banning of chains at that time screamed anti-Blackness. The banning was no different than future NBA commissioner David Stern's banning of baggy shorts following the rise in popularity of Allen Iverson. It was all in an effort to curb the growing legions of both players and fans who were bucking the traditions that catered to the status quo. Players were expected to behave a certain way on and off the court. Gold chains were associated with street and gang culture, and those things were deemed unfit, unsavory, and undeniably Black. But it wasn't until MJ donned the chain during the 1985 All-Star Weekend and Slam Dunk Contest that the gold chain took flight in a new way. MJ's signature gold necklace. It screamed defiant. It jumped into the stands, it got ghetto kids in front of their television sets, hyped off of Little Debbie and Kool-Aid, practicing moves in bedrooms with clothing wire hangers bent into circles and wrapped atop doors, mimicking not just the motions but the likeness of the man palming the Spalding and donning the gold. The cycle of the ball, hoop, chain, all gloriously embracing the dark skin, sweat beads, and hanging tongue of the man hanging in the air, Nike laces as wings. His flight was our flight. Wanting to "Be Like Mike," a likeness of his image, was in context as godlike as we could imagine—those who wanted to be fly, get fly in the projects and hoods across America could use Jordan's flight, gold chain shimmering in the glow of the stadium lights, as our means and way out just the same.

Jordan's historic rise was also a reboot for the Nike brand as it battled over street turf with the likes of Adidas, Puma, and Converse. MJ's ascension in those early years was also attached to his style of play: wagging tongue, the ability to jump through the rafters, his speediness running up and down the floor, crossing over defenders, his insane dunking ability. The image of MJ's chain tattooed to his neck while he jumped from the free throw line is an image etched in our memories. MJ in the 1980s was not only a talented ball player and a marketing team's wet dream—but he was also the reflection of the inner-city kids with hoop dreams playing friends and foes under dark blue hues, the sunlight still catching the cement

and brick walls, netless rims blending with the grunts of "AND
1!" while onlookers tabulate scores, NBA stats, and hood gos-
sip. While the MJ of the 1990s and early 2000s became everyone
else's, in the '80s Mike was ours and ours alone. He may have
been oohing and aahing crowds from the Midwest to the East
Coast, but he still belonged to us. The chain was a bat signal
for all the Black kids who were struggling to find themselves
on and off the court. We could find a small piece of ourselves
tucked away in the seams of the chest of his jersey, serving as
a beacon we could see live on TV via NBA games or commercials. There was a Jordan Brand before there was Jordan *the*
brand: sneakers, burgers, electrolytes, trading cards, and video
games. The chain would disappear as Michael grew older,
replaced with less obvious forms of luxury: cars, cigars, and
gambling debt. But to so many of us, Michael Jordan in the '80s
felt like Black freedom personified. Mike flying was us flying
with him, along with the aspirations we had carried over from
the corner back to the block, from the classroom to the boardroom. In those moments, MJ's Blackness was ours, too: a shared
camaraderie that, whether real or imagined, kept us buying the
sneakers and arguing with everyone and their mama about
who was the greatest player of all time. So, even while Mike
also became the poster boy for rampant Black capitalism, while
young Black men died over the sneakers, he jumped in. But
that history of flight didn't stop on the hardwood. And gold
has never stopped being the heir apparent.

Gold is a proclamation, a form of celebration and victory,
a proverbial comeuppance from those who have known desti-
tution and squalor. We, as Black people, who thereby are not
a monolith, have a common love affair with it. Door knockers.

Gold grills and caps. It is our attempt at the glory denied us. The resurgence of the chain today—wanting to look cool, be fly, seem important—is a return to the time where subtle beams of flashy were just enough to let others know you were aware of what money feels like on a body of Black. Even I, with my two little Amazon $18 chains on, feel like Hercules. And even though I can afford a more serious investment, the street culture won't let me. I don't want to ever run the risk of having my chain snatched or fought over. With two daughters, a partner, a family, and a village to love, being held up at knife- or gunpoint over pricey metals is not the way out I imagined for myself. But the purchase speaks to the want, the need, for Black acceptance and the need to be in close approximation to the wealth we've always wanted but have been blocked from accessing. The chains, oddly enough, can feel like the closest thing we have to freedom. The want for the gold is egoic, centered on the optics of appearing like we got it all together when we don't, the proverbial "keeping up with the Joneses" rearing its ugly, decently priced head. We want what we were told we would never have, could never afford. We also want what we feel we are entitled to—if we cannot get our forty acres, at the very least we can rock a stupid fat, gold chain. And even while wearing the chains, it's easy to imagine the glares from other Black men who I am sure in my head are questioning my wealth, my pockets, and my ability to put my hands on anyone staring too long. This is a trauma response, yes. And a response rooted in past harm. It also has not made me take the chains off. Because the chains make me feel as cool as I wanted to be. I'm Nas in the window with the notepad all over again. So, of course athletes, hustlers, and rappers alike have seen gold and gold chains as more than just adornments, not just as symbols of wealth, stature, and symbolic representations of cultures dating back to the earliest of Pyramids: their gold chains also have served as the embodiment of God, of life, of the circle. Life, death, and all of the living between all gold everything.

How to Make a Black Friend

Feat. Ty

Paul Rudd's *I Love You, Man*? Good movie. Paul Rudd's character is a hapless but lovable white man who does not have many male friends, and none he would consider a best friend. Pretty soon, he's going to be walking down the aisle and getting married to a racially ambiguous-looking, cool-as-a-cucumber Rashida Jones, and due to his lack of a strong male lead, he has no best man to help him get drunk, lose his ring, or have him end up in some post–strip club adventure. After a failed friend date, he meets Jason Segel. Hijinks ensue. They start a band, they go see Rush in concert together and do weird, overtly sexual air guitar things. Jason becomes his best man. The end. My bad for the spoilers. Take away the wedding, the Rush concert, the beer-chugging game scene, add in way more Black people (like way more), and you have my story.

Ty was my Jason Segel. The Black version. Tango and Cash. Bell and Biv minus the DeVoe. I didn't find Ty, Ty found me—literally. He runs a bomb-ass podcast called *Tea and Converse*, and over some Instagram chatter he told me he dug my latest musical endeavor at the time, "songs for charles," and wanted to sit down and rap a taste about my work and my art. I was all like, "Bet. Count me in." I don't really mess with tea like that, being a black coffee kinda guy (shouts to Heavy D), but the idea sounded fresh enough. By this point, I had begun really identifying what my voice was as an emcee, but my time and energy were more focused on my writing, and pushing the album wasn't a main priority. I was proud of it, and it was probably the proudest I had been of any project, so when Ty DM'd via Instagram and mentioned he had heard the album and wanted to chat about it, I was down for it. We agreed to meet and chop it up.

I didn't stalk his social media like I normally would when interviews and such come up. That's what nerds do—stalk, but on the low-low. And I'm a nerd. I'm what some might call a hood nerd. That awkward kid who read *Mega Man* books, got into fights with schoolyard bullies but always made sure to get indoors before the streetlights went on. It was some of this nerdom that would connect us both. I would also later learn that his father and mine were both somewhat estranged from our lives in different but similar fashions. We shared a love for White Castle, and a deeply reverent passion for all things hip-hop and rap related. My male friendships up until that point barely scratched the surface of what real intimacy amongst homies could look like.

I was a court jester until second grade, a straight-A student through my public school life, a dramatic actor, an incredibly good dancer. I held doors, I did gentlemanly things I thought you were supposed to do to get girls to like you—wrote poems, whispered sweet nothings, loved my mama, learned to clean, cook, be well-mannered. I did the things white people would approve of—did well in school, listened to authority figures, kept my pants at waist level, and avoided being too loud or aggressive in public. Whatever the right thing was, I adhered to it, and not reluctantly. No one told me Black was defiant, was the antipathy of anything that sat in normative, societal behaviors. Following the rules—rules that were never made for us or meant for us—could be categorized as anti-Black. I was trying to fit in. Blackness doesn't fit in anywhere, it just is. My Blackness lived in a construct, lived and lied in its limitations. My friendships did the same. My friendships upheld the standards, even if my friendships in grade school defied that: we were Black and brown overachievers fed by free lunch, ducking crack spots and gang wars along the way. We were connected by our lack of new textbooks, by being lower middle class, and, at times, downright poor. We were connected by the juices we drank for twenty-five cents after we played football in the streets. We shared the same streets, the same harassment from the police, the same feeling that our white teachers didn't understand us, judged our choices in clothes, in words, and in music.

The friends I made growing up were the homies in proximity. And we were all different. Making friends in elementary school was so simple. Everyone who went to PS 33 on Jerome Avenue in the Bronx was local to the block and neighborhood, at least within that three-block radius. We all were primarily into the same things: girls, video games, and sports. And getting into trouble. And because I avoided trouble like the plague, primarily because my West Indian mother would have snuffed the life out of my lungs, when I wasn't with the homies, I was with my other homie: my imaginary friends. After we'd all play tag, after we'd exchange X-Men trading cards, after we'd argue over if the Knicks would ever win a title, after the games of free tag and off the wall, after stickball in my mother's courtyard at 2435 Creston Avenue or two-hand touch football or parked car sitting or running to the corner store for quarter waters and Now and Laters, I'd head home and build my own world. In that world, I'd freestyle rap my days away in my mother's bedroom because it was easier to negotiate decisions with invisible friends than it would be with real-life six- and seven-year-olds who couldn't possibly understand how badly I wanted to be loved and seen. In that world I was invincible, easily avoiding the discrepancies that seemed to exist whenever my feet would hit the pavement, and I would learn to run and duck the pitfall of Black bones that exists when you are not born with much but a wondrous will to want for more, to survive where they have told you that survival is outside of the realms of possibility. So, you reimagine a way out. And it was not a concept I could readily identify with my friends. We were all preoccupied with getting out and finding different ways of what "getting out" could mean with very limited resources. My man E joined a gang. Rich focused on getting money. Some of us barely got by, focusing on the day-to-day ways we use to deflect. Some of us joined gangs, flagging and learning signs and colors with beads resembling tribes we would never learn the names of. Some learned how to roll weed, how to boost and steal their way into clothing racks and retail stores. Some learned the language of violence to marry themselves to a street life they saw their uncles and cousins and brothers and daddies emulate.

Having graduated from a high school with a majority white student body, it wasn't until my freshman year in college that I would have my first real taste of adult male friendship. Through brothers like Craig, Triz, G, Red, Q, and David, I could be all the parts of myself while not being in fear of ridicule. While some parts of this may have existed in middle school, our types of conversation were primarily limited to music and sports. That was probably most middle schoolers, but when you are a sensitive Black boy growing up in a world that deems your sensitivity as effeminate, it is easy to feel lost and be reminded of your facility—stare downs in train stations, shoves and words exchanged on crowded buses and hallways. In college, I was all parts rapper, spoken word poet, thinker, and clown. The depth I sought in Black male counterparts was accessible and in a cultural language that met me and others where we were. When 9/11 happened we grieved, we shared stories, we recounted memories, and we listened to Jay-Z's *The Blueprint* album on repeat and discussed it in the cafeteria for days on end.

As I got older, my friends got older, too. My brother D's friends became my friends by default. As I moved into more rap circles, I would see firsthand how softness was indeed interpreted as weakness. So much of masculinity at the time was defined off the strength and viability of physical appearance. Height and weight signified strength. A certain kind of confidence and aggression is what would get you labeled an alpha, and being labeled an alpha was as good as any sort of credit you could obtain in the hood. My friendships, while beautiful and fulfilling, would also be by default for most of my life: we shared commonality with location. And immediate community. After college, our deepest conversations revolved around our relationships with the various women in our lives, us scratching the surface with the barely functioning language we had on love at the time. We talked about feelings, our hurts, our struggles, but we never stayed with them for too long. The point wasn't to examine and interrogate, but to share and potentially duck and avoid accountability. And if you were a certain kind of man, you remained neutral. And even when we confronted each other with mishaps or mistakes made in love and with love, it was still with limited language, a language that felt too far from us to be able to reach for. The lack of real language, a deeper language surrounding vulnerability, about trust and the patriarchy and being introspective not just about our feelings but the feelings of those we may have hurt tended to shape how we held (or didn't hold at all) space for the complexities in those conversations. Mainly because we didn't even know it existed. My friendships were fruitful and meaningful. But I was looking for something deeper.

There is no handbook for making friends as an adult. And even though there are a number of friend-finding apps, they feel a little like the kind of app that shows up on 2:00 A.M. BET infomercials right next to Christian Mingle or Black People Meet. It's hard to imagine who I'd be talking to. But then, I worry that maybe the problem is that I don't know how to talk to Black men. I can't tell you the last time I sat and watched any type of sporting event. I cannot play spades, nor do I care to know how. The only dominoes I recognize are the ones that come with cheesy bread and boneless wings. I don't enjoy long talks while slathering barbecue sauce on a chicken. I mean, do niggas even say shit like that? I don't know, but I know I stopped smoking cigars years ago, I don't know how to hold a game controller, I ain't touch a barbershop since 1999 (I cut my own hair), and I don't got a car I can fix up or talk about how I'm about to fix up. I don't belong to no megachurch or anything like that. Not part of a community basketball league or work kickball team that plays on the weekends. No gym buddies. No fraternity to step with, get drunk with, or to haze or initiate via gangbang into.

As a young man, the social groups I joined or was allowed into were largely because of their proximity, or because I had cool toys at home or had access to hip-hop records that others didn't because my older brother worked at a record store. My adult male friendships generally fell into the category of "what can Joél do for me?" And I more than happily obliged. I scribbled out poems for friends to help them get girls. I helped friends with essays (re: wrote) to help them get better grades. I did these things, yes, surely out of the kindness of my heart, but also because I thought that's what it took to get people to love me, to see me as a friend, as an ally. I wanted to be invited to the birthday parties I would not go to because I couldn't afford the right shoes or had shaved off my eyebrows (true story) or wanted to avoid the perpetual state of awkward that is me in group settings when I have to engage with people I don't know in unfamiliar territories. My kind of charm works in low lighting, primarily in small groups where small talk is limited and we jump right into childhood trauma and our stances on abolition, liberalism, and *X-Men: The Animated Series* (in that order). Making friends as an adult is like having to listen to nails scratching against a chalkboard as ASMR. I kid I kid I joke, it's probably worse than that. Aiight, bet I'm exaggerating greatly. But you get what I'm saying. It was made doubly harder for me because whatever the status quo, neat box you're supposed to fit in as a cis-hetero Black man hailing from the Bronx is a feat my arms are far too short for. I fall too short in a number of areas as a Black man, I think.

So, for Black men, love is generally reserved for the women

in our lives. We are seldom taught how to embrace or fold into love, let along the idea of verbally expressing that love to our closest male friends because we are rarely taught how to love ourselves that is not in some way, shape, or form connected to how much we can produce in order to be considered worthy or exceptional. Praise for Black men is reserved for how well we perform our masculinity—in the bedroom, the boardroom; on the football field, the basketball court, the stage; for the ribs we grill and the tires we change and the cars we fix. How well we love is a relatively new barometer for a majority of us.

So when I was told by friends in high school that me wearing slacks and a vest on a school day that wasn't for a dance or prom or a funeral, that I was dressing like a white boy; or in elementary school if I did too well in class or got high grades on a test or read the books we were asked to read or did the homework they asked us to do, and have your friends call you white, you question not only your friendships and their integrity, but also your own Blackness. Those interactions, among others, distort your perception of your Blackness. Mix that in with being Afro-Caribbean, and no one explaining to me or really any of us, what that meant to us growing up—the layers, the nuance, the context of growing up in New York City amid so many different ethnicities, where also nationalities become tribal and sometimes take precedence over race, skin color, and class, changes the flavor of how we interact not only with each other but also with ourselves. When no one gives you the language to unpack your own intersectionality, how can you handle unpacking the intersections of your intimate relationships, including your friendships? Black males going into adulthood aren't given the luxury to unpack anything: feeling, trauma, hurt, joy, abuse, our language, our misplaced anger and misogyny, the ways patriarchy and white supremacy can at times share some of the same energy as certain rebellious elements of zealous Black Hebrews, Zionists, and Five Percenters. We are too busy busying ourselves with masculinity and the attempts of upholding the ideas of what it means to be a Black man in America. The idea that we must be breadwinners, we must work always, we must not be emotional. To question the rules, to question the language given to us, would mean to question our relationships to masculinity, to the men in our communities, and to our friendships.

As an adolescent and teenager, the social groups I was forced into made having Black male counterparts pretty much a breeze: proximity to a playground, to a ball court, to a bodega; an unlimited supply of toys, snacks, and video games; ghetto kids all attending the same public school and middle school; a shared drama class in high school and a shared dorm in college. When I look around, I see men who have held tight to the friendships and bonds started in their younger years. Men who look forward to a weekly hang over whiskey and cigars, beers and stories about broken homes and adolescent misfortunes. They catch up about who did what with whom, remembering so and so who has just passed, who just married, who just came home, who slept with so and so. Maybe they survey the neighborhood outside their steps or their homes or their cars, reminiscing on what was and looking ahead at what the potential could be. I don't have that. I lost that in high school. Some of us went to different schools. The ones who went to the same schools stayed close until we didn't, reverting to comfortable social groups and status quos until we figured out who we thought we were.

"Intimate friendships don't come with shared social scripts

that lay out what they should look like or how they should progress. These partnerships are custom-designed by their members," Rhaina Cohen wrote in the *Atlantic* essay "What If Friendship, Not Marriage, Was at the Center of Life?" Cohen wrote about a multitude of deep, complex, and beautiful friendships between women, friendships that expand the notion of friendship and their role in relation to monogamous, committed relationships such as marriage. And while the essay centered around women's friendships, much can be gleaned from the topic, as there aren't many ways in Western society where men can talk freely and openly about the intimacy involved in how we gather and congregate. The phrase "date your friends" is rarely if ever used within the context of male friendships, especially Black. The discussion would lean into the superficial components of what makes those friendships: how they met, what they share in common, the length of friendship. The emotional connection isn't drawn until somebody has to write a best man speech. Black men are not afforded the space to unpack our feelings about our personal relationships, let alone the dynamics of those relationships. We don't discuss intimacy, how we see each other, or even the stakes involved when it comes to the direction of those relationships. So, if you're in your thirties, and yet to land a secure Black men's brunch group, or Black men's church group, or Black men's fantasy league, or Black men's pickup game committee, you have to hope you find a friend or new group of them using old-school methods. Like, social media maybe. Social media has brought many of the friends that I still hold dear to me. But I would come to realize that there was a hole that I felt needed to be filled. Whether it was because of the lack of a father, or just based on the other friendships I saw out in the open, what I realized was that there was a strong desire to have connection that would bring all my worlds together—the music, the love, the appreciation of art, with a hood aesthetic—the ability to see things through the lens of the ghetto I grew up in. Frankly, I had been looking for a romantic partner to fill a lot of these things. I wanted to go to an art show with someone and maybe catch a flick and not have to explain any of the feelings I felt after. Or, if we did talk afterward, that it was a discussion and not an examination of who I was. I wanted to talk about the latest project while dissecting the angles of Bob's Burgers. I wanted someone who was like me but was very much unlike me. And, how I explained it, a friendship custom-designed for me. And I didn't know I needed or wanted any of those things until I met Ty.

After work, I cleared up my desk, packed my bag, took the 6 train headed uptown to what felt like a newly gentrified section of East Harlem. Google Maps led me to a somewhat seedy apartment building that probably served as a hookah refill station, and I rang the buzzer. I walked into a comfy-enough studio space—clearly someone had saved enough coins to build out the living room area to turn it into a recording space where I assumed rappers broke weed atop old vinyl covers and sat on thirteen-day-old Cheetos while writing and reciting scribbled bars from notes in their iPhones. I arrived with no tea offered or available, which was very odd to me at the time. He explained to me that he actually used to offer tea during the conversations, but now it was more about the vibe of the show. There were also no Converse shoes on display at all, but I did meet Ty. I was still worried about messing his name up because it's just spelled wild funny. Like, if you had a robot friend but it was from the hood and someone asked you to give the hood robot a name and instead of calling it Tyrone, you just took the *e* to keep it official. We dapped up and began the interview. But, before we started, he introduced me to his daughter, Xéla. Their rapport was friendly but combative, like two friends who have been friends for a really long time, except the friends happened to be a newly crowned teenager and a thirty-something father. While they spoke, she asked him what he did with her fish-eye lens. He chuckled and admitted he might have lost it. She kindly chastised him for his lack of remembrance. And in this exchange, I got a glimpse of what true fatherhood sounded and tasted like; in her I saw the joy of being loved by a father, a Black father. Their exchange as father and daughter, but also as friends, showed me a space I had yet to see. Both of my brothers had sons, but they always felt like dads that gave dad energy— the energy that is loving, yes, but also a bit more direct. In Ty and Xéla I was witnessing something different: they talked the way friends would talk. There was an ease, a love, and a certain kind of joy that lived outside of the norms that dictate fathers of all sorts should carry shotguns anytime their daughters stepped foot outside of the house. I had never seen a Black father with his Black teenage daughter in real life, only in TV sitcoms. Seeing Ty with his daughter was a Halley's comet of sorts. Plus, they were talking about photography. What that told me is that he and Xéla's mother had curated a space for her that allowed for discovery, to pick up and do the things that spoke to her, and to try them. No one just carries a fish-eye lens around in their bag unless it is intentional. And I thought, If I had a daughter, I'd want her to trust me with her fish-eye lens, too.

So, I trusted that he must be a good man. We sat down, and

with my water in hand, we talked for over an hour and some change about music, life, the hood, acting . . . the works. We left and dapped up, and I decided then and there that I was going to make Ty my friend—my new Black friend. And I did. Let him tell it, we sat on the steps of the Allen Street playground in our shared favorite neighborhood, the Lower East Side, and I spilled the beans about the struggles of early fatherhood. I don't recall any of this, because fatherhood and stress ages you, and calamity can subtract years off of your memory. But what I can remember is it would be not too long after that anywhere Ty went, I went, and vice versa. We'd share music. We'd share random voice notes about food, about dates, about rap lyrics and songs and albums; obscure liner notes and artsy shit that we knew only we could understand. When I want someone to know of some obscure thing—whether it be a food, or a place, an artist, or an idea—that has a credible buzz on the outskirts of nowhere, I go to Ty. He was the first person to put me on to Griselda. Ty played drums in a band in high school. Ty did the Black kid cool shit, even now, that I had always wanted to do back then.

When I became a father and co-parenting was pushing me to the brink, I called Ty. He was a voice of reason without being overbearing. He wasn't trying to doctor me with advice about what I should or shouldn't do, but was just a healthy sounding board. Male friendships often meant protecting egos. It meant brash and responsive behavior rather than patience and calmness. Often, all myself and other male friends would do is hide behind our insecurities, deflecting and posturing by projecting the best innate qualities we carried, leading with whatever would best hide pain—we'd hide behind our money, our dick size (how many "bodies" you caught a heavy topic of discussion), our knowledge of sports or music industry topics, our abilities or physical capabilities. These ways of being tend to not only influence our relationships and friendships, but also the spaces that we dominate by the sheer hierarchy of the world. Such pretenses didn't really exist with Tyron. But that was rare for me in Black male friendships. Not because I didn't want. But because we were operating out of trauma the majority of the time. And the freest I tended to feel, and be almost always, was when I was around Black women.

Some would say I have a rainbow coalition of friends, a group of friends that feels like home to me. And a majority of them identify as women. When I was growing up, the friends I kept close were mainly because of proximity, and that proximity was male. You just didn't have women friends. Women were for the male gaze only, used as a barometer of how cool you were: how many girls liked you, wanted to be with you; how many girls you could bag and get a number from. As we grew older that became how many women you had slept with. Women lost names, lost identity in those days. Women became body counts, became "ole girl with the fatty," became the butts of jokes or the butts we passed in the halls or the butts we slapped without consent or the butts we grabbed in the club when we were too drunk to know or care if we offended anyone. The posing we all did, the posing I took part in, was always for show. It wasn't until middle school when I had someone who I considered my first friend of the opposite sex, Fran, who I wasn't trying to secretly make into a muse or a girlfriend that I could parade around to show how much of a man I was becoming to my peers. She would become my confidante in a way, creating space for the kind of intimate sharing that was very unique and considerably different when compared to the male friendships I had acquired. It was in that space where I got to hear the details of young love and heartbreak; compassion and what authentic listening looks like. Fran was dealing with real life and love decisions in our teenage years, and my job was that of trusted confidant. Our friendship is still the most long-standing friendship I've had. We fell in and out of friendship owing to time, distance, and other relationships that shifted our dynamic over the years. Finding each other again was a beautiful reminder for me that love in all capacities gets to shift, change, and blossom, no different than the season and weather.

So many of the men I grew up with and around dealt with the surface level of feelings and emotions. Anything deeper than that we learned to hide or drown out in drugs, in alcohol, in sex, in violence. We draped ourselves in the armor of pain, the shield of misogyny as our war garments; the act of fist to face, mouth to bottle, becomes how we funnel the depth of our feelings, all drained into a vacuum none of us are privy to. My man Rich was my best friend for years, but a shift happened when I was writing rap songs to process and find my way through my heart, whereas Rich seemed to be more concerned with rap as a means to an end to make money. Our relationship in high school drifted more because proximity to each other also changed how we got to interact with each other. A long-term relationship turned engagement pulled me away from a majority of my college friends, as I was too afraid to let others into the depths of our relationship and the issues we had. As much as I desired closeness, I also pushed others away, unsure of myself and unsure if I was ready to allow my friends into my heartspace. My feelings I gave credence to through notebooks—a litany of words strewn together over pages and loose-leaf, full of rancor and desire, mischief and denial, heartbreak and longing. Even throughout high school, friendships with young girls were still opportunities to turn them into partners, or to turn them into idealized versions of whatever existed in male friendships: name-calling, jokes, sports talk. The affixed labels to gender roles and dynamics had been firmly etched into my programming.

College became where I would learn a new language of friendship. One that was not predetermined by gender. For so many of us, college became the place where we would try on new versions of self, with people who did not know the older versions of us—the tired, tried versions, the ones with the hangups and preexisting daddy issues. The scars blended neatly with the ramen nights and party sweat. Our shared living quarters, the stories we held against our chests and out in the world; the ones we buffered between classes and huddled over with meal passes in crowded lunchrooms and punch-drunk conference halls . . . these became the homes where the bodies mattered not as much as the spirit. I was sowing seeds of companionship; I was falling in love (for real for real). I would lose my virginity to Tweet's *Southern Hummingbird* album. I would make out with girls outside of dorms; would help my friend duck a charge and let him stay in my room over the summer. I would be given the gift of companionship from both men and women who looked like me, who knew what it meant to walk in a Black body as a young adult. We were dealing with shit, publicly, in the open and letting the nuance of our bleeding hit the winds and beat our faces, and each of us was learning how to be with each other in a way that was new to me, that would set the tone for how I wanted all my relationships to be.

However, there was something missing—commonality. Because for all the beautiful people around me, there was nothing, there is nothing, like the kinship felt from a fellow Black man. A grown, and consistently growing, kinship. I can't explain it to you if you're not in the know. It can feel like water. Nourishment. Kinship can sometimes be the only lifeboat we have available in a world that would rather watch us sit idly while loss, racism, and grief eat away at our lives and well-being. We lean on to and into each other for laughs, for words of comfort, and sometimes just a silent and shared experience of living that affords something that society cannot take away from us—peace. And the ground we get to cover runs the gamut of so much. Like, why Usher and not Mario? Why did B.I.G. blow up and not Craig Mack? What made you go left instead of right? Many variables, all unexplainable . . . it just is what it is. And it's a sincere, simple understanding that speaks volumes in crowded rooms; rooms that often don't fully represent our complexities and diversity of experience and thought. Black men are expansive, not expendable. Kinship teaches us that.

Meeting Ty felt like closure, a cycle of lack in male companionship and friendship officially over. I was looking for a homie in my age bracket who I could shoot the shit with. Granted, the wholeness I feel is a wholeness of self; the feeling of knowing I complete me, right? My Ram Dass shit. For upward of five years, Ty was a friend when I ain't even know I needed one. Birthday parties, family get-togethers, wack parties with weird dancing niggas at the Ace Hotel. Ty was at every show I performed at.

Every show. Sometimes he'd record them. We decided to start our own podcast and recorded at White Castle locations because we were both greedy hood niggas who loved White Castle. Anytime Ty had an event for a podcast or a book launch, I'd be there, barring any times when I'd have to watch my newborn, my first child, Lilah. I went to see Pink Siifu with Ty at a concert in Brooklyn and proceeded to get water thrown at me from onstage, literal water, like I was fifteen at a punk concert. When Ty typed "LOL" or "ha" it's because he actually meant it. The first time I heard the word *phô* was with Ty because he dragged me around Brooklyn looking for it. Ty was my best friend. Until he wasn't.

Unfollowing someone you love sounds trivial until you recognize it's part of the slow dismantling of what was. The unfollow generally is the last straw, the final straw before the mute. Some debate the merit of the mute function, but the psychology behind it rings true—an unfollow is more than just the click of a button. It's become a statement. It tells the unfollowed "I no longer care to know what's going on with you." And the functions of mute and unfollow differ, depending on the context of the relationship. Casual follows and unfollows from strangers can usually be attributed to a few things: 1. Following a person for one thing but then learning that one post was an outlier (e.g., you saw a Reel of dog content and then went to follow them only to learn they mainly post memes of Umar Johnson). 2. Following a person for their Umar Johnson memes, only to realize *all* they post is Umar Johnson memes at least four to five times a day. 3. You followed them for their Umar Johnson meme content only to find out they voted for Trump. 4. You thought they were single until you saw the shadow of a person who took their photo and saw their caption and knew *that* was a lie. When you unfollow a friend, there's generally only one reason: yawl no longer fuck with each other.

I couldn't tell you what ended our friendship even if I tried. But I can tell you the last time we had a full-fledged text conversation: January 5, 2020. My eldest daughter, my now four-year-old Lilah, was moving to Texas with her mother, with no known return date. As much as I tried to prepare myself for her departure, I knew it would be one of the hardest things I would have to endure. My daughter is the center of my world. To maximize the time before the move, I planned a going-away gathering at our favorite spot, the Children's Museum of Manhattan on the Upper West Side. I invited only my closest friends and family, a tight circle of folks that loved and cared for Lilah, including Ty and his now sixteen-year-old teenage daughter, Xéla. What I didn't know was, for whatever reason, Ty was anti the Children's Museum of Manhattan. A few texts went back and forth, and in my head I couldn't quite grasp how the person I considered to be one of the best people in my life was making what was a moment where I needed him the most into a moment that revolved around him and an issue he refused to disclose. Besides, he would be going with Xéla, even if he hated the museum every time they went there. Looking back now, I feel like it was selfish of me to be upset about something that was potentially triggering for him. But, in that moment, and the subsequent moments after, I was forced to reckon with the fact that Ty never was good at dealing with the uncomfortable. Most Black men aren't.

Ty never showed up to the museum. Or my birthday party show a couple of weeks later. Or to the hospital or our apartment in Bed-Stuy to see my partner and our new child together, our daughter, West. Nor did he respond to my texts. I thought back to the countless conversations we'd had about relationships and how dipping was also easier for him than confrontation. For a majority of Black men, confrontation for us results in death. Stepping on sneakers, scuffles in clubs and alleyways and desolate corners in front of dimming bodega lights. Confrontation is yelling, toxic words and emotions flung to faces with spittle and aggressive mannerisms to boot. The room to settle differences, to talk things through, to put the fragility of our egos aside for the greater good, is a skill we are rarely ever taught or shown. Public displays of admiration and affection generally wind up being turned into a game of the dozens against each other, with one trying to outjest the other. Passive-aggressive digs as a form of flattery, riling each other up a symbol of real love between friends. Black men aren't allowed to process, to feel. Feeling is too strong a signal of vulnerability, too easy to be spotted amongst wolves as a sign of weakness, too soft to be taken seriously, or soft enough to be taken in general. My entire being has been to be the antithesis of all that I had been taught. By confronting Ty with what I saw as a hurt, reflecting that and opening space to talk through it, what I was really opening up was the space seldom held for any of us: comfort. And comfort found in other men can be uncomfortable. I've gone over in my head what caused the rift. A few friends have asked me what caused the rift. I have no answer for the rift, or the fallout.

How do you break up with a friend if you are a man, a Black man? Our relationships are supposed to end in death: diabetes, or violence against each other, if you let the media tell it. We don't discuss feelings of loss or grief. We bottle things up. We refrain from speaking. We push the tension to the side and ignore it or walk away completely, battered and bruised and carrying the scarlet letter of shame on our chests to every function, every relationship, every argument and sideways glance and perceived insult and misstep until we are six feet under. We are tabulating, taking tally and accounting for every side-eyed look, every enviable and awkward glance, every unliked photo the algorithm forced, every unread email, text, and unanswered invitation.

The spring of 2020 Ty texted me after the looting that happened in the Bronx on Fordham Road about a block away from where my mother lives, to see if she was all right. At 11:30 P.M. I hadn't heard from Ty since January. No explanation. No text before or after acknowledging anything. Black men are not supposed to have emotions. I have a heap of them. We all do. The world has forced us to believe otherwise. In that moment, I knew I was dealing not with Ty's shit, but all of our shit: our inability to cope with and deal with hard, big emotions. We are not robots. We are not machines. But what if we could build machines to teach us what we didn't know?

I don't know. Sometimes, I sit at the living room table and imagine a world in which I could build us up a big, Black love machine. The kind of machine a Black man can walk into and cast away the hurt and fear that keep us from sustaining meaningful and intimate relationships with each other. The kind of machine that sharpens our empathy and compassion and makes way for inclusivity and intersectionality so that our triggers teach us, not torment us; that our trauma does not have to tear into us and tear us apart in the process. When I think of the Black male friends that I grew up with and the distance that exists now, a lot of it is me: not feeling Black enough, down enough, cool enough. I was the friend that had friends in varying friend groups, but never a consistent friend group of my own that would survive outside of the confines of the environments they existed in. Drama class friends, hip-hop friends, school friends, dorm room friends. It's like being invited to a party where you're friends with everybody, so you kind of forget that you aren't. You feel like an interloper, like you're eaves-dropping on the people with real friendships, real friendships that survive turmoil and fake school beef and distance; friendships that survive marriages, divorce, miscarriages, minor slights, and major setbacks. You don't belong to these friend groups. You are a bor-rowed friend. Even Ty had a friend group—friends he had since grade school, friends he kept from the days when he wanted to be a drummer in a band that played the kind of music Ty loved—off the beaten path, opaque, jarring, experimental. I don't know if that kind of machine is possible, the kind that can bring friendships back from the dead, the kind that can help us as Black men find the hearts society told us to stash away, but if I can make it come true, maybe I'll find some new friends in there, too.

Come to find out the machine wasn't very far. It was time. Time has a way of changing the framework of what was and what could be. The potential of anything exists in the construct and fluidity of time. It passes and goes. Hurts can shift, can bend like *Matrix* bullets in slow motion. Out and about in Chinatown with my girls and my partner after finishing some phô, I get a random text:

> Yo, were you just on the corner of _____?

It was Tyron. By that point, I had decided that I would faith-fully mourn the ending of our friendship. Grief is something

I had learned to embrace and simmer, like some witch's brew that has been sitting in a cauldron waiting to be used. Buddhism had prepared me for the pandemic and the impending grief that would follow upon not only watching the folks around me struggle with the loss of loved ones, of jobs and mortgages, but also grieving the transitions of life. A wave of seasonality many of us were unwilling to succumb to. The practice of mindfulness and nonattachment, so central to Buddhism, also would be how I would help others navigate their loss, while I was navigating the loss of my friend, and the long-distance relationship I would be forced to have with my child for the duration of the pandemic. So, to receive a text from Ty at three in the afternoon felt like a moment in time where a reluctant ghost had finally stepped through the portal. Because in the absence, I came to realize how much I needed Ty. The fear I had carried—a fear that had long made its way into my heart through the various times I'd learned to love and lose—was, Did he need me the same?

Black love does not have to be reserved for romantic partnership. Neither does it have to be exclusive to womanly companionship. Black men get and should be able to reap the benefits of what a multilayered, intimate friendship looks like, without being fearful of what even the use of that language in the outside world may convey. Romance does not have to be reserved for our partners. Romance does not have to exist in a box, in some sort of monogamous patriarchal way we identify which relationships matter the most. Intimacy gets to be up close, personal, real, and alive in all of our relationships, not just the ones we share a bed with. They get to expand like water within the vessels they're poured into. We get to pour into our relationships in a similar fashion. We have to. So much of what is seen as masculine is caricature, is performance art for the sake of optics and perception—so many of us don't know the real version of us because the real version of us is hidden by and informed by codes, rhetoric, and theory that was created without our consent or knowing. So much of what we deem to be masculine we have simply adopted as principle. If the pandemic taught me anything, it is how individualism and this idea that self-reliance is a virtue are the lies we are told in order to remain distant and detached from the goal of liberation. It takes a community to get free. And in order to build that community, there is a deeper level of love and vulnerability required across all of our relationships—even with the people we don't like; even the ones we loathe. This doesn't mean closeness and proximity in terms of communication. It doesn't even mean seeing the door open for reconnection, especially when there has been harm caused. But Black love and adult friendships require us to see things through the lens not only of reciprocity, communication, accountability, validation, and boundaries—a few of the pillars that help us maintain healthy relationships—but requires moving from a carceral construct and toward an abolitionist mindset when it comes to our friendships. We tend to punish the ones we love after they've done something we deem to be unforgivable or inadmissible. That is directly correlated to how we treat, or rather mistreat, our jail and prison populations. To be incarcerated is a forever scarlet letter, prohibiting you from enjoying and engaging in the normative ways of day-to-day life, based on the hierarchy of mistakes you've made and harm caused. No one is redeemable. No one is forgivable. Cancel culture is prison culture redux. Because there is no real accountability—public shaming is not accountability. Because accountability innately requires some way our pathway toward a future in which harm can be acknowledged. But no room is left for it in the ways we handle harm. A better model for love and friendship, for Black love, needs to involve someplace where redemption is possible, not some foreign act of kindness, shame, or guilt under the guise of reconnection. Abolition tells us harm will happen and can happen, even around those we love. But creating safety is a communal activity, one in which no one group plays the role of judge and jury over accountability but recognizes we all play a role in how we let (or don't let) others reenter our lives and spaces. Our capacity for love is only limited by our imaginations. Recently, Ty texted me:

> You got food at your house? Me & Xéla hungry. Not Popeyes though.

> But if you're tryna grab dinner with me & Xéla we'll be on Vanderbilt getting haircuts. ✂️

Tyron and I check boxes of what it means to hold space as grown-ass adults trying to figure out the world together. And that love does not live separate from the love of my partner or my children but, rather, adds to it. And the idea that male friendships don't get to be as special, as intimate, and as warm as other relationships is what leaves so many of us looking for and longing for things and vices that isolate us from the truest, most vulnerable and loving versions of self. When Ty texts me about chicken, about art, about big booties, about rap songs, about relationships, I'm here for it. Because that's what friends are for.

Homecoming

Feat. Nipsey Hussle

No matter how much loot I get
I'm staying in the projects forever.

—HAVOC OF MOBB DEEP, "SURVIVAL OF THE FITTEST"

And the streets say Jigga can't go back home
You know when I heard that? When I was back home.

—JAY-Z, "STREETS IS TALKING"

When Havoc rapped that he planned on staying in the projects forever, my immediate thought was, Why? What Havoc was really speaking to was the communal need to stay as close to "home," or the idea of what home means, as possible. "Home" being the obligatory location where street shit reigns supreme. Our proximity to it gives us the cred we desire, not only as Black men but as Black men who also need to be seen as alpha men in spaces where being considered less than alpha can get you disrespected or, worse, murdered. Hov was trying to tell us he can go home anytime he wants to. Whether that statement is true or not, what the Jigga man was speaking to was the same notion: home, the hood, the projects, the block—its desirability, no matter how desolate or distant from an ideal we may sometimes chase till our grave, is still the place to be.

For many, home is a physical location. Big mama's house on Sundays. The smells of warm, stove-topped food being cooked and stirred, searing our noses with the memories of family gatherings, drinking until the dusk eats the clouds, moments all congregating together like a symphony of love, all of us sitting with each other for a spell until we do it all over again.

Sometimes home can look like counting all of the ghosts in the rooms. The bodies en masse gathering for loss. The ones who didn't make it back home for whatever reason, without being granted the opportunity to move forward along with the rest of us. Other times home can look like forgiveness—it can look like seeing in the eyes of those no longer here and still present, looking for either a way in or a way out. And that version of home can shift; can expand; can become stardust in our hearts; can be the remembrance of raindrops that bring us back to play, a sweet humming for the heart. Home gets to be poetic. It does not have to be a footnote. Home can be where our imaginations go to roost. Home can be dead weight. Can be the fire after the insult, the place we run from where there is nobody or nowhere else to turn to. Home can feel like a new chapter or can feel like a chapter we are trying to burn. Home can rip at our cartilage, can feast on the leftovers, to make a plate out of our well-being, the last feed of fixings before the supper is done. I've spent a lifetime finding the language of home for me. And every time I ask, the answer to it changes. Home is fluid in that way. Home is a YouTube comment section, rummaging through and seeing the thoughts and responses from two days, two months . . . two years ago; a thread on culture crossing borders. For some, home looks like a bulldozer of buildings, of people, of feelings crushed by the metal grip of a Barclays, or some other industrial complex meant to harness the tears of Blackness for profit. Home can be where the heat is. Home can be with you, carried into the kitchen with the oven open, trapping in the warm of a winter spent with the help of a radiator, can also be the heat under the mattress for the cold wintry nights where ashy knuckles grip things we wish we wouldn't remember. Home can be fraught with more questions than answers; a series of avalanches.

For most of us home is a location; a place we can come back to over and over again. For me, my home has almost always been the Bronx. The body doesn't forget home—every argument, every beef, every slammed door; every bacon, egg, and cheese; the time we stole Hi-C and Pringles from Caldor, playing with the last remaining action figures before the store would be replaced. The blocks surrounding the area, a museum of nostalgic Bronx relics that speak to what feels like a forgotten time, would change, too: Sammy's would be no longer be the epitome of hip-hop fashion; Buster Brown's would give way to Porta Bella, the home of reasonably priced fashions that would serve as everyone's prom, wedding, last-minute club fit, and quinceañera option.

And for others, home is the block—a long stretch of buildings, houses, corner stores, gum stains, fallen soldiers, fallen leaves, names and gang affiliations keyed into the ground, debris from parked cars, cement cracks, dry pavement. It is the first and fifteenth, it is layaway and store credit; it is a statement made after a life taken, a mistaken identity turned sour; the hours shopping up and down with Aunty KK; it is Bon Bini and Rainbow and Strawberry; it's nicknames like Pookie and Tee Tee and Boola and Biggs; it's slap boxing and elderly Black women sitting in lawn chairs selling candies for a penny around the way; it's Ms. Shirley doing your mother's hair upstairs while her cat stalked the hallways. The block is mythological. Everyone's block is different, and yet so much the same—a domain we would return to after school, after the playground, after summer vacation, after watching MJ score forty, fifty, and sixty; we'd regroup, we'd plan and strategize: Whose crib we going to? Who got the Sega Genesis? The Xbox? The PlayStation? Whose moms not home? Whose moms gonna let us bring friends over? Whose moms cooking tonight? Whose moms got the fatty? Whose moms whose moms whose moms but never the daddies. We rode bikes, played skellies, freeze tag, off the wall, stickball, two-hand touch football, manhunt; we shot dice, we had block parties, we played until the streetlights came on, we played spades, we played dominoes, we played basketball with the milk crate; we ate ices, ran for the Mister Softee truck, ran from gangs, drank quarter waters, drank nutties, drank Olde E'—all on the block. We melted and melded into the block, a Voltron of synchronicity, each one of us becoming together . . . growing, laughing, learning. Some of us cling to the block like it is the last thing we have ever loved. And sometimes, the block is a metaphor, an idea. Because there is also the culture of the block; the things that connect us back to the feeling of whatever home is. We chase it, the rush of nostalgia flaring our nostrils. And if you happen to accrue a certain level of fame, success, or notoriety, then the call beckons you back to the block and will break your back, the pressured weight of returning to the all too familiar.

We as Black men tend to reach for home in so many ways—in pussy, in our mamas' arms, in our cars, and in our jobs. And for those Black men who lack the stability of any kind of home, there can be a want and need to snatch what sense of home others may have right from their throats. Home, more clearly defined as shelter, is a necessity. It is not trite or overblown to think that a home is as needed as food and water. And if you lack the bare necessity of home, seeing others frolic in the safety of that state is a crushing blow to the ego and heart. And to see someone, say a Black man, fully living in whatever version of home they have cultivated for themselves, can be triggering; can make you run up on them, pull a trigger, and take their comfort away and make it your own. This is how Stack Bundles lost his life. Stack was on his way to stardom—an affiliate of Jim Jones's ByrdGang who had also worked with the likes of Lupe Fiasco, Lil Wayne, and others—but was shot in front of his Far Rockaway Projects holding a White Castle bag. A month before his murder, his Porsche was vandalized. Far Rockaway was Stack's home. He stayed home, even while his home was a hotbed of violence, a mirror to the same world he rapped about, the same world he was also seeking to climb out of. Chinx Drugz, a close friend of Stack's, was murdered in a drive-by shooting over a years-long feud that started on Rikers Island. It's alleged the shooter was also an aspiring rapper, jealous of Chinx's rise with French Montana and their crew, the Coke Boyz. Unbeknownst to Chinx, he was being stalked the night of his murder by someone looking to trade a life for a life. Like Stack, Chinx was killed back in his old stomping grounds of Queens. Coming back home has a price. Choosing to stay home and rebuild it? A potentially bigger one.

Maybe you were making breakfast when you heard Nipsey Hussle was murdered. Washing your car, walking your dog, running a mile, or two. Hitting the gym. Hitting up the homies. Normal stuff. You were somewhere, in some urban city tagging up walls with a name or a set or an avenue. Somewhere with nets missing from the rims in the playground, where thick spring air meets project building decay in a town close to home far from yours. Somewhere, someone parked a car with Chucks on the dashboard and lit a smoke, rolled down a window, and poured out an ounce or two for a man they never met. Some of us lit candles, and convened at our versions of the Staples arena—a corner, a condo even, posted up looking at the sky-line. We shut down convenience stores. We pulled out old CDs; we reminisced and made phone calls and sent texts with jittery fingers. We broke bread, and in between the crumbs and open mouths and laughter, somebody sobbed until the clouds did, too. Some of us may have run to the Marathon Clothing store. Somewhere in that day you sat down and said a prayer for Lau-ren. For Kross and Emani. For Blacc Sam. Maybe you made salat, found a stereo system large enough to fit all the sounds of the ancients, of the ancestors, and dedicated music to the sounds of California, playing "Victory Lap" until everything besides the sun melted from the vibration.

If you were anything like me, you cried and yelled. Cried like a loved one was just lost, like a close friend was no longer here; cried like something was stolen from me, from us; cried for

Lauren, cried for his babies. Cried for parents who had to bury their son. Cried for the city, for the future . . . cried for the culture. If you were anything like the author, you hustled to the Marathon Store online and, if you hadn't already, pulled out your wallet and posthumously purchased your Crenshaw jersey. If you were also anything like your author, you had to wait over a year to get your Crenshaw jersey shipped to you. And you may have even worn it when you had the opportunity to rock a stage and maybe channel some of that Nip energy into a crowd. And rocking that jersey, you knew you would have waited a year longer or more. Any amount of time would have been the right time to wait for Nipsey. If you had the time, maybe your body got itself from its love seat and ran to Crenshaw and Slauson. You could have knelt there. You would have seen a mural or two, faces with floodwater tears on them, everyone washing away, waiting for an answer. Years spent grappling with his death have shown me this—Nipsey reminded me of home. He felt familiar and as close to the block, to the corner of 188th and Creston Avenue as Slauson did to him.

The moment I found out Nip died, I was in bed. I'd had an enjoyable day: a typical Sunday, before the baby and bills, included coffee and breakfast somewhere in Bed-Stuy. Eventually, our little family came back home, our physical place of rest. And looking at my phone that afternoon, I struggled to make sense of what I was reading on Twitter, what my partner told me to read. What seemed to be trending didn't make sense. Rappers get shot all the time, right? It has become the rite of passage for successful artists who came up in the streets to have their credentials tested, to have their music serve as a mirror reflection of the ones back home they represent. Except, Ermias wasn't a normal rapper. Ermias wasn't a rapper, at all. Ermias Asghedom could have been anything—a lawyer, a doctor, an engineer. Calling him just a rapper belittles the work and the energy. The same one who sent kites and care packages to the ones coming home from a bid. The same one who created STEM programs for the community. As a father, and as a Black man, my heart was in shambles. When certain folks move on, you can feel the energy pivot—something changed.

I wore a blue bandanna in my blazer when I stepped on the TED stage in December 2019. Not just for Nipsey, but for all the Nipseys, for Ermias. I wore it because at best, I knew there was something to be said of a father who no longer could be physically present like me. A man who, on any given day, could have been my cousin, my brother, my bodega-bound, strip mall hero. This man talked finance and trap and spoke about legacy like they were next-door neighbors; drug talk, street talk, Wraith talk, Rolex talk. Nipsey was all of us. But with that, we have to be careful to not make this man into a myth, a mountain of an image to attach our dreams to. His homophobic comments were a reflection of so many other Black men who use masculinity as a way to interrogate and question the masculinity of others who choose to love differently and, arguably, more proudly and honestly. Nipsey's being was a contradiction. Nipsey was as real and as tangible as the block of the strip mall in Crenshaw that he rebuilt, creating businesses to benefit and support the people in the same community he grew up in. He didn't have a chance, a chance to do all the things; a chance to be a grandfather, to walk his daughter down the aisle. The chance to grow old with us. Unfortunately, a lot of Nipseys never do. Thirty-three years is far too limited of a time for anyone. Imagine Hov not making it past forty. With all the flaws, all the humanness in his experience and language, age and experience allow for growth, for reflection. A life brutally snatched away. If you come from where some of us come from, we *all* know/knew a Nipsey. We lose Nipseys every day. Some don't make a blip on the news or social feeds. With the passing of his life, we create a memorial of his message at the gravesite, each of us leaving a wreath or a piece of memorabilia as a memory. What will we do with this time? What will we do at this moment, now? How do we want to be remembered? How do we remember Nipsey? What does a legacy look like and mean? How do we celebrate life? How do we mourn it?

It is so scary to think and believe that we don't have control over what happens tomorrow. That our existence, that people and the homes we make in places can be snatched from us so quickly. That our belief in a divine order does not ensure a decisive path to end on. A beautiful, young, flawed Black man was murdered—a father, a partner, a businessman, an artist; gone far too soon. I don't need to remind you to keep your loved ones close. We can't control the when, or even the how. All we can do is show up as the truest versions of ourselves, intentionally, with the love our hearts are afforded and make amends and peace with the self we no longer remember. Each of us walks with a piece of Nip somewhere inside of us. That is why it is okay to cry over Nipsey, today. It is okay to pray about Nipsey, today. It is okay to have unresolved feelings about Nipsey, today. It is okay to love Nipsey without knowing Nipsey, today. It is okay to miss Nipsey without knowing Nipsey. The sound of death in our homes, in the places we return to and frequent, is a loud one.

That same sound can travel through walls, both literal and figurative. Fred Hampton was murdered in his home by police in his own bed. Sean Bell was murdered the morning of his wedding day. Amadou Diallo was shot outside of home forty-one times. As much as our community violence can start and end over unwarranted beefs, silent stares, and never forgotten grudges, law enforcement has a stranglehold on the heat and tension that exists in the very spaces we collect and break bread in. Statista tells us that in 2022 alone, there were 1,096 fatal police shootings. In 2021, there were 1,048 fatal shootings. Additionally, the rate of fatal police shootings among Black Americans was much higher than that for any other ethnicity with a staggering 5.9 fatal shootings per million of the population per year between 2015 and March 2023. And having Black men on the force seems to not make much of a dent. Legal scholar Amara Enyia told AP News in a February 2023 article highlighting the brutal murder of Tyre Nichols at the hands of five Memphis officers that "being Black and a police officer does not undo the inherent anti-Blackness in the policing system." So much potential taken from us far too soon.

What books did Nipsey have in him that he will never write? Who would Sean Bell have been as a husband and father? How far would Fred Hampton have pushed himself and us? How many seeds of inspiration would Amadou have planted with the breaths remaining before they were stolen from us, the collective us? "Us" because each Black man lost at the hands of violence is a loss we all suffer. The sum cannot be tallied, cannot be weighed or scaled or measured on a chart or with a visual illustration of a data point. I see Nipsey everywhere—in tweets and memes and video clips on Instagram where we are seeking solace and inspiration for the road ahead. When I see Lauren, his beloved Lauren, my heart breaks every time. Because we all move on but death does not. Death stays. It is stagnant, stiff, stifling the ones who have to absorb the true impact of the loss. I miss Nipsey like I knew him, like I needed him. And I did. We all did. Because of the layers. Would Nipsey have grown to apologize for his comments surrounding the queer community? And would we have given him the space to grieve that former version of self that was insecure, lacking in understanding? How does age and experience also lengthen our life span? Nipsey will never know. The clear and present dangers of staying in the same places where the homies and the 12 know our names can be a prison in and of itself. Because home always calls us back, no matter how much we try and drown out the sound.

I am sure PnB Rock heard the call—Roscoe's House of Chicken 'N Waffles is no place for a murder or a premeditated funeral. A father and son murdered PnB Rock—a father, and a son—over a chain. And while the South Central, Los Angeles, Roscoe's House of Chicken 'N Waffles where he was killed is a far cry from his hometown of Philadelphia, the clarion of the home has a long reach for many of us, who either came from squalor through our own lived-in experience or acquired the squalor by association, borrowing from the experiences of others. Roscoe's House of Chicken 'N Waffles is an LA staple for those seeking something that feels and tastes like home. Something that harkens back to the block, to a place and time tied back to memories that feel as close to our skin as the wind can be. Even at home, whatever home may be, we die different. Every death, a tally mark, a reminder of what you can't come back to. The losses become murals that color the bodega corners. They catch us walking to work to catch train lines, our headphones in while we take in the death like fossil fuel fumes, each colorfully

tagged death artful desensitization. We are tethered to the procession, with each burial, each RIP announcement another white
noise segment waiting to pass over. The hood is a hornet's nest
and yet we are fiercely drawn to the noise, to the overt and discreet
ways it silences the shrills and cries of the evening. Not a drill, no,
more like a summoning of the spirits that are laid, casket upon
casket, chalk outline to white sheet. In the Bronx, Ortiz Funeral
Home is the road map back—countless others, all of us each other's wings, rocking the shirts with the colors of our gangs, doves
flying above the fracas of a ménage of sad, the face of a loved one
too soon gone living in the memory of an RIP emblazoned on the
front. The Ortiz Funeral Home is parallel to the Edgar Allan Poe
home, the same place where the master storyteller crafted some of
his greatest works. The visual can be stunning—the home of Poe,
nestled in a park surrounded by grass and benches, meanwhile
across the street others who have met a fate, not as poetic, come
home in a different way. A home can break your heart.

I stopped calling Kareem "Kareem" and started calling him
Buc because that was his DJ name. Everybody else on the block
called him Buc, and nicknames have a funny way of sticking to
us. My brother D still calls me MaG, the rap name I forget at times
I once carried with so much pride. Buc was a year older than me,
and I remember feeling a burst of pride seeing him in the halls of
PS 33, our elementary school. There was always a level of calmed
cool that Buc possessed. And he was funny as shit—his laugh
was the infectious, hand-over-mouth, bent-over type. Boola, Buc's
older brother, is D's close childhood friend. Once getting my haircut at Tony's, the same spot D would frequent on Burnside Avenue, got too pricey, we found an alternative for me: Boola. For $5,
Boola would either come to my crib or I'd come to his, sitting in his

living room in front of the Ninja Turtles trunk. There, if Buc was home, we'd play with toys and watch cartoons. Sasha and Kia are kind and warm. Ms. Dayton, the matriarch, holding court. Earl Sr., his father, outside of the building. Earl worked security at the Loews Theater, another home for so many of us. I saw *Masters of the Universe* and *Spaced Invaders* with D there, having to lie about my age to get the reduced-price tickets. On one of those occasions, we went and got Popeyes after and D got an extra biscuit because the girl attendant thought he was cute. Earl would let the neighborhood kids in through the Loews's back door. For what it's worth, Buc and I's closeness wouldn't start until I prepared to leave home for college and returned home soon after my failed attempt at higher education at Temple University.

I wanted to leave the neighborhood I grew up in. Up until high school, all I ever knew and all I ever thought I needed was in the Bronx. Every school, every friend, and everything I loved existed within a three-to-four-block radius. That radius expanded in middle school when I was accepted into Pace Academy, located at MS 118 on Arthur Avenue. Buc attended our neighborhood school: IS 115. It's the same school D attended. Some of my elementary school friends went to IS 115. But I wanted to be different. I also weighed the odds: IS 115 looked like a prison. Most public schools in New York City, past and present, still do. And even though I was starting to shed some of the husky weight I was teased for, I was still aware enough to know the levels of safety I felt in my previous school would be no match for the intensity of what middle school could look like. High school would take me even farther—out into the unknown of Manhattan as I traveled by train (the panic!) to Fiorello H. LaGuardia High School of Music, Art, and the Performing Arts as a drama major. My love for theater started in elementary school and was fermented by Ms. Piotrowski, my sixth-grade elective teacher, and seventh- and eighth-grade homeroom and English teacher. In LaGuardia, Adeel would have me try scallion pancakes for the first time on his dime, us staying late after *You Can't Take It with You* rehearsals with John; white Ken would show me what pomegranate looked like while Black Ken would be my source of friendship and hurt: the same Crip who I would share train rides and M.O.P. tapes with would also chastise me for having a white girl sitting on my lap in the lunchroom; we'd later not even acknowledge each other while walking on the same block, us walking different paths; James and I would perform *Waiting for Godot* together; Jen would put me on to tuna melts; Jessica would teach me how to kiss with my tongue; Will would bring me to Spanish Harlem, him rolling up and me catching contact highs while he made beats with the MTV Music Generator on the PlayStation that we would free-style to until the wee hours of the night. I had to leave home to find a new one. When I graduated, the choices were: A. Stay in NYC and join a talent agency that would have me audition for roles on *Law & Order: SVU* because there was someone who looked just like me who "was getting a lot of roles playing drug dealers"; B. Try and head to Moscow with the help of my former acting teacher Mr. Yusim; C. audition for Juilliard, with a strong inclination that I could get in; or D. Go to college. Moms told me Moscow was too far, and Juilliard and real auditioning felt scary. After applying late, Temple University was the easiest and best choice: it was the only school that offered me a grant, and it was the only school that responded with a "yes."

I spoke to Buc before I left, my $2,500 scholarship Award for Drama from LaGuardia was almost already spent on fly gear and necessities like an iron and fake silverware copped on Fordham Road. And we talked about our dreams: Buc was getting into deejaying and he knew I was nice with the mic; me and my old friend Rich had been harnessing our rap skills in my bedroom, using D's job as a then associate at HMV Records and his love for finding new music to our advantage—I'd find the instrumental B sides and I'd challenge us to freestyle rap over and over again. I encouraged Buc to leave, to take a leap of faith. Buc was no different than me. Both of us knew our homes well. I wanted Buc to find a different home. I remember this conversation most. I was teary-eyed because I wanted Buc to be anywhere but the place we had seen so many get swallowed whole in Creston Avenue.

Located in the area of Fordham, Creston Avenue was home to so many of us. My home at 2435 Creston was right across the street from Buc's building, which was right next door to the former Loews Theater. If you walk by the building, Buc's candles and emptied Henny bottles still decorate a corner of the building. Rasheen, Robbie, Jose, Ms. Murch, Ms. Ethel, Ms. Shirley, Miguel, Tony, Trevor, Tee . . . the first drive-by I ever saw—these were the lives, the loss, the love on Creston. After two humbling years at Temple, Biggs, the oldest and most mature member of the crew of D, Boola, Sess, and friends, was also the neighborhood plug—he got D a job at Oaktree before it became Structure before it would become Express Men. He also got me and Buc to work in the stockroom. I parlayed the gig into a sales floor position as a customer service lead/co-manager. Sharing a back room and sales floor with Buc was a day of shenanigans, girlie-watching, and laughter. Myself, Buc, and C Live danced on the floor and in the back room. Buc also added a layer of growth to the mix: he was a father. We talked about me laying a verse for the Tryizzy mixtape that never happened. I've got the verses somewhere in an old notepad. Opportunities, memories, moments . . . home. When Ms. Dayton passed away, one could say a part of Buc left with him. A lot of Creston left with her, too. She was loved and adored by everyone, a face I loved to see on the way back home from work—always a kind word, always a wonderful smile, her voice, her hug. A few years later when D called me early in the morning and told me Buc died of a heart attack, I knew he had found a new home, too. At Ortiz Funeral Home, Boola asked me to read the eulogy because he knew I was good with words. I said his niece's name wrong. I felt like a fraud. Later, after we drove to Jersey to throw dirt and flowers on Buc's casket, we'd all convened at Earl Sr.'s apartment— pictures of siblings, of parents, of loved ones. I hadn't been in that apartment for years. Sometimes I wonder if I would have tried harder to pull Buc out—more time, more calls, more words—he wouldn't have stayed. But he loved home. The block will grip us until our lungs are gone.

Tamir Rice was murdered in the same city he was raised in. So was Mike Brown. Takeoff didn't die in his hometown, but he died venturing into parts of a city that felt as familiar as his verses did. Young Dolph got shot buying cookies for his mother in the same city he rapped about. Jam Master Jay was murdered in the same studio in Queens he built for up-and- coming Queens rappers. Freaky Tah. Big L. Bankroll Fresh. Mag- nolia Shorty. Soulja Slim. Drakeo the Ruler. Scott La Rock. Half a Mill. Miguel got stabbed in 2435 Creston—the same building he was raised in. Tee Tee and I went to 33 together, too. Tee Tee, now in a wheelchair, got shot around our old stomping grounds.

Home can be unforgiving. Home can be as sterile as a bullet wound, as stiff as a corpse. Home can be as hard as saying bye, or overstaying your welcome.

The Sound a Slap Makes

Feat. Will Smith, Chris Rock

I hate to admit this out loud, but I am always late for things. Well, that's not entirely true. I am late for most things. Things that are deemed important. Trivial things. I am not egregiously late, and I generally am good about letting it be known that I will be late. But late, I am. And some of us define late differently. One might argue that five to fifteen minutes before the agreed-upon time is actually on time. And arriving at the predetermined time is late. Heck, some (me) might even say five minutes after is still on time. But, I guess time is subjective. The moments captured in that time, too, can be subjective. Because the context of the time and timing matters—maybe the lateness doesn't matter as much if you have nowhere else to be. If time is not a commodity to you. For others, your lateness speaks to a lack of respect for the commodity that is time—Malcolm X once proclaimed a man who does not wear a watch does not respect the time and therefore does not respect me. What El Hajj Shabazz would say about a world of cell phones and Apple watches that tell time, blood pressure, and Kardashian news is beyond the scope of this essay. But in the end, I'd probably be late for whatever El Hajj had to say anyway. It's my nature—

I've been late to dates, to ceremonies, to tests, to auditions. I'm the next-to-last one there. I'm sweaty, and I'm annoyed. It's not from a lack of caring. It's just that I sometimes get stuck in the moment of whatever it is I'm doing. I like to prolong moments, squeezing the juice out of them until there's nothing more to give besides the remnants of what's already left. But I'm always missing the moment when the moment happens because I was busy doing something else—another moment, another day.

So, it came as no surprise to me that I was late to the slap heard around the world. As with most things, I stuck to my script and I missed it while it happened. Because everyone now can have a take, stake, and say in the matter. If you have a Twitter, an Instagram, a Substack or Medium, a trendy TikTok thing to be beholden to, then you, too, can materialize an opinion out of thin air out of a thing you may not have had any sort of correlation to until it was on your screen, in your feed, in your mouth, waiting to be exposed and expelled. We are now all critics, all of us right on time for the moment at hand, because we all are now sharing in collective moments. Or are we? We'd like to think because we are all seeing things at the same time, hearing about and talking to culture with also the same metronomic heartbeat, that we are all just as well thoroughly engaged and present with the moments. But we're not. We are hyper-focused and glued to the screen, tuning in to a thing until we are not. Because another moment will come that will be just as grief-stricken, as heavy and humbling, filled with hubris and the humidity of shock value quantified; we are all click-baiting ourselves and each other. And then the moment passes and we wait, tongues hanging, the dogs of the universe, panting and wishing for the FOMO to come onstage and slap us in the face.

Anyway, I was there the day after. After the storm, after the ruckus, after the stillness and quieting down of the violence, is generally when I am making my entrance into the space. Maybe it's my upbringing in the Bronx, seeing how heavy hands to faces and fierce fingers to triggers could incite a riot in a home, in a community, and the bare-boned ways we deal with the violence that gets perpetrated on Blackness daily. I would much rather run from the violence than subscribe to it. When I woke up at whatever time the day after the Oscars, I saw the Will Smith hashtag trending with Chris Rock not far behind. I won't recount the moment except to say that I was very curious and shocked. Anyone with a pulse saw it, heard about it in a podcast or out loud in a too-loud coffee shop, or read a think piece or a group chat text thread about it. I was in a lunchroom having a conversation about it: two Black men and four white women. And in that context, a slap sounds very different, doesn't it? It echoes maybe a bit louder, as loud as one would imagine it would when there is a Black comic onstage poking fun at a Black woman with her Black husband sitting next to her. Men have been shot for lesser slights in the neighborhood I grew up in, in the many hoods I've frequented. Niggas get shot over stepped-on sneakers, over too-long stares, over mistaken identities and old beefs thought to be forgotten but reminisced over chalk outlines, yellow tape, and reluctant drive-bys. Niggas get slapped every day. Literally. Get slapped for not looking where they're going, or going left when they should have gone right. Except those slaps happen in rooms and on blocks that a white gaze is never privy to. Even with gentrification running rampant, whiteness tends to cover their eyes and shield their ears from what lives on the parallels of their peripheries. Black men slap other Black men all the time. Masculinity asks us to. It beckons us to defend a shadow honor, something that feels very fixed but also very unspoken. It is the indirect disrespect we are called to acknowledge. It has an undercurrent that is both loud and physical, physical because it is felt in our bones. Violence lives in our bodies. Our cells, dying and undying, born and born again; viruses attacking organs; the electricity of nerves crackling to a charged brain. Everything in us is a call toward an extreme thing or another; another moment waiting to happen that exacts a sort of rage, incites a certain kind of response. And sometimes that response is something that inflicts love. Or harm.

No one prepares for the sound a slap makes, the echo, and how it reverberates across touch points—families, communities, and individuals. The impact lingers, stings, and bites at whoever is close enough to hear, see, and feel the aftershock. And sometimes the slap is not even a slap at all. It is a burst, a loud, shrill pitch of aggression that shows itself in a multitude of ways, both physically and emotionally. Sometimes, it is language. Sometimes it is a father who whispers insidious things in your young ears. Either way, the context and cultural accessibility of the slap, or a slap, is clearly defined. A slap at a Waffle House in Crenshaw in front of Black eaters has a very different sort of ramification than a slap onstage in front of nervous whites. And the ramifications of that slap depend on your proximity to the context and culture—a theoretical slap of me in that Waffle House in Crenshaw affects my ego but not street credibility—see, I have none. Slapping a Piru in that same Waffle House may mean a gun gets involved, or an escalation of the violence that exists in the Waffle Houses and exists in the rooms, in the homes, and on the blocks of those involved. When you're fighting over avenues and colors, or just a carefully crafted reputation, the stakes are dramatically different. Life-changing or life-ending, dependent on the roll of the dice. Will's slap happened in the vacuum of white capitalist patriarchy: the consequences were more financial, more for the show, and a slap on top of the slap already witnessed by the viewer. Banning Will Smith did not affect his ability to pack a movie theater or sell streams, but it will impact how whiteness sees him. And for a Black man whose presence has been shaped by how whiteness sees him, this too can be life-changing or life-ending, in the egoic sense.

Some watching may have thought it a ruse, an act, a part of the programming that is much the mess whiteness has prescribed their Black entertainment to be: raunchy, aggressive, blatant. Violence is entertaining in that way, no? Roman gladiators, battling to the death at the bemusement of a captivated audience, waiting for the next death, next mass shooting, next hanging. Civil disobedience is normalized—after your favorite team wins. After your favorite team loses. After your favorite president loses. The violence is exacting. It always has been. And yet, there is always a surprise when it happens live, front and center, in the spaces we have determined are exempt from the barbarism of the moments of the day. Because there is no amount of scrolling away from the doomsday that can change what is in our faces. We feel far removed from the violence; a distant cousin. But if you were a Black person, the slap was not new to you because we are forever Black, forever dealing with slaps at home, slaps at work; whether they be emotional, physical; the ingrained slaps that happened on a day-to-day basis in the forms of assault, police, state-sanctioned violence, media portrayals, caricatures of

Blackness, the perpetuation of AAVE have some sort of cultural phenomenon, etc., etc., etc.

Slaps come in waves. We have all been Lupita in that moment, albeit not as beautiful. But definitely, mouth left ajar, wondering if we caught everything that led up to the moment at hand. We sit or stand, and watch. Sometimes we're captivated. Sometimes we're in fear. Most times we're frozen. Most times, we'd like to think we'd be the ones to admonish the Wills in our lives and our neighborhoods after the violence, after the harm. We'd like to imagine ourselves being as "heroic" as Will, standing up valiantly to right a wrong, sitting back down feeling justified for our actions. But most times, we're as shocked as Lupita. And the stage on which the violence occurs changes the flavor and feel of the violence, too. Because we expect this on the back block. We expect this on the corner somewhere that we know in Anytown, USA, where the violence is part of a long summer or a cold winter. We expect to see this violence in certain homes: either the ones we group in or the ones that surrounded us. It was your aunt and uncle, too many drinks and seventies classics in. And then there's the shouting. Maybe other relatives start chiming in. A shove here, a curse word flung there; a hand raised, followed by more screams. We know that violence. It interrupted our homework. It made us turn on the TV and watch, not out of curiosity, but out of fear. But this is the sort of violence we were tuning in for. We were Lupita. But this is America.

Because America has been slapping Black men around for generations, without so much as a Brad Pitt eyelash batted. We will easily lean on the likes of Roman Polanski as an example of the Academy's lack of urgency when it comes to those who have caused harm, but it is childish to believe this stance is solely an Academy position. This is not unique or happenstance—the institution itself is only an apprentice to an America that wields its insufferable behavior like a badge of honor. But this is the history of the greatest democracy in the civilized world—slap then hide the hand. In this instance, Will Smith's behavior is the most un-American thing he could ever accomplish. His slap—loud, cold; a cupped hand caught on camera—an affront to all things white picket fence and single-family-home orientated.

However, after decades of watching his carefully curated and calculated career the most human thing I've ever seen Will Smith do was smack the shit out of Chris Rock in front of a bunch of startled white people. It was giving WorldStarHipHop. It was giving "I've been waiting to smack somebody, anybody, for too long." Some of the debates online also questioned if Will would have tried to slap The Rock like that. Or 50 Cent. The answer is no. Because masculinity is also about sizing up, even subconsciously. A nigga walk in a room, and a nigga knows who is to be played with and who isn't; you know who can be slapped and who cannot. Alpha machismo on steroids. This assessment is made based on the size of the person, the type of gear they got on, the way they talk in a room, the way they walk into one. You guess how much money they have or don't. And history also plays a role. Every slight, every insult, every joke shows up in the room with us. And if we have acclaim, a certain kind of fame that is almost regarded as legendary, then the stakes become even higher—could be Gucci telling Jeezy he smoking on a loud pack of a dead homie of the latter that was shot by the former, all while live on a streaming platform watched by millions. It could be a rapper telling a former rapper friend turned foe that he fucked his old lady on a record, only to see both rappers murdered in sunny California. Or, it can come in the shape of a slap on national television. Masculinity does not offer humility or forgiveness—it offers violence and vindication. Masculinity is at your funeral, violins stringing together a symphony of sounds, mourning a loss that is all too familiar to so many of us: T-shirts with RIPs and colorful screen printings; images of dead homies sprawled across with wounded angel wings flying into the wind in the background. Black masculinity wouldn't let Will or Chris off the hook, both men playing the roles masculinity defined for them at that moment—court jester and perpetrator of harm. Some may ask, Why would Will choose to respond on one of the biggest nights of television? I think the better and more important question to ask is, As a Black man, did he have a choice, to begin with?

I've been a fan of Will Smith since I heard his voice-over vinyl, the grooves telling tales of misunderstood teens and girls causing trouble wherever they could find it. I aspired to be like Will: a rapper turned actor who had found success in both. He was funny, bright, and boisterous. I also saw the caricature. I saw the picture of perfection and the leading man he portrayed so well. That level of acting takes years of work, years of shape-shifting and changing to meet a moment. Will was never late. It was almost as if every decision was strategically on time, placed symmetrically for a camera, adoring fans rushing to their seats to not miss a moment of a toned body chasing bad guys, chasing aliens, chasing the love of a partner, a role, a father. But with that kind of armor, along with the kind of ascension that happens so quickly in the spectrum of the devouring American public eye (an eye that does not let successful Black men, or any marginalized person for that matter, become invisible. Because capitalism), there requires a certain attitude, a certain level of sacrifice, to keep the charade going. The mask is worn, to the point you cannot tell the difference between the maskless you and the version of self you carry around for protection; the mask becomes your identity; becoming the thing you wear when everyone and no one is looking, all to remain sane. The mask is a prison, and if you wear it well enough, for long enough, the mask becomes an appendage. The level of attention paid raises the stakes. There is a family to raise, people are counting on you. So, the mask doubles as a cape, allowing you the ability to become whatever idea of alpha male that feels to be most fitting to you. Will is from West Philadelphia, born and raised in Wynnefield, a middle-class neighborhood that became largely African American in the 1960s. The neighborhood was predominately Jewish American starting in the early 1920s. By the time Will was born, the neighborhood had begun a serious expansion, led in large part by Katie B. Jackson, known in the community as the "Queen of Wynnfield." When Will was growing up, his father was both his hero and harm. Will watched his father physically abuse his mother, punching her in the head when Will was a mere nine years old. While his sister fled, his older brother intervened. Will froze. In that moment, Will was Lupita, too. Willard Smith Sr. was a refrigeration engineer and air force veteran. Interestingly, while sharing his father's namesake, Will Smith himself never went by Junior. One can assume that while Will both loved and feared his father, there was somewhat of an acute sense of a need for detaching himself from his father's shadow. I know that feeling. Even outside of my home, I know the feeling of a tenuous relationship with a father who still had all of his demons in the front row. It begs the question if having a Black father as a body present in a home is better than having not seen or heard from your father at all. My brother Kelvin didn't meet his own father until his adult years. I never knew my man Rich's father. Never saw him at graduations or parent-teacher conferences. Never really heard Rich mention him at all. My father was home sometimes, and the sometimes he was I always wished he never was. Black fathers, unlike fathers from other races, carry their trauma around like a mask. And in every institution and space a Black man may be asked to show up in, a Black man who also doubles as Black father bears two weights: Black adulthood, filled with the fears of police violence, potential neighborhood violence, and systemic violence, along with the real fears of living up and beyond any of the lack they may have encountered as children being passed on and through their children as they assume the roles of father. Will's father may have worn this as both badge and time bomb. Responsibility can be crippling. And, rather than expose the wounds and scars, sometimes we mask.

I recognize masks when I see them. I wore them often. The mask is a box, a way to wrangle away freedom into a package neatly tucked away for adoring friends, family, and social media acolytes, to open and cling to. I was the "nice" guy, the "soft" guy, or the poet/artist, romantic type. I leaned into the tropes because the tropes allowed me to avoid any work on healing whatever inner child was begging to be given attention. Similar to Will Smith, I had a father who could be both physically and mentally abusive; a father who loved but also did not have the language or tools to express that love in healthy ways. And in those environments, you learn to wear a mask not out of convenience, but for safety. My mask made me a master performer. It was in this way I was able to refine who I was based on the citations. This was no code-switching but survival; my attempt at being everything to everybody while also single-handedly ignoring anything that would force me to face a mirror and deal with myself. The mask made me a bad partner, unable to deal with my internal struggles in healthy ways. I'd grow defensive when challenged. I would avoid accountability. I would lie, I would cheat, and use my niceness as a weapon? Shield? You learn when and how to tiptoe across land mines of conversation; the moments where a sudden shift or gesture could provoke a rage. I learned best to bottle everything. Will's slap was the bottle shaken and stirred and opened in front of a televised crowd. The mask was off.

But we are all responsible for the Will slap. No one's palm is clean of the muck. The lead-up to the slap was built up by every tweet poking at Will and his family's life. Because celebrities are not humans to us. And if they are nonhuman, the inhumane ways we treat them exist in imperfect harmony. Celebrity culture is all about hiding, isn't it? Mainly hiding from ourselves—a self that has a bloodlust for the extraordinary, that can pull us away from our simple, mundane existence, an extraordinary we can glue ourselves to our smart phones and television sets for. They're also hiding from themselves. Michael Jackson. R. Kelly. O. J. Simpson. All running to and from the public eye; asking us to be voyeurs to their talent and to immerse ourselves in their art while giving us shadowy glimpses into their own peril and distraughtness. The image becomes the mask and the mask becomes the shield—a shield from the adoring public and also the shield from our ego selves. Is there ever truly anyplace that is safe to hide from either? I will never forget the photo of a

bikini-clad Rihanna at the beach and a swarm of paparazzi wagging their tails doggedly, each capturing the Bajan with their
cameras, fangs out. How much better are we? We are capturing
moments, barehanded, trapping them in our mobiles, keeping
them in our photos to post, share, and scroll the empty away.
And there is no better way to do that than to capture moments of
those who have more money, more access, and more entitlement
and show the rest of the corners of our world that celebrities are
human, too. Some of us capture the follies in different ways—we
write them. We write them in a hurry, a flurry of viral words to
reach the population en masse, willing ourselves to the front of
the line to be the first with the original thought to lead the social
conversation. We want to breathe the internet, or at the very
least break the spirit of those we judge so callously, carelessly,
caressing each keystroke with the finesse of a sniper, pulling
on all the triggers of our waning feelings and emotions about
any and everything we are now forced to unwittingly engage
with. We play to the written rhythms of the algorithm, too. For
each action that happened in either public or private, for every
single Will Smith–delivered slap, there will undoubtedly be an
article, a tweet, an Instagram post, a TikTok dissertation assert-
ing our knowledge, and our ability to be above the fray and to
exist outside of the harm done by others. We eat our celebrities.
We are addicted to their well-being and their failures. And if
you are a Black man, the crosshairs of our appetites are meaty.
We starve for, we seek those big moments where big personalities are reduced to a headline under a wedding or art piece
live in direct alignment with the tweets, posts, and blog posts—
they all are preceding the moment that allows us to make fun
of those we deem to be not human; those that live outside of

ourselves and are so far removed from our loss stories. Their distance allows us to so easily toss away words and phrases that we are not connected to, yet we are also so connected to the subject whose feet we are holding under the fire. We have captured them so easily. Will's slap was an indictment on all of us, an impenetrable us that would so readily dismiss others as having feelings worth remembering or considering. It was like Will wasn't just slapping Chris Rock, he was slapping his father, the social media landscape, and the Academy . . . he was slapping everyone and anyone who felt that their masks were better than his. Even Chris Rock's comedy is a mask.

There's no more revealing of a mask than someone who jabs, pokes, prods, and makes fun of others in order to hide whatever pain, fears, or traumas they have yet to settle with. Chris Rock's father, like Will's, was a working-class man, holding down jobs as both a truck driver and newspaper deliveryman. Unlike Will's father, however, Chris's father would not live long enough to see Chris Rock become a star—he would die in 1988 after ulcer surgery. Chris was bullied by white classmates in the white schools he was bused to following his family's move to Brooklyn from South Carolina. When looking at Chris Rock's career in comparison to Will Smith's, we can see success but also can see how—though close in age—comparatively they have lived very different lives. Will, the handsome, light-skinned, charismatic jokester and action star adored by both white and Black America. In comparison, Chris Rock has never been seen as cute or attractive by media or by white standards. He has never been decidedly suave or smooth, seen as heroic or endearing. Chris Rock, skinny, lanky, and dark, has been the jokester and butt of the joke. Chris has made a career out of not only being funny but also of being scathing. His ill-timed joke about Jada at the Oscars would have been ill-timed at any moment, considering it was a Black woman he was pointing a finger at. Black women in the oral history of Black comedy have often wound up being the scapegoats of Black male comedians. Whether it's about hair or the lack thereof, sex drives or lack thereof, Black women remain the constant butt of the joke searing in the background at any upstart comedy club in any Black neighborhood you may patrol. The contradiction between Black women as the mothers of the earth and existence while also being the bane and whores of it is an uncomfortable paradigm that Black male comedians have leaned into for years. It's why Chris Rock was so ready, so prepared to make a joke about Jada on one of entertainment's largest stages. Chris Rock is a master of the fine art of Black woman bashing. He is also a genius of a comedian. Which makes the Jada joke even more disappointing. Which made his stand-up rebuttal to the slap, his Netflix live special, even worse. Chris spent the latter part of his special on a verbal tirade lambasting both Jada and Will. It was the kind of anger that someone who is masking learns how to hide behind. Chris knows and knew he could never beat Will in a fistfight, an image fight, or a money fight. But what he can do is engage in a way that Will won't ever be able to. Chris can live and play in the world of ugly truths. He gets to call things out, to say what he feels and means, even when it is shiny veiled and disguised as a critique, an assessment, or a dig. As a Black comedian, he gets to play in these spaces of reality in a way that Will cannot because Chris Rock's mask is not his image, but his comedy. And while a majority of Chris's stand-up in that special is highly debatable, it's his truth. And it is a truth he owns consistently. It is also a prime example of the reason why so many of us wear masks around each other. Because the mask keeps the ugly at bay.

We are all masking something; we are all hiding from something, from someone. Paul Dunbar said,

We wear the mask that grins and lies,
It hides our cheeks and shades our eyes,—
This debt we pay to human guile;
With torn and bleeding hearts we smile . . .

Our response to that hiding, to that role-playing comes across in many forms. For many of us, the dogpiling that happens after a seismic event that we all get to indulge in, heating up whatever preexisting hurt or hate was already bringing itself to the surface, is often masked as cultural analysis or criticism. But left unchecked, the criticisms are jetpacks of projections, fueled by the incessant need to be heard.

The same ego Will Smith felt the need to defend, is the same ego that fuels our tweets, our likes, our comments, and our essays. It is also the ego that allows us to deflect blame, to hide behind our presumed perfection, while pointing a finger presumably to those who are getting it wrong more often than we are, we presume. Will Smith was our wrongness personified on center stage for us all to love and indulge in, if even for a spell. His reign on the top, taller than leprechauns sure, and still he returneth to his large, beautiful home and his beautiful children and beautiful partner and beautiful bank account and beautiful things, but where will the ego go? The ego, the thing that we as Black men hold up like a trophy, a crown of thorns for us to bleed unto, where does that tarnished emblem of masculinity go to hide when the whole world could see all the shattered pieces that lay beneath it all? Will slapped Chris, yes. We also slapped Will back. We gawked, we chuckled, we pointed our melanated and nonmelanated index fingers at our TV and phone screens and said "Look at that man shatter" and we tweeted and wrote and chatted and spoke about it like Will was our best friend gone rogue; he was the one we made fun of at the barbershop or the girls trip; the Academy said you are banned, you are shunned—thank you for giving us your blood, sweat, and tears all these years, but you are not enough. Will will never be enough for them, for us—insatiable vultures for the demise of Blackness, of a fragile masculinity that can be torn paper thin by cameras and a public feening for another moment to judge.

I can't overemphasize that Will's slap wasn't just a slap of Chris, but a slap of all the masks he's been made to wear to keep his sanity and his career. Every Black man you have ever known has wanted to slap the shit out of someone—their boss, their parents, their partners; to embarrass them, to make them feel the pain we feel at every microaggression; at every loss, at every moment we were told was meant to humble us when we didn't need it; meant to deflate, dehumanize, deafen, and dim our presence. Chests too far poked, mouth far too big; boardrooms and classrooms we were etched out of. The slap was also conducted with a smidge of privilege. Many of the other conversations held online were a chorus of "This is how I want my man to stand up for me." And yet, not every man is Will Smith. Not everyone can slap anyone, a celebrity at that, sit back down in their seat, win an award, and make a speech following, and then proceed to go to an after-party. The justice system does not work that way for a Black man from a level of poverty and class. Even a certain kind of Blackness is exempt from carceral punishment to a certain degree. Unless of course if violence has been enacted against a white man or white woman. A Black man slapping another man in public like that would potentially be something far greater than a slap, depending on who is on the other side of the slap in question. And every Black man has to think about the consequences of returning the favor of violence, or risk whatever cred that may have existed floating away into the ether. But Will knows better and knew better.

Chris was an easy target. Chris spent his early years dodging the kinds of slaps Will willfully gave that night. Will spent a lifetime ducking the same kind of slap he offered to Chris, albeit a more privileged, potentially more sanitized version. Black men like me were literally raised on slap boxing. We would play fight by slapping each other senseless . . . for fun. It is in this way that Black masculinity so often is about perpetuating the same violence we spend our lifetimes attempting to avoid. And that violence lives on in our day-to-day interactions. Will's response to a slight that had everything and nothing to do with him (the Rock joke, it can be argued, had less to do with Jada's alopecia, an assumption many made with the notion that it was a widely discussed topic amongst the Hollywood elite, and more to do with Jada's proximity to the stage along with Rock's awareness of the cultural significance of mentioning G.I. Jane amongst a sea of whites). Looking at the layers of it all, the audience saw onstage not a moment but a series of moments collected and bottled and stored to be used at a later date. A far lesser slight would have been a joke poked at Will by Chris. But masculinity also means defending your property by any means. And property is inclusive of your woman. And within the framework of patriarchy and masculinity, *your* woman needs and requires protection, requires saving. It is not so much a trope as it is an identity for those seeking to lead the imaginary pack and for those who identify as women to identify who the leaders are. Just a bunch of identities exposed and open, bandaged wounds wanting for air. The Oscars were just the format. Will would have had the same response in a grocery store; on Rodeo Drive inside of a posh shopping center; or in VIP, where cameras are prohibited. Neither the Oscars, nor Chris Rock or Jada, were the reasons for Will's response. Masculinity was. It was Black masculinity he was beholden to. The larger issue is that Blackness, both as an identity and terminology, has also become synonymous with culture. Thereby Black masculinity is not even allowed its shape but has become a certain kind of symbol, with its intersections leading so much of what we talk, think, and how we show up in the world. Hip-hop and sports are Black masculinity's playgrounds, with chicken vs. egg played between the industries and the environments that create them: the hood.

So much so that Will Smith, even with all the money, fame, glory, and accolades, is still a light-skinned nigga from West Philadelphia with daddy issues like the rest of us. Which makes him human.

Like us.

For Black Boys Contemplating Suicide

Them boys ain't no good
that's what everybody say
them boys misunderstood.

—MEEK MILL (FREESTYLE) ON KNXWLEDGE "ROUNDHERE"

Being born a soft Black boy in the Bronx can get you killed. And, to Meek's point, being Black and being misunderstood can serve as an underlying cause for the harm done. Even worse, being born a soft Black boy in the Bronx can push you to kill yourself. You learn this early when we call each other faggot because that's what you're supposed to call anyone who cries too hard, laughs too much, plays too nice. And it's funny and cool and a catchall for all things that we consider wrong or unruly or dangerous, things we don't really have all the words for. Until someone not in your circle, not in your crew, calls you the *F* word, in broad daylight, without provocation or warning. It is a mutter, and if your earphones were maybe two to three decibels louder you might have missed it. It could have been a wind of a whisper almost, how quietly loud it was. When I heard one of the boys say it, it started me down the rabbit hole of how many ways I could kill them—poke their eyes out with my house keys, stab them in the neck with my house keys. It would make the burning in my lungs, my chest, stomach, and eyes go away. Because hurting them with my hands would feel fundamentally better than whatever scarring was happening in the moment with the flippancy of the words they used to call me what I knew I wasn't or wasn't supposed to be. Because to be soft, to be fragile as a Black man in this world, is not safe. So, when I look at my life, I can see and sense all the little ways the world has hurt me. And I can also see all the little ways I've hurt myself, too.

I pick my bottom lip until it bleeds. It has always been this way. Since I was a child. It's called dermatillomania or excoriation disorder. The relief during and after is what a skin picker craves and searches for. My mother was a nurse for over thirty years. And there were two things I could always depend on her to bring home after working the night shift: Ensure and Bacitracin, or what we called A + D ointment. The ointment was greasy. The ointment would be splattered all over my face during the winter NYC months, and even more so on picture day at school, which would normally be commemorated with a clip-on tie or some sort of crewneck or turtleneck situation. The ointment was also used as a balm for chapped lips. My mother would complain incessantly about the lip-picking. Eventually, partners new and old would, too. I've never been diagnosed. But I know I have it. The bleeding does not stop the picking. I am a Capricorn, so being stubborn is my default response—I will not only do things, but will also do them until there is nothing more to be done about them. I pick until I get to a point where picking no longer feels necessary. It gives me pleasure, even if it is not cosmetically pleasing. I have to avoid doing it in conversations, but sometimes I do not. Sometimes I wonder if the person across from me, watching the corner of my bottom lip being tucked gently into my mouth, knows I'm stopping the bleeding or in the process of starting it. If it is not my lip, it's razor bumps that appear from time to time on my neck a little below the jawline. I will always find something to pick at. For the most part, it's just one of the many things I've been relatively good at hiding. I hide things well.

This isn't where I meant to start. I always think I know how I will start a story. But once I start, it never begins the way I thought it would. Sometimes, it is a mild storm, where I can see all the debris around me, floating about, each piece of another layer left from some fallen rain cloud, now sullen and wasting away while I wait for the next thing to develop. Sometimes it comes like a gust of sun, simmering itself around me, bringing out the shimmer in me. I don't try to predict where stories will go either. The outlines live in my head. I only write and say what I can both feel and swallow on my tongue and in my body. What is home but a human archive in flesh form anyway? The flesh and sweat mixing together, I no longer mince words but blend them in preparation for the rapture. And I don't quite know what the rapture is quite yet—but I know it's abolitionist in both its framework and spirit. I know it is loving and forgiveness. I know it is romantic, platonic, fluid, and polyamorous in the way that it shows itself to all of us and especially to me. The rapture can be freeing, the feeling I hope can be carried into the next generation of writers, organizers, activists, influencers, athletes, and everyday citizens working and striving toward a better tomorrow. I truly do believe that language can be the salvation for us all. We talk about tools and access but not enough about helping folks understand how to engage with the tools and access they have been given. To my mind, the rapture looks like our ability to let go and surrender any preconceived notions on what we think will get us free, and more time and energy spent as a collective with the ways we can find malleable solutions daily. Because the truth will set us free, but the truth changes as much as we are willing to change along with it. And our language gets to be that way. Why cling to a standard of etymology that was created? Why do we think words created within the context of an Anglo-Saxon, Eurocentric standard still hold weight and value to us now? And why do we judge others and their stories by not aligning with a truth that once was held to be the vanguard but can no longer stand up to the weight of the society we live in now? The only way to deconstruct the present is to construct new ways of thinking and being. We need language for that. And that language comes from going within, first.

I want to be better with words. I want all of us to be better with words. I want things to be sticky, and easy. And not easy in the sense that it is void of challenges, but the kind of ease I am referring to requires an effort that is not taxing on the heart-mind or soul. The previous iterations of my Black self will hopefully thank me later for this work. This is the work of reimagining and deconstructing the language and the energy that grounds it, while also building anew. This pathway is also a patchwork of hope and healing, across the varying spectrums of Blackness, from the diaspora and beyond. And in that fabric lies the curiosity that I strive to continue to align myself with. There is indeed a deeper questioning, a probing that I have been doing as early as I can remember. Not in the ways that some children would tinker with electronics and gadgets to inspect their inner workings. Mine tended to be more surreal, more existential. I wanted to know what things existed. It's why I read so much, I think. To learn better why things were the way that they were, to find some level of reprieve from a world that constantly made me not question itself but my role or need to be in it. If you are a Black boy "Why are you here?" is not the question others may think it is at first glance. It is not a question rooted in philosophical theory meant to encourage exploration; it is a question rooted in death and murder—a removal from belonging. "Why are you here?" is really "Why are you taking up space that should belong to someone else?" It is why we are so enamored with dystopian fiction and Afrofuturism as a means to explore other worlds that don't bother us in the ways America can and does daily. I am asking myself, "Why am I here?" I want to make space for a new me, and better versions of me that my daughters will be. That story has to start somewhere.

This has always been the story I have been scared to write the most. But this, this is not about that, if I'm being as transparent as I want to be. No, this is about the aftershock. There are levels to my detachment, to my distance from the past. The elephants in the rooms I inhabit, the cobwebs on the skeletons neatly tucked away and compartmentalized in these closets. But there has always been the incessant nagging of feeling like the story would need to be told, if there would be any unity in my heart or spirit, it stayed where it stood, far off in crevices collecting up the pieces of me I seem to leave behind where I go, with whomever I walk toward, or from.

The first draft of this got deleted. I asked myself then, I am asking myself now, and will ask myself later, if that was the intervention of Yahweh or Jesus or Selassie or whoever the spirits may be, keeping me from a recording of this. But, I trudged along anyway. A little piece of me flew away when the text was scrubbed. But, I will push even when pushing seems like the last thing that is needed.

I had planned on calling Dwain, first. Had planned on it for some time. The first time Dwain read this was probably the first time a decent number of people had read the first inception of it as well; Jon in Seattle and Sheryl in Maine would be reading it at the same time, too. D found out before Mom, for sure. He knew before Skee, Skee who would be locked up during the time the story started. The conversation I planned with D would have started with small talk, light circles of dancing around dad shit, life shit, art shit, and love shit—the things you share with your bigger brother/best friend. I would jog around the central issue, the issue he would not know existed until it left my mouth. Five-year-old me who always felt too small to be in such a body adorned with all the feelings of the world, trapped inside of wishes and dreams.

Secrets are a funny thing, no? How they intrude into our space and de-filter the angles and corners and make the quiet obsolete. They come and disrupt, they take our hands and make us grab for things—ears, bodies, warmth, guns. Sometimes, they come to us in the form of a phone call, a daydream, or a nightmare. Even now, as I type I wonder about the moments after "Publish" after "Send," after the conversations and questions, and the heavy that sits and will proceed to sit and cloud the areas and parts and corners and closets. Secrets, like moths, are hidden in the nether regions of the cabinets we tend to frequent but forget about, the crevices and corners. They stay there, festering and growing. But they show themselves eventually. They make grand appearances at the least favorable times: family gatherings, and romantic road trips. In IKEA aisles and while shopping for produce at Key Food. Secrets are never meant to stay that way. They break things open and leave the pieces there for you to either start anew or put back together what is broken. But things will never be as is. That's not how secrets work.

We start here: I was molested when I was five years old. I couldn't tell you the date or time. But I know it was summer. I know that because I can remember the sun setting and the TV blaring in the bedroom, the kind of way our TVs would do when we weren't in school and weren't too concerned with what sleep was or wasn't. It was by the younger brother of a friend of D's on Creston Avenue in the Bronx. Their family would move away a few months after. I will trust that there was no correlation between me and the leaving because that makes it easier to digest, and easier to throw away. Did I make this up? Was there blood? If your innocence is stolen, does it return in the form of an angel, a hallucination? Did you want what you were given, or rather, did you ask for what was stolen to be taken? You remember things. You remember the open window on the third floor. You remember the fire escape in the two-bedroom apartment. You remember him climbing through the window. You remember him whispering. You remember him climbing through the window because he could because you knew him and his face and his smile because you are five and you remember faces and people. You remember more whispers. You remember a finger to his mouth, mouthing "Shhh." You remember your pants. You remember the sweat and a drinking glass falling off the top bunk and breaking. You remember your mother waking from her early evening work-couch-sleep, walking into the room after things had already broken, and the ghost of a teenage boy had already climbed out of you, out of sight, down fire escape steps, exiting. You remember your mother asking "Is everything all right?" You remember sobbing after she left, more about the glass than about the other thing that shattered. You remember the air, how it sat against your small skin, and how everything would taste different. When we moved from the building, it wasn't because of that: my mother was tired of the loud parties with the Budweiser cans all over the hallway and the used condoms in the stairwell. But this story, this story is not about those things. No, this is about the aftershock. This is also about the recoil and the echo that follows.

The story I get to tell now is equipped with words that I didn't have before. That language is owed to me being in therapy. Therapy initially was the consolation prize for getting back together with my fiancée. This was around 2012, when she and I had started getting our bearings after moving from Brooklyn to Florida to Atlanta, back to the Bronx to live with my mother and stepdad, and then trekking all over New York City, looking for anything and anywhere that felt like home. My agreement to therapy was a way to maintain hope and peace, to balance out the pain inflicted and endured. I had cheated, twice with the same woman. It started with an impromptu encounter during a work trip where we introduced ourselves and held each other's stares for way too long. It felt like the first time in a long time that a woman, especially a Black woman, looked like she wanted me. We then moved to casual emails, where we shared how much love we each had for the person we were engaged to, while also confessing that we were both attracted to each other.

The emails got more and more sexual, more adventurous and flirtatious. It ended the first time when I sent my partner a text that was meant for my emotional fling. Hands full with pizza boxes and a two liter, I held my phone in one hand while I sexted my partnership away. Getting back upstairs to our Upper East Side studio apartment with my fiancée's brother and his fiancée waiting for our game night, my partner confronted me about the text in the kitchen. Since lying came readily to me, that was the easiest and most reliable language I could muster in the moment. The energy in the whole apartment shifted to a moody fog that would soon force her brother and his partner to vacate.

"YOU AIN'T SHIT!"

The words flew out of her mouth effortlessly. She yelled. I cried. I walked around the neighborhood aimless and hapless for three hours before returning to the couch. I packed my things the next day and headed back to the safety of my mother's home. Three weeks later, after a string of apologies, acknowledgments, faults and flaws, I desperately tried to own without any real interrogation behind the whys of my missteps, my fiancée and I reconciled . . . until I cheated again. As soon as she was on a plane headed to Los Angeles, ring still on her finger and dreams of being a writer and actor in California heavy on her heart, I sent an email to my former fling from another email address that my soon-to-be ex-fiancée just so happened to check. The next time I would see her, no more than a few days or weeks later, she would be standing beside me ringless while I read a poem at my Aunty KK's funeral.

When I'd see images on TV or in magazines, the people sitting in the therapist's chair never looked like me. And that always seemed to be intentional. They were white and balding, or white and neurotic, or white and muscular. But not like me. Niggas don't do therapy. The stigma is real. And it isn't enough to just *go* to therapy. There is a level of honesty and transparency that is required to be able to show up in ways that can actually alter the behaviors that are causing so much mayhem and madness. It's with therapy that I was able to step inside my inner child, map out the hurts of yesteryear, and find a path that felt less like a roadblock and more like an entryway to some level of healing that had never really felt possible or tangible. Niggas don't do therapy. They don't have to tell us. We're told we ain't shit, not fixable, expendable. We are told we are broke, we are broken, we are nothing without the people in our lives who made us. We live in that space, sit with it, and that guides and directs what we reflect back out into the world. Therapy is for white people. Talking about your problems is soft. No. We have to hold ourselves and each other accountable as Black men in ways that also hold space for softness to be a prerequisite for how we love each other. I learned that in therapy, too. And because of that, I can look at my past with more gracious, tender, and clearer eyes. Eyes that have aged, have seen things: at the age of five is when I would start walking into our 3B kitchen and started poking my stomach with the tip of my mama's kitchen knife, the same knife she'd cut mangoes, cut strawberries, cut her famous meat loaf with, that same knife would also find itself against the chubby flesh of my belly, me wanting to find a way to dull whatever felt like too much. I would never do it hard enough to draw blood, but enough to feel some sort of pain. Was I testing my threshold? I don't think so. My tolerance for pain is relatively low and always has been. This was deeper than that. A part of me felt like I deserved the pain. Where that deservedness came from, I wouldn't be able to tell you. When I hear doctors and sociologists talk about genetics having some sort of connection to mental health disorders, I am reminded of my father, his brothers, and his sisters—all in a household with an abusive father of their own. The extent of the abuse is hard to say. According to the National Institute of Mental Health (NIMH), mental illness is usually caused by a combination of four main factors: genetics, biology, environmental, and psychological factors. I can look at my father and look at my face in the mirror and see just how apples do not fall far from the trees they grow from.

During my freshman year in college, my white girlfriend had found out I cheated with a girl in high school who I would playfully call my friend in the hallways but secretly would kiss by the lockers in the hallways. My world fell apart. I was Mr. Nice Guy, the kind boy who everyone liked and who could never hurt a soul. I was a romantic. I was a poet. And I was acting like an irresponsible eighteen-year-old asshole. My ex-girlfriend and her best friend called me on the phone to grill me about the accusations. After the back-and-forth, I unplugged the phone from the wall and desperately looked for anything that would get me out of the sinkhole I was falling into. I searched around my empty dorm room, eyes sore from crying, and sought anything that could be easily tied around my neck—a rope, maybe? None to be found. My Andis T-Trimmer cord? This could work. I needed something, anything strong enough to carry a body. I placed a chair in the middle of the room after my roommate left for class, and placed the cord of my Andis T-Trimmer tightly around my neck, trying to get all the blood out. The same chair my roommate and I used to study and lay our legs on, I stood on while trying to figure out how to tie the cord to the ceiling, measuring the distance between ceiling and floor, jumping from the chair while simultaneously choking myself like, How do I do this? It felt too hard. I dumped my head in a sink full of water in our bathroom, holding my breath, waiting for something to happen. I was too scared to take pills. And slitting my wrists felt too messy, too much of a scene. But I knew at that moment that I would rather have died than be seen as the liar when everyone back home thought I was the nicest guy and could do no wrong. My ex-girlfriend would call the resident assistant of our floor, who would proceed to knock on my door and call the room, and I would proceed to not answer, but then I would. And she would mention a phone call from a young lady who sounded very frantic. The young lady had mentioned the possibility of me "harming myself." I would chuckle. So would the resident assistant. Deny, deny, deny. She would believe me. Who wouldn't believe me—a happy-go-lucky, cheerful, outgoing eighteen-year-old? I realize it has always been easier for me to lie than to confront my lack: a lack of comfort in my skin; a lack of money; a lack of food sometimes; a lack of confidence. But what was abundantly clear was: running from my truth was harder than leaning into the fiction in my mind.

For years, I used my sexual trauma, more as a point of deflection rather than an opportunity to reflect on the harm caused and how it had crisscrossed itself into my life. I would hide behind it, use it as both a shield and an excuse to not be held accountable for the ways I showed up in the world as a man. I got off on being the nice guy, the tortured soul, the beleaguered man who only needed a chance to prove that he was different from the other men. My diet of *Love Jones* and 1990s R&B songs led me to believe that a sensitive man who could also be manly was the most loveable sort. I would weaponize my trauma to gain sympathy, to get attention, to have my scars loved and held, without doing any of the work required to understand my trauma and how to not have said trauma show up in my relationships with others, mainly because I lacked the tools required to unpack it, and also had no desire to acquire them. I was hurting my way through life. I was lying to myself and others, mainly because I thought the truth of me, the real me—scared, anxious, dejected—wasn't worthy of love. And I played the role of the scorned, lost, and woebegone Black man in need of saving from the systems and the world looking to keep him down. I had become the damsel in distress, ready to place my burdens and woes on any woman who was willing to lend an ear and a shoulder, while I got to the *real* work of creating art and trying to change the world. I had convinced myself that I was noble because of hurt. Staying in the hurt, in the lying, was easy. Holding a mirror to it all was the hard part.

The summer that my daughter Lilah still sat in the womb, I walked past the trees I would normally pray to her with, and briskly made my way through St. Mary's Park during the work week, contemplating how to leave—jump in front of a car, or a train; pills; a bullet; start a fight I would plan to lose? I was not ready to be a father. And looking back, I now know no one is. My father certainly wasn't. Nothing and no one prepare you for a phone argument that sends you spiraling on the bus ride on the way to pick up your child from day care where you have to debate between checking yourself into the nearest hospital's psychiatric ward or just jump off the bus and run into traffic and let the rest of the details sort themselves out later. Nothing prepares you to then call the suicide hotline, where you hear the voice of a woman who sounds like she could be your aunt, all to have her tell you, you are enough. How would I create enough pain so that the pain would no longer be? Where do you go when the pain of staying is sharper, stronger, than the feeling of leaving it all behind? I would never cut myself. I was too scared of the marks. The fear of leaving would always be the strongest. That energy needed to go somewhere. It needed to be channeled into something that felt bigger than me, bigger than the humming of death gnawing my ears away; louder than the weight of my daughter's dreams resting on my chest and shoulders.

Art would save me. In the times and moments when I felt like the world and the bones inside of me would collapse under the weight of it all. It was after that walk in the park when I would begin writing the pieces that would make up the bulk of my soon-to-be one-man show "Jamal Wanna Build a Space-ship." Because art was my savior before Mary's son was. Writing has always been easier than death, and performing has always been better than breathing. And so, here I am. Trying to heal me. This is about healing. The "me" that recognizes that the tears of a Black boy who grew up in the spaces I grew up in, could be chased by gangs (eighth grade), robbed (sixth and seventh grades), or murdered, made to feel hunted and prey-like, could be so much more than what the environment/white supremacy tells us we deserve. Art gave me expansion; it gave me freedom. Freedom to process and sift through the hurt, the pain, and the sense of loneliness that seemed to always cast itself alongside me like an unattractive shadow that would follow me no matter how far I tried to distance myself from it.

I have always wondered if what transpired on that top bunk bed in 3B was the catalyst for the shame that I felt about the feelings I carried around with me: the need for want, the desire for more than whatever I held and had, because those things were always too small, never enough to keep the empty from devouring my whole. Black boys are taught to expect very little from the world but coldness and the responsibility of masculinity we have to shepherd into existence without a real road map or rule book. The rule book we've been given, passed down to us by the Black men in our neighborhoods—the barbershops, the corner, the churches and mosques, in our homes—dictates that our masculinity needs to show up in certain ways to be authentic. And if it doesn't fit into the narrowest of boxes, then it doesn't count. We are so much more than that. Surrendering to that, succumbing to that, redefines what masculinity gets to be. It also redefines what Blackness gets to be by default.

I am a man now, but my five-year-old self is here, too. He is here, along with the names and bodies and selves of others seeking closure, redemption, or a hug. He is not so far removed from the adult me. Adult me still sees where the light starts, and the dark breaks. Adult me still chokes and suffocates and wonders why I cry so easily and break so hard. Adult me wonders and prays and hopes that he can guard his children against the things they deserve to be protected from. I want to preserve their innocence for as long as humanly possible by giving them alternative scripts and different rule books to adhere to. There were no missteps here. My mother did not fail me; nor did D or Skee, relatives, or friends. God did not abandon me, I have learned. And neither did my father. I have leaned on shoulders and arms and hearts; on words and books and lovers, and the quiet chain-clanking of my ancestors, at times weeping at their feet, looking toward skies, pleading for answers that may never come. We want to tie up the loose ends, but that is Hollywood fiction at best, manufactured toxicity for the sake of deflection at worst. Sometimes, the ends remain just as loose and tangled and as dirty as when they first arrived. Sometimes you pick your lip to survive, just to tap into the pain that lets you and your body know that you are alive and yes! you are still here. This story is about all of these things.

Good Art, Bad Art, Black Art

Feat. Donald Glover, Jerrod Carmichael, Tyler Perry

If I don't like I don't like it
I don't like it
It don't mean that I'm hating

—COMMON, "THE 6TH SENSE"

Common's statement is plain—we can comment and have opinions on art without it meaning we have a dislike for the art or the artist. But what is art to begin with? Black art could be finding the curve in a straight line really, so long as a Black person is doing it. But that's debatable. Black art isn't stagnant. Nothing is. So, what is Black art? Art with a name tag, maybe? What and how do we articulate it? My man Jeary and I, Jeary works at the Metropolitan Museum of Art—beautiful Black man, uber-talented—we was kicking it at this very healthy spot in the Lower East Side I used to go to when I wanted to feel like a writer on the white shows I used to watch that featured white writers going to places that looked like the one we were sitting in. Jeary and I got to talking—talking about Black love, Black art, Black music; talking politics and money or the lack thereof. Just two Black men, sharing a fondness for the worlds we inhabit and the kindness we shared for one another's journeys—I, a thirty-something father at the time and Jeary, newly hired associate educator, Teen Programs, at the Metropolitan Museum of Art. In our conversation, he used a line from Kanye's "Spaceships" in reference to a story he was telling, and I finished the lyric. I think that's Black art, too. And I know there is a term for the thing Jeary and I did but I can't tell you because yes, I am well-read, but I did not go to a doctorate program nor did I major in African American Linguistic Studies. I have a high school diploma and two years of college, and I learned who Kimberlé Crenshaw is from Twitter, the extended conversations led by Black women on intersectionality gaining real and invaluable traction following the murder of Breonna Taylor at the hands of police. I say that not with pride and also not with shame—the shame I let go of a long time ago when I realized the theatrics required to say you understand Black culture are too performative for my liking. Because knowing everything and everyone who ever made or said anything is the mark of the elite, of the promised. I never knew all the poets. The poets I loved the most were murdered in the nineties or were busy climbing rap charts. Black art is making new dances to replace the old ones white people keep stealing two years too late. I write essays like I write raps, to be honest. You know what's Black art? Black Thought. He been rappin' his ass off. Donwill and Von Pea of Tanya Morgan. Jean Grae. Anytime I see my man Fred, we give each other hugs like two niggas who just came home. That's Black art to me. I can say *came home* and if you're Black you'll know what I meant. And if you're Black adjacent, if you've absorbed enough Black culture via Instagram influencer campaigns, or

Insecure, or ads, been to CultureCon *and* ComplexCon *and* Afrotech *and* are friends with Morgan Debaun *and* have an LLC and were featured in an Afropunk photoshoot for the *Cut* (because no one goes to Afropunk for Black, afro punk music amirite?) *and* have an AAVE library card, then you probably knew what I meant, too, though. Same difference, I guess.

Teddy Riley gave us a whole new genre. George Clinton made us a whole new genre. Nelson George redefined Black critique. I don't fuck with drill music, but it is a sound we've never had, which is saying a lot for hip-hop, which has sounded the same for about fifteen years. And so what Black art is and was are largely determined by who you ask and when. The context in which we engage with the art matters. Amongst the intersections the brilliant Kimberlé Crenshaw has written and spoken of, an intersection I find to be most important but rarely talked to, is the intersection of culture and region, and how and where you were born and raised can often determine what is considered to be art by some and trash by others. Geographic location, and even so far as your block, your town, your city, your borough; the college you went to, the sorority or fraternity you pledged; where you choose to get your news. All these things and more have a profound effect on how we show up in the world, and also on how we engage with art and media. Me being born and living in the Bronx with my two older brothers to a West Indian mother from Dominica and African American father from Pensacola, Florida, has so many implications—it shaped the kind of hip-hop I heard, the kinds of music I heard in the house, what I was allowed to watch, who I hung out with. Because my uncle Vincent immigrated from Dominica and stayed with us for some time, I heard the Counting Crows, Tracy Chapman, Ace of Base, and Shinehead. Because my mother was of a certain age, I heard Billy Ocean, I heard Chris de Burgh, I heard Club Nouveau, and Bobby McFerrin. Because D listened to a certain kind of hip-hop, I missed the early years of backpack rap—no People Under the Stairs, no early Slum Village or MF Doom; no pilgrimages to Fat Beats or Bobbito and Stretch late nights—D was a hardcore East Coast fan who would later have some southern leanings. D listened to Suave House, so I did. I heard the *Mr. Scarface Is Back* album because that's what D listened to. I heard Mary J. Blige's "You Remind Me" not because of *What's the 411?* but because of the *Strictly Business* soundtrack. After that, I would hear the song again on a Kid Capri mixtape—even now during the song break, I hear Kid Capri's shout-outs. I saw Kid Capri in an airport during a brief layover and walked over to dap him up. Because culture. D flooded the apartment with deejay mixtapes from S&S, Ron G, Doo Wop, Dirty Harry, Tony Touch, Chill Will, DJ Jazzy Joyce, and SupaSam. What I gravitated toward largely depended on what D would make me tape on our VHS while he was at work: Brand Nubian, Lords of the Underground, Group Home. So much of how I defined Black art was defined and influenced by others around me. And with that, how I view and consider art to be good or bad is very much still guided by the era and cultural context in which I heard the music and saw the films. I was a latchkey kid. Many of the ways I would engage with certain kinds of art wouldn't happen until high school, where I met kids who were listening to shit, reading, and engaging with shit that had never been remotely close on my radar—the Grateful Dead, Pearl Jam, the Cranberries, Nirvana, the Smashing Pumpkins.

Having cable TV was another level of expansion: I could see videos from Goodie Mob on *Rap City*, see other Black teens on *Teen Summit*, and hear R&B on *Video Soul*, all on BET. There were no art galleries, no Afrocentric Black parents who had traveled the world. No sneaking subway tokens and cigarettes from my mother's purse onto the train to head to SoHo or the West Village to see some band whose flyer we saw on a parked car somewhere, meeting up with friends, sipping from a vintage flask on the top-shelf whiskey we got out of someone's liquor cabinet. Our parents were doing what they could to keep us alive while surviving in the process. When my cousin Leah let me borrow her college textbook of African American writings, a book that's still in the closet of my old bedroom in my mother's apartment, it was my first, real intensive journey into Black writing that wasn't condensed into Black History Month lessons: the likes of Frederick Douglass, Booker T. Washington, Amiri Baraka, Fannie Lou Hamer, Zora Neale Hurston. It is through that lens that I was taught about art.

No one is the Columbus of language. Our taste buds aren't ours. They are given to us. We think our opinions are ours, but they're not. We are an amalgam of all the people, places, and things we've engaged with—everything is shaped by everything. And so even how we see, think, and feel about art, especially when we're talking about Black art, is not only how we as individuals are engaging with work, but also how others in our surrounding community have engaged with the work, and are even now influencing how that work shows up or doesn't in our lives.

White art isn't called white art. It's called art. The way we weigh conversations surrounding Black art has so much to do with our history as a people; people who have long attempted to maintain ownership of our art, only to see that art be bastardized and stolen for the greater good of capitalism, commerce, and the rising entertainment economy. White pop culture gets to be weird, zany, and avant-garde, without the microscope of race or authenticity being forced down the audience's throat. White art also gets to be mediocre without it hampering the opportunities for more mediocre white art. To truly support Black art means being open to the fluidity of Blackness as a whole. Black art, much like the current conversations surrounding sexual orientations and binaries, gets to be as open as our existence as Black people is outside of the margins and scope of definitions. That fluidity will also force us to ask ourselves if proximity to whiteness makes Black art more palatable, more avant-garde. Art that pushes boundaries, that lives against the norms, tropes, and stereotypes of what is considered to be true Black art, opens the door for a wider, deeper conversation about what defines Black art. And while that feels like a subjective conversation, the ways of the world lend themselves to a more objective clear answer, separating the art we love and loathe into very specific categories: good art, bad art, and the art that can sometimes be a catchall for the spectrum . . . Black art. In my mind and heart, one of the best pieces of good art to show itself to the world in quite some time wasn't a movie, a stage play, a streamable album, or a TV show, but a comedy special. By leaps and bounds, *Rothaniel*, Jerrod Carmichael's incredibly intimate and hilarious stand-up special, was not only the best piece of art released in 2022, but may also be the best stand-up special since Chappelle's *Killin' Them Softly*, and probably the most honest since Pryor's Sunset Strip set.

Directed by Bo Burnham, the white comedian, director, and actor who also directed one of Chris Rock's most personal stand-ups to date, *Tamborine*, Jerrod Carmichael's stand-up is a searing, beautiful display of genius platformed in such a streamlined and simple way it's hard to not feel like you are also at the Blue Note at one of their rickety tables toward the back where on any given night you are just as likely to see a jazz trio, Bobby McFerrin, Robert Glasper, or a jazz brunch choir. We open up on a scene of crestfallen snow, cueing in the wintry blues of New York City. We hear chatter and seats filling. Bo is setting us up to get cozy. The setting is in and of itself an invitation, a solicitation to the viewing audience to gather around the imaginary campfire. The stage, red chair defiant in the center, is also a provocation of sorts: I dare you to dive into the sensuality and intimacy of this moment. In comparison, Jerrod's NBC show *Carmichael* wasn't the proper vehicle for Jerrod's immense talent. His two-part video HBO diary slash docuseries HBO Home Videos, if anything, gave us a glimpse into the Black experience of Jerrod's upbringing—the love of his mother, the absenteeism and strain that is the dynamic between himself and his father. Really, *Rothaniel* is the evolution of Jerrod not as a comic or an actor, but as a fully fleshed human who also happens to be gay. While much is made of Jerrod's coming out as gay during the fifty-five-minute show, the star of this special was community, particularly Black community. Jerrod's almost call-and-response-like methodology with the crowd in attendance speaks to a higher caliber of Black art that calls back to the Black church, to hip-hop, the mmms and aahs of an audience seemingly as comfortable as Jerrod is onstage. Jerrod's subtle wardrobe—gold link chain, red satin shirt—as soft and easy as his presence onstage. Jerrod spends the show seated, slumped, sometimes arching forward, ready almost to walk into the crowd with mic in hand, willing them to invest in a kitchen table conversation. And the fact that the stand-up felt more like a conversation than an hour set of comedy is what makes this a piece of Black art worth interrogating. Jerrod, like so many of his generation and those before him, remixed what we expect in the binary of a construct. This was a conversation between himself and the audience, a fourth wall not available for dissection. And the conversation, just by its mere presume of being, is a Black one. Yes, because Jerrod is the one leading it, but also because of the juxtaposition of the artist and the art shared: the closeness of it all. Whiteness in art tends to be distant. Whiteness in anything tends to be distant, removed from the subject and the object. Capitalism in its purest transactional form removes warmth from rooms just by its sheer need to distance us from the products we engage with. Jerrod's whole approach onstage was an apolitical, artistic master class on what happens when we remove ourselves from the boxes we place Black art in, with commerce serving as a distraction from the main point of art: to move, to inspire.

This is also why to best understand Black art we have to watch it. Albeit this sounds simple, in a world where streaming and binging are king, we often are left to critique work based on the critiques we receive from others. So much of the art and content we are engaging with is removed from the context and nuance in which it was created and is also being featured. Our thoughts are now third-party sourced, a game of artsy Telephone where each person's judgment of art is first processed by someone else seeing it for us. To truly understand art, especially Black art, we have to sit with it. D'Angelo's *Voodoo* is one of the finest pieces of musical art ever recorded. The album was everything his debut album *Brown Sugar* was not—it was raw, eclectic, and funky. It pushed the neo-soul genre in an untapped direction, digging itself back into the roots of funk, blues, R&B, and gospel music. But the only way to truly know that would be not only to listen to the art but also to sit with it. We don't sit with things anymore.

As a self-professed 1980s baby who went to college in the 2000s, who will almost always fawn over anything '80s and '90s (including anything that falls in the neo-soul era of art and music) related and created, the notion that anything was created after these periods can sometimes feel like a foreign concept. I can readily admit and see my biases up close, front and center. But also, as much as aging continues to shape my views on contemporary art, much in the same ways how those who heard the blues, heard bebop, saw Thelonious Monk perform live for the first time, heard Sam Cooke turn secular and Marvin Gaye turn sex symbol, what defines good art and bad art is a blurred line. I realize that I have also always been an art snob.

I have always firmly believed there is good art and bad art. Ever since I was my eldest daughter's age. I remember being five years old and knowing "Around the Way Girl" was a personal favorite, that *Teenage Mutant Ninja Turtles* were fresh; that New Edition was dope and New Kids on the Block were the Walmart version; that Reginald Hudlin and Spike Lee deserved their flowers then and they deserve the flowers now. There were music and films and the artists behind them that not only stood the test of time but also pushed everything else that would come after them, forward: Tupac, Chuck D, and Denzel. Even now, knowing how we all have opinions and the freedom of choice, but choosing the Bluefaces and Brent Faiyazs of the world feels to me like a poor decision based primarily on a lack of care for your well-being and your ears. I am fully aware of how this reads. I know exactly who I've become: the jaded, beguiled, and beleaguered old head who critiques art with a fine-tooth comb. I am fully prepared to tell my daughters they "don't know about this" when they get older, because they don't. They never will be able to fully understand what the crackling sound of a needle atop a longed-for vinyl feels and sounds like; the feeling of the freedom of sweating and dancing with everyone in unison when *All About the Benjamins* first came out. There was a feeling of epicness in that time in the early years of the nineties that can never quite be duplicated. I imagine a similar feeling of a Motown classic hitting the airwaves for the first time in the sixties. Time and place and context have so much to do with the ways we engage with art and artistry. To be fair, I will never understand what it means to them when the latest YouTube celebrity or TikTok star shouts out their city in a video or drops into town impromptu and shares it on their IG Stories. Those moments will be as sacred for them as my moments were for me. Our feelings about the art we both love and loathe are subjective, conditioned by the shitty street blocks we were raised on, the inherent biases that have grown in us, that we cling to and are attached to by heartstring and hip: the sounds of a voice, the melody of a hum or hook; the bounce of a beat. Art is no different from how we speak about the human experience—there are people we hate, people we despise, and there are also people who can do no wrong. My fear with our tendency to avoid mindfully critiquing Black art is that we will not take risks, instead leaning on tropes to tell stories rather than trying to find the truth and intention behind the art we are attempting to create.

We get to push our art and the artists who make it to be better. Not solely by taking on and tackling a challenging and daunting role, but also by pushing them to discover what is underneath that role, that tension. I've made bad art. Really bad art. My attempt at bad art was needed to make good art. The plan for me was never to be a writer per se. The plan was to perform. The plan was to theater, film, rap, and poem my way to a career that would reach Yasiin Bey heights, André 3000 proportions. I wanted to make scalable art. I grew up reading the *Source*, *XXL*, and the inside covers of CDs. I would tell myself, often before this moment where you the reader are reading this, that I would never be good enough for a major publishing book deal. Or a *New York Times* opinion piece. I knew my writing was not readable for, say, the *New Yorker* or *New York* magazine. *GQ* used to return the emails then they stopped. At one point I was close to an *Atlantic* writing opportunity to include in my bylines, but that fell flat. So much of my voice has always been mine, and my unwillingness to contort or change that voice to fit into a space has often left me in the background, watching my peers both booked and busy in the editorial bylines I used to salivate over. But none of that matters to me much anymore. Primarily because, even while being pretentious about art, I can also recognize how corny it is to be pretentious about art, especially Black art, especially when we consider the bar is so low when movies like *Boondocks Saints* are hailed as classics and will never hold a candle to *Do the Right Thing*. Even the more heralded films in what's considered to be popular film—*A Clockwork Orange*, any Woody Allen flick, are considered to be a burgeoning film-maker's supposed wet dream fantasy. *Gone with the Wind* is still heralded as one of the greatest movies of all time if you're to be considered a true film buff. Same with *Citizen Kane*. Nowhere in these conversations is *Shaft* or *Blacula*. The bar is set to a monotone whiteness. When a film that exists outside of that shows up in the Black community, it tends to stay there. Because Blackness is not considered the norm. Whiteness is.

The stickiness of good art is that it outlasts the time in which it was created. Frank Ocean's *Channel Orange* transcends its genre. *Rocky* is a classic because the story will always come back to two star-crossed lovers who were opposites of one another but found themselves in each other. Serena Williams makes art on the court; the same way Kobe did, Lebron. Good art is seldom up for debate. Bad art always is because no one shows us how to critique work. While gatekeeping as a whole has kept many a Black artist from pursuing a career in art, the sudden lack of gatekeeping has made it possible for so many of us, myself included, to make art and decisions about our art that are uninhibited, free of recourse and tone policing. Meaning, anyone can create an album without the need of a record label. Anyone can publish a book without a publisher. Anyone can share their art for the world to see online. The lack of gatekeeping also no real way to measure whether the art created can stand up to the art before it or the art that will follow. Without a community of those tied to the work, what we see is a work unbound and unregulated that feels unsettled and not refined. That rawness can be great with the right cast, or bad with the wrong ones. For so long I wagged my finger at Tyler Perry movies, often comparing him and his body of work to his contemporaries—his characters lacked range, and the stories felt sophomoric and pulled right from a soap opera series. Until I began to realize how much my mother loves Tyler Perry, and how much my brother and his wife love him, too. And I had to stop being elitist and realize how much of what Tyler does isn't for me. Madea is indeed somebody's deceased auntie in drag pulling stunts from the grave; the grandmother who is still standing proudly as the matriarch holding court—skillet in one hand, a pistol in the other. It's for an audience that craves to see these stories and can hear their mothers and their brothers in those stories. And that there is as much room for a Tyler Perry story as there is room for an Ava story, a Spike Lee, a Spike Jonze, or a Scorsese story. What Tyler Perry has done and continues to do is speak to a Black experience that feels close to self, to skin, for many. Because if you are a churchgoing, southern Black, Tyler's creations offer up pure pleasure and entertainment that feels less convoluted and multidimensional than a *Sorry to Bother You*. Tyler's work is not attempting to make a political statement. And revoking that being a bad thing has been a part of my evolution. Because if my West Indian mother, who worked incredibly hard to make a way for her children in spite of the odds, can see a part of herself not only in Tyler Perry but also in the movies and shows he makes, I can find something about him to love, too. Tyler's story is what makes his art important. Because we as a Black audience are always rooting for him, even when the attempts feel forced and dramatically stereotypical. My mother also loved *Days of Our Lives* and *Santa Barbara*—a genre of soap opera that Tyler leans into heavily for his work. The exaggerated circumstances are no different from the plotlines seen in the conventional daytime TV dramas my mother spent her afternoons viewing after work. Oftentimes, as Black viewers, because we have been offered so little room to try stories that live outside of a studio's expectations, the feeling that

everything we do must be exceptional is a feeling all too familiar—in film, in music . . . life. Black art gets to be bad. If we are
progressing, if we are truly practicing and preaching equality as
a society, then our art gets to run the gamut, the full spectrum of
excellent to mediocre to horrid. One show that mixed a highbrow
approach with current Black culture sensibilities is the Donald
Glover show, *Atlanta*.

I read the pilot to *Atlanta* consistently after the first season.
I know countless others heard and saw their voice not only in
the characters but also in the speed and pacing of the writing
and dialogue. What Kanye did for Black, backpack rap hipster
culture with *The College Dropout* is what Donald was able to do
with the entirety of *Atlanta*. Donald Glover created a space where
quirky Blackness could cradle the line of cool while still remaining relevant to culture: Black culture. And it didn't come off as
trite or fake or even contained. Donald also was smart enough
to assemble a team of writers he knew he could trust with the
vision. *Atlanta* always felt like an experiment of sorts, a "how far
are they gon' let us take this" kinda energy. Experimental but
connected. And in that experiment, scenarios that were normal
and at times funny and sometimes traumatic were stretched out
not for comedic effect but because they could be. Which one of
us hasn't got caught rocking something that wasn't name brand
in front of the homies (*Atlanta*, "FUBU": season 2, episode 10)?
Which one of us hasn't been at some expensive-ass party we probably weren't supposed to be at ("Old Man and the Tree": season
3, episode 3)? How many of us had a tepid relationship with our
barber ("Barbershop": season 2, episode 5)? Further into the show,
you got the feeling Donald and crew were playing with us in that
they continued to push the boundaries of what surrealism could

look like. Season 3 moved in and out of plotlines. The glue of the show was race, primarily Blackness. And the journey seemed less and less about the audience and more about the folks creating the work for the audience. The careers of the actors on the show have all skyrocketed, primarily due to their talent. But the show also elevated the standards not just for Black art, but for art in general. The show never felt like it was trying too hard, even when the notes took us way out there ("Alligator Man," "Three Slaps," "Teddy Perkins"), but also kept it tonally even, providing humor, social commentary, and real-life shit. As a father, Earn's struggles to make ends meet while being a dad felt too real and at times too close to home. Albeit not the same dynamic as on the show per se, but there are plenty of Black men who I know can relate to the unnerving feeling of not knowing what the fuck is going on with your life, putting two sticks together to try and make something happen. And that is Blackness in a nutshell, right? Our entire existence is doing extraordinary things with the bare minimum. We are almost always capable and almost always willing, but life throws endless curveballs and has been since we were brought to the American plantation. There was a four-year gap between season 2 and season 3 of the show, a lesson if there ever was one. In a world where art is expected to be churned manically and mechanically, bending and contorting to the needs and whims of those who consume it, forcing the makers to make things for Instagram feeds, Donald Glover treated the show like a musical release, each season an album's worth of music. And with that thinking, the D'Angelos and Princes of the world would be quite pleased with the output—long stretches of breaks between albums have consistently remained the norm for musicians solely focused on the art of making, as opposed to the commodified way we tend to create nowadays. Creativity, especially Black creativity, is not a sport of consumption but an act of prayer, of love. And sometimes, if we're lucky enough, that love gets channeled through the vessel of art. The way that art gets communicated to the audience is what sets the tone for how the art proceeds to be translated for the masses, even if the intent starts within the framework of Black identities.

Some may argue that *The Chappelle Show*, *The Eric Andre Show*, and *Key & Peele* were *Atlanta*'s predecessors—sketch comedies on the surface but also using Black vernacular, along with varying degrees of weird, nerd culture blended in—with each one taking what it means to make art as a Black person on their heads. *Atlanta* is inherently Black because its star characters are Black, much like *The Chappelle Show* before Chappelle himself went off the rails of bitter and enraged transphobia. But the art in both *Atlanta* and *Chappelle* would just as equally be consumed by non-Black persons as well. Because it gives the audience an insider's look into the minds of Blackness. While we are not monolithic, that art is a way in for some non-Black persons, who are much too eager to see and seek Blackness as a barometer for how culturally adept they can become, to acquire their knowledge of Blackness. Here, being Black is not a race, but a tool; Blackness is now seen as a persona, a character that can be pulled out of a magic hat whenever the next dance craze, the next BBQ shows itself. We see this in the rise of the use of African-American Vernacular English, better known as AAVE, which is now being adopted as standard language, hip in its use, which provides the non-Black user the feeling of cultural cachet without having to be responsible for understanding the context and framing of the language. Non-Blacks engaging with Black art is no different: without the subtext that is almost inherent in growing up as a Black person who may generally be exposed to a certain kind of adaptable Blackness that moves in and out of Black communities and spaces, the heart of what is being spoken and created gets lost when you are not fully invested in understanding what makes Black art Black in the first place. And that can be scary for a Black audience that craves things to be solely ours—solely for our unpacking and discussion without the gaze of whiteness bearing down on us from afar. So much of everything that was once ours, our stories and our families and our bodies, has been taken and commodified to the point where it is almost unrecognizable in certain regards. The white gaze distorts Black art merely by existing. Its callous tendency is to co-opt and make the art something that needs to be for everyone in order for it to be successful or worth being a topic of discussion in the mainstream, which matters greatly when we are thinking about how projects get funded and see the light of day. Donald is making art for Black people, but for which Black people is probably the more complex and important question. And not all Black people will engage with the art in the same ways that they may engage with *Think Like a Man* or a Madea film or a *State Property* release, much in the same way Black culture is now everybody's culture, and this is not new—from blues to jazz to hip-hop, Black art starts as an art primarily consumed by Black people and is then slowly and aggressively co-opted and consumed by white audiences until Black art becomes everybody's art unless it's "too Black." *Atlanta* is beautiful Black, but it's also safe and digestible in the ways that MLK up until his later years was safe and digestible, in that it pushes just enough boundaries to request us to ask questions without forcing us to do so. There is something interesting in that regard when compared to an Eric André show, which is so experimental it removes any conversation about Blackness because it is so void of archetypes but is so Back because of it. That's also not Donald's fault. From *Watchmen* to *Lovecraft Country*, the bounds of safety have been stretched primarily because the world is so unsafe for Blackness that a re-creation of the Tulsa Massacre would trend on Twitter following the first episode of *Watchmen* but would still not feel shocking enough. Blackness has already been shocked, to the point anything that seems to call attention to the Black Death and atrocities against us all feels like dog whistles to leftist white liberal allies who feel guilty and want to be complicit enough to support the next season of Black art, the next Black artist, the next Black attempt at making something meaningful to Blackness. Black art becomes less of our own when everyone can be in on the joke with a quick Google search, a mimicked voice or borrowed slang term, a click on a hashtag. One could argue that Black art can at times be diminished when the vehicle it is administered through is owned by whiteness and white people. *Malcolm & Marie*, the Netflix feature that was Sam Levinson's post-*Euphoria* attempt at a black-and-white-shot romance noir, stars an out-of-her-comfort-zone Zendaya and an unsure John David Washington muddling over what feels like a forced interaction in both dialogue and correspondence, all of which is guided by the gaze of white Sam. Shot beautifully but led poorly, it leaves us wondering if white people have a place in helping Black people tell a story that is not solely a Black story: a lovers' quarrel.

But one could look at Bo's guidance in *Rothaniel*, also seeing that Jerrod served as a producer, as a way to illuminate what happens when, rather than owning the direction, Bo seems to be assisting Jerrod to usher in a certain kind of vision. And while Zendaya served as a producer on *Malcolm & Marie*, it is clear that Sam's vision is in the driver's seat. When we choose narratives that don't see race, we eliminate whole parts of a story that are never dormant. Black art is just art, but the Blackness in it is what makes it readily available to us. To ignore it, especially when left in the hands of someone who may not be conditioned to see Black stories as worth telling, we get art that is unclear and misguided in its direction. Because our language, by offering us the subtle subtext of Blackness—how we move, talk, and deal with each other—is what also helps our words jump out of the page and onto something worth engaging with.

I think good art takes risks. I think good art needs bad art to exist. I think Black art exists because we are inherently risktakers. Our whole livelihoods are a risk in themselves—living, breathing, running. I think good art is Westside Gunn, knowing a collaboration with Black Star, the duo of Yasiin Bey and Talib Kweli, would never have been possible in the era of the nineties when Biggie, Nas, and Jay-Z reigned supreme. Primarily because the intersections of capitalism, luxury, and conscious rap felt far too divisive a line to cross. For better or worse, those lines are blurred. And I don't think that's a bad thing. I think good art is Kendrick Lamar doing what he did on his *Mr. Morale & the Big Steppers* album: dissecting and investigating the different ideologies of Blackness and the tension that exists among them all. Good art continues to ask questions of its audience and, rather than seek answers, is creating space for curiosity in a reimagining of sorts. And even if I told you what bad art was, you wouldn't believe me because we've known thoughts on art to be subjective. I have never thought that to be true, primarily because I think there's a difference between what we consider art and what is just entertainment.

There are things that we consume that bring us joy that I would not necessarily consider art. And while we need room, levity, and lightheartedness as a Black community, our art should be changing the public discourse surrounding the culture and context in which the art was made. My favorite art doesn't just avoid binaries. It deconstructs, dissects, and plays with preexisting paradigms. It disassembles and contradicts and, in contrast, it dissects us in the process. If we are not prodding each other to be conscious of how we use art as a gateway to a higher form and state of being of Blackness, it's a waste. And through that concept, Black art is undeniably Black just by being itself—raw and authentic. It takes up and holds space in a way that defines itself for the audience that engages with it and those who make it. Black art is as much about the intent as it is the outcome. Good Black art challenges our norms and stereotypes, confronts them without comfort, leaving bare little room to squirm away. Bad Black art does the same through a different purview, its insistence on relegating ourselves to a certain kind of expectation and predictability that can also challenge what we think is supposedly true about good art in the first place. By that distinction, Madea is just as much an art piece as Mars Blackmon in that both characters shifted the landscape for how we show up for Black art. In some cases, art and entertainment get to coexist. And I will watch *Atlanta* in another ten years and it will be just as good, just as resonant, funny, profound, and just as Black. *Rothaniel* will be just as impactful in 2042 as it was in 2022. Because no matter how many limits, litmus tests, and caveats, no matter how many definitions or labels we try to place on Black art, Black art has none.

Black Republicans

Feat. Jay-Z

All these lies that America told us our whole life and then when we start getting it, they try to lock us out of it. They start inventing words like "capitalist." We've been called "niggers" and "monkeys" and shit. I don't care what words y'all come up with.

—JAY-Z, VIA A CLUBHOUSE CHAT, CIRCA 2002

Capitalism is violent. Capitalism maims. Capitalism burns everything to the ground. Capitalism fuels gentrification with a blowtorch. Capitalism tidies up imperialism, makes it a nice bed to lie in, to sleep under stars nestled by the backbones of slave labor. Capitalism builds a Barclays. Capitalism funds police and military activity more than it does education and services needed for suffering communities. Capitalism is undemocratic. Capitalism takes turns fucking you over. Capitalism does not value your body, only the work your bodies do in service of servitude, of more capitalism, more high beams, more billionaire boys clubs, tycoons, and venture capitalists, who would rather eat the poor than risk their pockets starving for another millie. Capitalism makes poverty a poor people's problem. Capitalism will look to build a better Mars and not a better Bronx, or Bed-Stuy, or South Philly, or Compton, or Palestine. Capitalism loathes anything that doesn't feed the machine. Capitalism will dupe you into believing that Black wealth is the key to our liberation, as opposed to Black wealth being the key to fueling more capitalism.

Capitalism feeds on the insecurities of Blackness—you will never be fit enough, fly enough, or Black enough; you will never be able to accrue enough. In response, we buy more things that closely resemble the kind of Black we are and aspire to be. Take me, for example. I am a hoarder of books. I buy books often. I buy books because I am indeed an avid reader. But also, I buy books to prove to myself and others that I am astute despite only having a high school diploma and some college under my belt. My books plant me in the Black intelligentsia. So it goes if you are someone whose beauty is your brand, then you and capitalism embark on the nerve-ending journey of Sephora, of Ulta; bags of products of Drunk Elephant and Youth to the People. And even when we point the finger to the sky or point our jagged fingers to our neighbors, to gluttonous celebrities, even when we point and pout and say "not us, we are not you" we buy into it. We buy into it often without choice because what else is there? How else will we post our vacation flicks to increase the FOMO on everyone's radar? How will we get our groceries in the frigid cold while we sit, seated at our tables watching the screen, streaming the latest thing to screen, and fawn over them from the comforts of our rent-stabilized existences? Who will stitch the tongues of our Nikes, sew the lining of our Fear of God sweats, fold the soles of our Air Force Ones? Who will fill our newsfeeds, fill our stockings, feed our urge to find the latest fight to share, the latent shootings of unarmed Blackness, the latex hidden under a Balenciaga?

Y'all was in the pub, having a light beer
I was at the club, having a fight there

—JAY-Z, "YOUNG, BLACK, AND GIFTED" (FREESTYLE)

I fell in love with Jay-Z the rapper before Jay-Z the business-man. I love Jay-Z so much I started a weekly column in 2021 titled "What Would Jay-Z Do?" where I would answer questions from the community with the help of Jay-Z lyrics. Jay-Z was the first poet I fell in love with—not Nikki Giovanni, not Sonia Sanchez, not Saul Williams or Gil Scott-Heron or Staceyann Chin, or June Jordan or Amiri Baraka . . . Hov. And, no different from the aforementioned poets, he spoke to the realities of the ghetto, of life and living and dying in between the margins. He brought a deep sense of understanding in a sort of complicated simplicity that made sense to me. We were poor but we weren't that poor. We might have been the last ones on the block to have cable, but we had cable, you feel me? I wore hand-me-downs, but they were the good kind. Jay-Z not only understood my struggle but also was giving us an invitation to make it out the hood and make it out for good. As Hov, shorthand for his play on Jehovah, Jay also calls himself the God emcee. So much so that on "H to the Izzo" he explains:

Like I told you sell drugs, no, Hov did that
So hopefully you won't have to go through that.

Hov, forever the quintessential prophet, and profiteer, both guiding us toward the light by showing us the way forward by being the martyr for our toiling while explaining what he had to do for us: make money by any and all means. Jay, our modern-day Black Jesus! Here, Jay-Z is the sacrificial lamb, dying for our sins as hustlers, as nine-to-fivers, go-getters, LLC Twitter, and the like. He essentially went through the fire, hustling, as he told us with "Crack's in my palm, watching the long arm of the law." I would play Biggie and Jay-Z's collab record *Brooklyn's Finest* over and over again until I could recite each bar verbatim. The once-upon-a-time Roc-a-Fella affiliate Sauce Money's *Middle Finger U* was an almost interlude but not quite a certified banger. "Pre-Game," which would be featured on the *Belly* soundtrack, is still one of my favorite Jay-Z verses. When Jaz-O and Jay-Z were still close, his verse on "Foundation" (another B side) was premium Hov content: drug talk, wordplay, versatile flow. The ways he manipulated the English language—double and triple entendres, similes and metaphors, alliterations galore—could make Shakespeare do a double take. I didn't know or understand capitalism, neither its mechanics nor functions nor how it applied to my worldviews. My parents weren't teaching us Afrocentricity or Black economics at home—my mother worked thirty-six years at Jacobi Hospital in the Bronx.

The first time I got my hands on some real money, I bought jewelry. Because nigga right? Niggas get money, we buy flattering shit. Mainly because if you never had shit, looking like you have shit becomes the way to show to yourself and others that you've come up in some way. They were the jewels in the backs of the rap magazines I loved—*Rap Pages, Don Diva, SLAM, Honey,*

Black Men Magazine, the *Source, Vibe, Scratch,* and of course *XXL.*
In the backs of those magazines, you'd find ads for wave caps,
durags, fake callouts for fake photo shoots for aspiring video vixens who don't mind the taste of Belvedere as hair product. The
jewels would be Jesus pieces plated silver in the shape of grenades,
tanks, or teddy bears. The jewels the dope boys wore into the barbershop when you were still sitting on the Yellow Pages for Tony
to reach you (if you were lucky enough to get to Tony, or at least
be in Tony's Barbershop right off of Burnside Avenue before Tony
moved to Puerto Rico because who wants to cut hair in the dead
of winter in New York City? Not Tony). In those jewels there lay a
false sense of proximity to capitalism—the idea that I can give off
the impression that I've accumulated a level of wealth at a young
age that would distinguish me from others. And that urge grew
increasingly more important once I realized I would be heading
to college. Because I was coming from a place where money did
not feel accessible to a place where you could feel it in your hands,
could rub it in between the index and thumb like a thin, green
clitoris—because for men money and pussy go hand in hand with
the things we crave and desire that we tend to abuse the most.

Around the time I went rummaging through those magazines, I had just gotten my scholarship check from LaGuardia
High School: $2,500. I cashed it immediately. I spent months plot-
ting on the back of the *XXL* magazine's fake jewels section, hoping to grab the same $30 Jesus piece I had been eyeing for months.
Or at the very least, something that looked close enough to one
of the pieces I saw my favorite rappers wear in their over-the-top
music videos, the ones with video vixens splattering their bodies over foreign luxury cars like sexy paint you're not supposed

to touch until after the Belvedere poured on their new hair has already dried. At that time, the block was sharing space with the men selling watches, the men selling oils and incense, and the men selling bootleg mixtape CDs. Dwain would cop the mixes, and when he was inspired he would make his own. Shit, I started making my own mixes on the blank cassettes and CDs Dwain wasn't using. This was at a time where I could recognize the value of money but wasn't too sure about how I would get it, have it, or use it in the same ways the rappers I loved had. While you were copping a mixtape from a popular New York City deejay, you'd also maybe grab an album that hadn't hit the stores yet. The streets were the source before the digital market ever was. The CDs would have somewhat distorted album covers. The track-listings would be out of order, or sometimes, the tracks wouldn't even have the right names. Dwain, who'd started working when he was fourteen, was my plug, primarily because I didn't have a source of income. D worked because he wanted money. Skee sold drugs because Skee wanted money. The moral of the story was: you hustled to make money. You hustled so you could order the #14 combo with an egg roll, pork fried rice, and a Sunkist and watch the Knicks lose another playoff game because capitalism feeds off of your hunger for more. D became my guiding light for all things hip-hop and life—what D listened to I listened to, what D did I wanted to do, what D wore I needed to wear. And D was not of the backpack variety. There was no Stretch & Bobbito, no Slum Village or Lootpack, and no conversations about Dilla and drum patterns. D was strictly radio and B sides. D was a FUBU, commercial and hardcore rap kinda guy; Triple Fat Goose and Timbs clean and neat and tucked in the back of the closet. So, if it wasn't on a Doo Wop mixtape or at Jimmy Jazz or Sammy's, D wasn't messing with it and neither was I. If Kid Capri, if deejay S&S, if Ron G wasn't playing it; if deejay Dirty Harry or Chill Will wasn't blending it or mixing it; if deejay SupaSam wasn't passing us the tape or the homie on the corner of Fordham Road and the Grand Concourse by the D train was selling it (along with incense, sunglasses, watches, and Black Bart Simpson T-shirts); if Ralph McDaniels wasn't talking about it or playing the video for it; if Dee Barnes wasn't interviewing them for *Pump It Up* or Kool DJ Red Alert was mentioning them by name, then none of it got any play in the Daniels household. In those days, De La Soul, ATCQ, and the Jungle Brothers were cool, but they weren't going to get more play than Big Daddy Kane. Sure, we appreciated Queen Latifah, but it was Das EFX and EPMD all the way. This would shape my upbringing: upward mobility, rising from the slums, and doing so by any means would be how we got by. We listened to music that made us want to aspire to be better in the margins, not in the knowledge of self, like so many Five Percenters were preaching. When my sister brought the X Clan album cassette to the crib, we spun it once and let it collect dust. We were about dope lyrics, dope clothes, and dope money. The same allure Jay-Z would wax poetic about on *The Black Album* is the same allure we were plugged into every day. We chose Bad Boy over Slum Village, steering ourselves toward commercial rap over the toiling of the underground that seemed to be way nobler and way less profitable.

But by the time my mother was okay with letting me work, the bootleg was slowly dying out, too. My mother wanted me to focus on schoolwork, not job work. But when the opportunity came for me to work as a TV host for a New York City Board of Education–sponsored program, it all made sense. The hours weren't long, I'd get on-camera experience, and I'd have a check. A check I could spend on the things that mattered: rap magazines, rap music, and porn. I'd take my little check and the little dollars that came with it, and I'd head to the bodega and I'd shuffle through. And after I'd rummaged and flipped through the pages of reviews, stories, and interviews, I'd head to the back pages. And these back pages were close to the *Village Voice* back pages but not quite. Before Craigslist, if I wanted to find a sex worker or a turtle, a used bicycle or a used sofa, I could go to the *Village Voice* to find all things deemed invaluable to the community that could find a *Village Voice* in the local neighborhood, aka white people. But if, like me, you happened to be the type who burned the ends of Jansport book bag strings to keep somebody else from stealing them, more often than not, you'd have *XXL* or *Source* magazine tucked somewhere on your person, like the magazine itself was an extension of whatever classwork you would have been given if you had made it to class in the first place. Scrolling those pages, with the rappers and the chains and the ads for Lugz and Timbs, Karl Kani and Esco and FUBU made you feel like you were just close enough to the cool shit you could never afford unless you hustled for it. Capitalism dripped from every page.

There is a proximity to coolness that exists within hip-hop—in both the masters of ceremony who come together with one another to create, collaborate, and corroborate the stories along with the experiences that fans bear witness to. The commercial appeal of hip-hop runs deep. And with that so does the opportunity for commerce. A large part of that stems from the cross-pollination of cultures within the art form. You see it in the early years of hip-hop, when Fab Five Freddy brings Basquiat to the Bronx via train to hip him and school him to the new way culture is being made, and he then also brings Afrika Bambaataa to Blondie not too long after and Chaka Khan then features the same dancers from the 1980s-era defining film *Breakin'* in the video for her hit song "I Feel for You." What we were also seeing come to life is the chokehold of coolness and how a culture becomes a mainstay. Being fly is imperative: being the one who gets to share in the air that comes with having your person being visually appealing to the masses is intoxicating. And it can also make you rich. Because in that space exists a sort of transactional currency, where folks with the currency of cool are paid for their services of coolness, sharing their knowledge and presence for a fee for those who want to be just as cool to get to engage with the attitude, the culture, and energy of it all.

I was made fun of in high school for wearing sweater vests to class because I thought I was going on a date to the movies with a girl who unbeknownst to me already had a cool boyfriend. He was cool that her cousin (who also unbeknownst to me had a crush on me at the time) would tell me directly, after me delivering the note confessing my crush, that I indeed was not cool enough for her. The brand of cool she was chasing was also chasing a dollar that could afford a movie and dinner, and could probably afford the train fare or cab to get them to wherever they needed to be and wanted to go. Uncool me was struggling to get the money needed to get myself to some sort of capital of cool that I could not procure on my own. I would find it through rap. Rap made me look cooler to my brother D when he found out that I could freestyle off the top of my head to a beat. It was a practice I had cultivated years ago in my mother's bedroom, forgetting lyrics to my favorite rap songs at the early age of six and compensating for my lack of memory by making up new words to songs repeatedly. As an underground emcee during the early blog-era years, I was bubbling to the surface—underground showcases at 2:00 A.M. with J-Hatch, me rapping with the passion of someone who was never quite sure if they'd hit the stage again, to an audience of twelve. In those days, you were given a surplus of physical tickets to sell. Oftentimes, I'd just pay out of pocket rather than risk the embarrassment of the "nah, I gotchu" tagline that would normally follow a no-show that originally started as a confirmed purchase. If you got lucky, you had other rappers you'd befriend who would stick around after their sets to watch you perform. Cats like Toare, Vega Benton, Gif, Chaundon, Emilio Rojas, and others at one time or another supported the process. But it was finding my way through rap and through adulthood, chasing some kind of fame or notoriety, that would get me out of the depths of obscurity. Working as an HIV/AIDS case manager or discharge planner for a nonprofit wasn't going to do that.

Being cool in rap is less about having money but looking like you do. It's why we buy the sneakers or used to buy the fake Jesus pieces from the backs of the magazines. You don't have to be cool, just be in proximity of it. Rap was the means through which so many of us—young, Black, white, old, poor, rich—found a newer, hipper version of ourselves. It's why white people still love saying nigga in muted whispers when the radio dial is cranked up with their other white friends, or why 50 Cent's "In Da Cub" still gets burned at every Mexico resort that allows the less rhythmic the chance to feel like they get to participate in the glory of knowing explicit rap lyrics, where they can hum the bad words to themselves, which gives them the feeling they are blending into a crowd, rather than being the blender that disintegrates it. We chase the feeling, the high of the fashion, of the high-stakes tightrope edging that happens when virgin ears get to lean in to hear tales of street lore rattling across sound systems. It is that calling that keeps us pressing Play even now.

Several years ago, amid a pickup for my girlfriend's birthday, I hopped on the C train back from Spring Street, arm-cuddling a bottle of Gato Negro Cabernet (because nothing goes better with expensive-ass sushi than cheap-ass wine) and decided to google "Jay-Z London." Jay pops up in my head from time to time, a stranger-friend I know too well. Mainly because there is so much happening in what he is not saying, both in interviews and verse. I, like so many other Black men in my life, see a bit of Jay in myself, even if we can't master the art of triple entendres or know how to properly weigh baking soda on a scale for just the right amount of crack cook-up. There is always the feeling that there is a Jay bar for every situation you may encounter in life. It's that skill that has made him arguably one of the most successful artists and businessmen across any industry, second only behind his wife, Queen B Beyoncé.

I already knew what the answer to my Google search was before I looked it up because I am what some would classify as a Jay-Z stan. I'd argue with some that I am a Jay-Z stan within reasonable measure—I can discern between Jay-Z the mogul, the father, the shrewd businessman, the GOAT, and the emcee who sometimes underdelivers, depending on who is in the booth with him. I won't argue if his verse on Khaled's "God Did" is his best ever. I think we can argue if it's the best verse a fifty-year-old rapper has delivered while being thirty-plus years in the game. If you were asking me, I'd tell you his first verse on

"Where I'm From" is Hov rap at its finest. Jay paints an incredibly poetic, dark, and twisted narrative of the streets and the Marcy projects he came from. In the opening bars, Jay-Z lets us know quickly the environment he was born into that set the stage for the Shawn Carter we know as Jay-Z: "I'm from where the hammers rung, news cameras never come / You and your mans hung in every verse in your rhyme."

Back to the story of thought: if you decide to humor me when you click Return on your keyboard after entering your Google search term, the first image you'll find is a color photo of a young Shawn Carter in the driver's seat of a Benz from a visit to London, circa '89, based on Jay-Z's memory—a memory that has served him well in his career of platinum hits written without a pen or a pad in sight. It's a characteristic that both he and B.I.G. shared before it became the modus operandi of any and all aspiring rappers to say they're writing without a pen, to the dismay of many who have to hear the raps and rhymes their practice elicits. Jay mentioned the London trip in his feature verse for Pusha T's "Drug Dealers Anonymous," where he lets the listener know he was in "'89 in London pull the Benz up. Type it in, Google's ya' friend, bruh." The record features a sample of the voice of Tomi Lahren, a 2016 clip pulled from her former show *Final Thoughts*, where she wags her finger pointedly at Beyoncé with an emphatic, "Your husband was a drug dealer. For fourteen years he served crack cocaine." The record also features a sample from, coincidentally, the song that speaks to the ascent of Black capitalism in the world of music and entertainment: "Bling Bling" by former Cash Money Records superstar B.G., a word so ubiquitous for flashiness and capitalistic excess in the late nineties that Merriam-Webster recognized it as part of the English language in 2006.

Hov's verse on the Pusha T record is quintessential. Hov walks us through his history as a drug dealer in very plain language, while also waving the gaudiness of the lifestyle he has curated right in your face, assuredly. His guest verses tend to extend beyond 16s nowadays. He spends most of his time in cultural icon mode, not in album mode. We are more likely to see Jay in the news now not for a *Billboard* record he is currently breaking, but an investment in crypto, marijuana, art, the NFL, in whatever is going to advance his chase for the almighty dollar and, in the long game of life, a legacy for his family. And somewhat earnestly, if you're watching Hov carefully, he displays a desire to have all the things whiteness has attempted to deny him. We can look no further than his 2008 Glastonbury appearance to see what kind of time King Hov is on. After Oasis vehemently criticized the festival for letting Hovito into the lineup, but failing to give him headlining status, Jay-Z showed up to Glastonbury with a guitar in hand and began his set by singing an Oasis song. Not just any song, but their most enduring record, even now: "Wonderwall." The performance also speaks to a big part of how Shawn shows up in the world. His mere existence as a Black man in America has been a middle finger to whiteness. But when does the middle finger turn into a handshake?

There are many iterations of Shawn Corey Carter. I have been and continue to be fascinated by all of them. Mainly because, when you grow up poor or lower middle class as I did and are surrounded by other poor and lower-middle-class people like I was, ascension is attractive. Jay-Z's first, Hype Williams–directed solo video "Can't Knock the Hustle" from his debut album *Reasonable Doubt* was dripping with aspiration: Hov is already setting the scene for how he wants his audience to see him. Champagne on ice in buckets, laughter amongst friends at tables, cigar smoke, and flying cars, everyone dressed like a scene out of *The Godfather*. We would watch *Scarface*, and movies like *New Jack City*, *Sugar Hill*, *Juice*, and *Boyz n the Hood* . . . movies about success, money, power, women . . . excess. These films were also about access, and it is a product Jay-Z sold and has been selling—he's been selling water to wells since his inception into the spotlight. It's this "hustler's spirit" that is in plain view throughout *Reasonable Doubt*. Jay recounts stories of his past, from Dehaven and State Street dealings, to shooting his brother over drug dealings, the works. The freshman debut rings like a *Miami Vice* episode, a manifesto for hustlers much in the same way Marx's manifesto would pave the way for revolutionaries worldwide. But, more than glorifying the trappings of the drug trade, Hov spoke to the pitfalls, the pains, and angst; to see this is to also see Jay-Z's struggle with capitalism: how much it builds and also how much it destroys. To paint Jay-Z's politics and capitalist leanings as a one-sided affair ignores the complexities of not only Jay-Z, but also of all of us.

When the billion-dollar Barclays Center was finally built in Brooklyn in 2009 amid much chagrin from the community, environmentalists, and others, it also removed homes and businesses in the area, while forcing many residents in the Prospect Heights/Fort Greene neighborhood to relocate. The last holdover from the $4.9 billion Atlantic Yards Project, a sprawling endeavor that was to include 877 units for affordable housing and a glass-enclosed public plaza (neither of which has yet to be built) was resident Daniel Goldstein, who was paid $3 million to step down as spokesman for Develop Don't Destroy Brooklyn, a group that fought vigilantly against the building of Atlantic Yards. In all the commotion, what wasn't lost on many in Brooklyn and across the city who were fans of hip-hop was the fact that Jay-Z became the face of the Barclays. Hov was recruited by the developer Bruce Ratner to make the building of the Barclays Center more appealing to those who knew the Brooklyn-born star to be the poster child of the city—a shining example of the borough and community getting it from the mud, hustling crack on State Street to hustling tracks out of Madison Square Garden. His appeal would make selling the Barclays to the community of Brooklyn easier to digest. Whether his $1 million investment (along with the one-fifteenth of one percent stake of ownership of the Brooklyn Nets team that calls the Barclays home) played a large or small role in the arena's development, his cultural cachet made it easier to convince tenants that the move would be legitimate and worthwhile. Some could argue that the gentrification of the neighborhood, as in most parts of Brooklyn, was bound to happen. But the building of the Barclays ushered in a new era of consumerism and capitalism that was accelerated by the building's creation. We could look at Jay's entry into the NFL business and the use of social justice language as the entry point for a relationship with Roger Goodell for what it truly seems to be: a side hustle to acquire an NFL team. The moves made are not good business for the community, but good business for cash flow. Something Hov is extremely good at.

But I've also been able to find community through a love for Jay-Z as the rapper and cultural influencer. Seeing the Paper Planes logo in any picture on Instagram is an indicator that you've gotten the Jay-Z stamp of approval. It's the Roc Nation bat signal for someone looking to find where the fly shit is landing. I can also look at my upbringing and see how the lyrics of Jay-Z and the romanticism of those lyrics steered how I wanted to show up in the world. The songs were, for lack of a better phrase, a blueprint for how to navigate street life in ways that felt congruent not to the life I myself was leading and living, but to the environment I was surrounded by. At a writers' retreat in Marrakech I got to kick it with Yahdon Israel, the creator of Literaryswag and an editor at Simon & Schuster. If you're even remotely close to orbiting the industry, you more than likely want to be friends with Yahdon. We found ourselves, along with a few other brothers on the trip, having a pretty well-rounded conversation about being "trauma adjacent." It's the idea that while we may not have been the physical victims of, let's say, police violence or some of the more blatant crimes committed against Black bodies in urban neighborhoods, Yahdon and I both understood that we came from similar environments. His area in Brooklyn and mine in the Bronx were close enough to the action to feel the impact viscerally. It's like catching a stray that wasn't intended for you. Jay-Z's lyrics bring you to the bullet, the gun, and the body being hit, the person aiming at the target, and the passersby watching it all play out. Hov brought you into the kitchen, in the way that Kool G. Rap did so masterfully, in the ways that Roc Marciano, Stove God Cooks, and Pusha T do today.

Trauma adjacency also brings you directly to the source of the money flow: Jay talks about money. A lot. And within that money talk, there are seedlings of the pain endured in order to reap the rewards of capitalism. You can follow the trajectory of Hov's albums and see how the trauma flows effortlessly in an almost highly detached way. Jay was bringing you into the world he was very much a part of, but offering it to you in a way that immersed you, the listener, in it actively—residue still on your sleeves and fingertips long after each track. His relationship with his estranged father ("Moment of Clarity"), the women who left and lost hustling ("Song Cry"), selling drugs to fiends (almost any Jay-Z record off of any album), shooting his brother after finding out he was stealing his stash ("You Must Love Me"), friends lost to prison or the cemetery ("Regrets"), donning bulletproof vests in videos ("Where I'm From")—Jay-Z talks about the perils ad nauseam. He offers us both a blueprint and a warning label. But my fascination with Hov was part admiration and FOMO of the lifestyle he offered through the music along with product placements. Steve Stoute famously asked Hov to help him plug the Motorola pager. We got the lyric and image of it in "Give It 2 Me" off *The Dynasty: Roc La Familia* album. Pretty soon, every dope boy, fashionista, college student struggling with financial aid, and around-the-way girl had the pager on their hip. In "Change Clothes," Jay-Z told men to wear button-up shirts. We immediately moved our throwback jerseys to the back of the closet and were getting button-ups at Porta Bella and other hood dresser establishments. Following the emergence of T-Pain's brilliant and subsequently heavily copied use of auto-tune on records, Hov recorded and released "Death of Auto-Tune" and auto-tune proceeded to die a very fast death. While we were seeing his ability to drive and push culture (and sales) his lyrical dexterity was out on display. Fans would also develop a curiosity and interest in his maturation. Put Jay-Z's "Super Ugly" response diss to Nas side by side with any single off of his widely celebrated album *4:44* and therein lies a very deep chasm between the Hov of yesteryear and a Hov who has reconciled his feelings for his absentee father, and who had become a father while also dealing with his cheating scandal in a way "Song Cry" Jay-Z would be proud of. Younger me, however, could care less about growth in artistry. I didn't care about politics. I wanted lyricists doing gymnastics over beats. And in my head, nobody was better at that than Jay-Z.

> *I feel like a Black Republican, money I got comin' in*
> *Can't turn my back on the hood, I got love for them*

> —"BLACK REPUBLICAN" BY NAS FEATURING JAY-Z

A Black Republican—the phrase spoken out loud feels like an oxymoron. While the demographic and flavor of the parties have changed, the flow of money hasn't. And neither have the flows about money. So, when Jay-Z and Nas, back friends again after the hip-hop beef that shocked the world, chose to trade bars over barbs over the L.E.S. and Wyldfyer–produced track, "Black Republican," what we're listening to is Hov and Nas rapping over two sides of the same coin. So fast-forward to 2022: when we see puppets like former Heisman winner and retired NFL player Herschel Walker masquerading as a viable Republican candidate or Ice Cube playing the role of mega-don MAGA pawn to Trumpism or Killer Mike standing next to Governor Brian Kemp in what feels like an aimless attempt at a faux representation no one asked for, it is not shocking as much as it is disappointing. What we're seeing is an attempt to be able to take credit for getting the masses free while simultaneously giving Massa some feeble legs to stand on or kneel with, depending on who we think the victim of photo-optical violence is. Black liberation is a profitable sport for some. Similarly, witnessing Jay-Z's ascension is admirable but then becomes disappointing. On one hand, you have a sizable donation to Black Lives Matter, his financial support of the family of Kalief Browder, the young Black man who died by suicide after spending three years at Riker's Island for a stolen book bag. You can look at his helping Meek Mill's case in Philadelphia. You can see the ways that Hov sees himself as "Che Guevara with bling on, I'm complex," a Black man existing within a multitude of layers. One can also look at Hov and see someone washing away their sins with every dollar poured into every Black business and person he supports.

In Chicago rapper Noname's 2023 album release *Sundial*, she raps, "I ain't fuckin' with the NFL or Jay-Z." In 2019, Jay sat at the NFL table and brokered a deal for a Roc Nation league partnership, standing side by side with NFL commissioner Roger Goodell for a photo op to solidify the union. In light of former NFL quarterback Colin Kaepernick's kneeling stance during the 2016 season and his subsequent blackballing from the league thereafter, Jay-Z's deal seemed more like a money grab than a cause for celebration. Looking at this through the lens of social justice and advocacy, the heads of hip-hop seem to have missed the memo. Or rather, their politics have seemed to shift with access and money. We are disillusioned to believe that working within the confines of the system will yield any results that differ from the reality of what so many disenfranchised folks grapple with daily: capitalism. As Hov stated when speaking to reporters about Kaepernick's protest during the Roc Nation signing of the deal, "We're past that." A move like this is exactly why Black capitalism is still capitalism, no matter how many superstars attend the procession. Money keeps you away from poor people, so far removed from their everyday struggles, that the politics surrounding how to lift Black communities gets muddied with anecdotes that are less about actual people with lived experiences and more about data and stats that tend to be disconnected from the reality of people's lives.

There is a difference between believing in capitalism and surviving it. A majority of us are just getting by. My tax bracket has changed considerably. And I feel guilty about it. Because there is also another contingent of those within the framework of capitalism: those who benefit from it. I am one of them. While I can point a finger at Jay-Z, when Lilah needed a swim cap with less than a week to go before swimming lessons, Jeff Bezos's Amazon was the place I turned. As I write, I listen to Spotify playlists, even as I know as an artist myself their royalty payments are the worst in the industry. Capitalism is also about convenience. Capitalism is really about inconveniencing others for the benefit of others' convenience. The way we order food, order groceries, order clothing. The way we date, who we date. We buy into the idea of it all with the small actions we take every day. The work required to choose differently feels like too much labor. We choose to order our Ace of Spades from Drizly and the man driving the car to deliver it will also be delivering someone's pizza and someone's nectarines and someone's tampons and someone's ramen to get by because we are all just trying to get by.

I almost lost the $2,500 scholarship check. I had it in an envelope that I dropped in my mother's bedroom trash can while she was away with my stepdad over the summer in Barbados. The amount of panic I felt I can recall even now while tapping back into the memory—looking everywhere in the apartment. Checking under my mother's bed and behind. Looking under the bed in my room. Checking the closets. Retracing my steps. Thinking of all the things I wouldn't be able to get because of the money I no longer had. I eventually was able to find the envelope, all the money intact. It's wild to me how fast that money went. An iron, some South Pole sweatshirts from Jimmy Jazz. I thought I was rich. I thought I was Hov. I would later, after an unsuccessful two-year run at Temple University in Philadelphia, find myself working a retail job at Express Men, followed by a social services gig working with HIV/AIDS clients after my godmother, Hyacinth, passed away due to complications from the virus. The money made would not go to savings but would go to a Nokia Sidekick, to sneakers, to studio time.

Hov told us once to buy outright instead of lease. He would later change his stance. He would later tell us he could have bought a place in Dumbo before its valuation rose. The interesting part is Hov can still buy a house in Dumbo if he wanted to. But it wouldn't be good business for him. He told us so on "The Story of O.J.," plainly speaking:

> *I coulda bought a place in Dumbo before it was Dumbo*
> *For like 2 million*
> *That same building today is worth 25 million*
> *Guess how I'm feelin'? Dumbo*

That's what capitalism does, especially when Black wealth is involved. Everything feels accessible. Because the music makes it feel so. The ones making the music know they are selling us dreams we will never be able to afford. They are selling the lifestyle that makes you want the things you never had, for the things you never thought you needed until somebody told you so. It also teaches us what is beyond our tax bracket. If you ever get the chance, flip through an old issue of *XXL* magazine. And while you're at it, flip through it, read some of the articles, and stop at the back pages. Do the same with the *Source* and *Vibe*. Jay-Z's coming-of-age era was mine, too. Jay-Z became a parent in 2012. I joined the club in 2015. By the time I moved to Bed-Stuy in 2019, the Brooklyn that Jay-Z grew up around had changed significantly. Ramen shops, CBD stores; French cuisine living alongside bodegas and Chinese restaurants. Capitalism is everywhere. And so is rap music and its culture. It's in every commercial, it's in every advertising deck where the word *culture* is mentioned, an inherent nod to Black art and Black music. Biggie asked us if we ever thought hip-hop would take it this far. That was in 1994. By 2023, hip-hop's generated revenue lands somewhere around $7.7 billion. That's a lot of Ace of Spades. Hip-hop turned fifty years old in 2023. That same year, Shawn Carter turned fifty-four years old. He's come a long way. So has hip-hop. So have the fans, myself included. We're renters and homeowners. We're C-suite execs, we're parents, we're caregivers. The maturation of Jay has also been the maturation of us as a culture and fan base. More than one thing gets to be true at once: Jay-Z is one of the greatest poet laureates we've had in the history of the art form that is rap and also, in general. Jay-Z is a capitalist, which is a real word. At the same time, he's a shining example of the possibilities of Blackness. When a wave of nostalgia hits me, I'll watch an old Jay interview. Even now, he's still as charismatic, charming, sharp, and witty, on and off the mic. We leave so little room for the nuances of our humanity, of masculinity, and of art. I can still love Jay-Z and still hate his politics. Thanks to my big brother D, who had already seen Jay-Z at the Roc the Mic tour, I went to see Hov perform live for what was supposed to be the last time, by myself, at what he called his retirement party in 2003, following the release of *The Black Album*. Dressed in complete Rocawear regalia—jean jacket and jeans, T-shirt and bucket hat included—I stood in my section and rapped and sang my voice away to every single song, medley, and freestyle he offered. The intro to "What More Can I Say?" borrows a sample from the film *Gladiator* where Russell Crowe's character, after a brutal battle, asks the audience in the Coliseum, "Are you not entertained?!?"

Yes, Hov. Yes, we are.

The Postpartum Tree Whisperer

Feat. Q, Camille T. Dungy, Gary Martin

"I let things die." The words sat in the air, rotating on some sort of imaginary axis around the sun. As a semipracticing Buddhist, the casual toe or two dipping into the dharma and whatnot, the line was as succinct as it was potent. Because really, what ethical botanist Gary Martin was talking about was the process of surrender: surrendering to the moment, to the truth of what is obvious if you are at least somewhat attuned to the seasonality and fragility of nature and the life it begets, spawns, and, toward the end, lets die. The garden we were standing in was bleeding life, brooding over it, huddled around each of the various forms of plant and animal life to nurture the land in the ways it was intended. It didn't occur to me until I started writing this that I was standing in my Air Max 95 Pineapples, made from recycled pineapple as part of the fabric. Came to the realization out loud that my feet were planted firmly in the ground, as connected as I could be to the earth sans bare feet for even a second.

Camille T. Dungy told us everything starts with trees. At least that's what I thought I heard. Between the crunch of the dried leaves, whistling and humming of the birds above, the whispers of wind tickling the backs of our necks in the moderately cool out-door feels of the gardens we were standing in, all the voices and sounds together felt like a lo-fi symphonic experience. And when I heard what I thought she said, I could feel my chest expand with air, both lungs full, heart out and open, willing to receive whatever godly message was floating around the grounds of the garden. I know what I did hear her say for certain though after: I heard her say we were in the gardens in Marrakech staying at the Jnane Tamsna Hotel, a black-owned boutique experience owned by Meryanne Loum-Martin and her husband, Gary. I was at a writers' retreat alongside some other phenomenal Black and brown folks, and Camille was leading us through a workshop involving our senses and nature. Part of the conversation involved us walking the grounds surrounding the hotel, acre upon acre of lush, living organisms in the gardens, all while we learned more about the life and death of the plant life around us. Trees are the earth's first parents. They provide and offer us so much for so little in return from our species. Our oxygen, our shade . . . our books. Camille also reminded us of that. Even the book you're reading right now (hopefully. No knock on the Kindles or audiobooks, but the tactile, page-turning variety is what does it for me) has life in it: a tree gave this to us. What a gift. Something born from the ground continues to bear more fruit for us in so many ways. In that birthing, I can also see some of my parenting journey, too.

Growing up, I never heard the term "co-parent." I heard a lot of other things: absentee father, sperm donor, deadbeat dad, and my personal favorite: baby daddy. Baby daddy, for those not in the know, refers to an individual who helps to conceive a child but does little else. A baby daddy is also someone who is not married by law to the mother of said child. A co-parent was a term I assumed was reserved only for white families that star in televised prime-time dramas. It wasn't a term used to explain the role of a parent—either you had kids, or you didn't. And no one was having explicit conversations at the dinner table about the role fathers played in the household. Shared responsibility in the household, a balanced and more open parenting approach, was not a topic of discussion in our social circles. A majority of the time, the fathers I knew of growing up were barely present or completely nonexistent. Co-parent wasn't a phrase used or heard of where I came from.

I was born in the American Reaganomics era, coined after Hollywood actor turned profiteering president Ronald Reagan, whose trickle-down economic policies helped ring in a new industry of financial propensity: crack. So I should know—my eldest brother was locked up in state prison for ten years due to the harsh drug sentencing penalties that were issued out like peanut M&M's in the eighties. His father wasn't around. And whether or not that dictated the choices he made growing up, one can look at those choices and see the want and need to be seen, to be loved, and using the pursuit of money, and notoriety in the circles he navigated at the time, and the alpha-male need for our presence to be felt and acknowledged at all times. I remember my big brother Skee coming home in those early mornings with a bag of White Castle in hand, grease saturating the bottom of the bag. I'd be asleep but was always greedy and hungry, a constant state of being for me. Between the door unlocking and the not-so-quiet opening of the white paper food bag, I'd be in the kitchen right alongside my brother, he sharing a bite or two of his mini fish sandwich with me. Those were the days and nights when Skee was outside hustling. What I tend to remember most from those days of Skee prebid were as follows:

- ☑ My mother's tears
- ☑ Our trips via car and bus to whichever facility he was at
- ☑ The letters I wrote

As a father now, I can't help but think about how much of his life would have been different had his own father stayed. But he wasn't alone in that. There were a few cases of fathers living in the household with their children, but we rarely saw them in person. Those fathers were fictional: either living in our collective imagination or the ones who appeared on TV sitcoms like *Family Matters*, *The Fresh Prince of Bel-Air*, or the once thought to be an infallible classic now turned almost impossible to watch, *The Cosby Show*. Even *Sanford and Son* and *Good Times* allowed us to see Black fathers, as imperfect as they were, present in a way that may have felt fairy-tale-like for a majority of us who didn't know what it looked like to have fathers present in a real way that felt constructive. And the dads we knew of we barely saw: they were working two jobs to help put food on the table. But even if there weren't many tangible examples for us in real time, data gathered in the mid-2000s paints a very different picture surrounding Black fatherhood and co-parenting. A *Los Angeles Times* article from 2013 featured a National Center for Health Statistics report based on a federal survey that included more than 3,900 fathers between 2006 and 2010. And this survey found that among fathers who lived with young children, 70 percent of Black dads said they bathed, diapered, or dressed those kids every day, compared with 60 percent of white fathers and 45 percent of Latino fathers. Furthermore, nearly 35 percent of Black fathers who lived with their young children said they read to them daily, compared with 30 percent of white dads and 22 percent of Latino dads. And a lot of other fathers were doing time upstate for doing the same things my oldest brother got caught up in. But when the fathers we never knew we needed or wanted weren't around, there was only one person we could all turn to for food, shelter, warmth, love, and discipline: our mothers.

My mother, who I playfully call Linda T., was my first example of love, and what showing up as a healthy parent looked like. She was a hardworking, devoted single mother, a woman who would have benefited greatly from having a stable and secure partner as a co-parent. Linda Theresa Daniels was and still is my matriarch, my Band-Aid, my salvation, and the closest thing to a personal Jesus I know. My father, God bless him and his courage, was a Vietnam veteran suffering from bipolar disorder, paranoid schizophrenia, and alcohol dependence. It would be 3:00 A.M. on a weekday before school, and while the lights were out, my brother D and I sharing our twin-size bottom bunk bed in the dark of night, the top mattress a suppository for Skee's clothes, since the mattress was broken, and we'd awaken to radio static or a vinyl needle scratching and the soulful sounds of whichever station or record our father had landed on, and we'd have to lie in bed and wait. We'd wait until the commotion stopped, until the noise ended, until the cigar smoke cleared, until the last bottle or can was emptied. By the time I was in first grade, my parents were already divorced, my mother choosing our safety and her life over maintaining a very dangerous status quo. My mother often retells the story of sitting her boys down in her bedroom and asking us both if we wanted to go with our father. If you ask my mother, she'll tell you she gave us the choice because she did believe that boys should be raised by their fathers. Our answer, a resounding no, quelled any and all debates henceforth. I dreaded my father. The days when my mother had to run to cover a shift at work and my father had to pick me up were the days I dreaded the most. I was embarrassed and scared. Skee remembered a time when he kept a gun under his pillow just in case my father tried to hurt Mom or us. The presence of my father felt more like monster than male role model. My brother D was like a father figure, but even his example is an unfair case study. Eight years my senior, D was as ill-equipped to be a man of the household as my own father was at the time. I didn't necessarily learn how to be a man or a father by direct influence. My whole life has been a series of masculine trial and error, throwing my dick to the wall and hoping I didn't smash myself up in the process. The person I knew I could count on, without fail, would be Linda T.

My mother accepted no child support, choosing instead to continue working her job as a medical surgical technician for Jacobi Hospital in the Bronx, accepting help with groceries from family and hand-me-downs from Ms. Helen, her coworker at the time. It wasn't until a freshman seminar class in 2001 while at Temple University, when I was asked to write about some of my earliest childhood experiences, that I was reminded of how my uncles would bring groceries to the house. At the time it seemed like only a loving gesture from family until I realized while writing that it wasn't only love: it was survival. My mother never asked my father for child support, very aware that my father had

nothing to offer us financially. She lived the superhero trope of
Black women—bearing the weight of all the failures and misgiv-
ings of their Black male counterparts by bearing the pain in utter
silence for the sake of family, a salve for whatever is ailing the
home, absolving all others from the responsibility of solving the
issues that are a result of the systemic conditions that harm us
all. My mom, like most Black/Afro-Caribbean mothers, was the
one person to turn to for food, shelter, warmth, love, and discipline. I'm now a parent and can't imagine she was just one person
being responsible for all of that, while still maintaining her own
life as a woman, as a daughter, sister, and friend; as a potential
partner to one, a colleague to another. My mother, like so many
Black women before her and after, held her hurt, struggles, and
pain from us. If we caught glimpses of any of it, it was by sheer
accident. My mother gave me softness, tender hands, trying to
glue and keep my world together. The strings pulled, countless
times and often invisibly to my unknowing and sheltered eye.
My mother has lived a million lives, and in every single one of
them she is a supernova of a human; a woman hell-bent on pushing her children to the next layer of good that only comes from a
devout faith in something bigger than ourselves. My mom was
not a practicing Catholic, in that Sunday mass was never a part
of our upbringing. We prayed to Jesus, and my mother would
invoke the saints from time to time, rosary beads and candles
cradling the bedside nightstand. It was her loving foundation
more than anything that would steer me to Buddhism as a more
formal practice. Buddhism would also ground me as a man and
as a father. For in it, I was able to tap into all the versions of self
without judging them. That kind of vulnerability not only deep-
ens our practice but also has the potential to deepen the love we

have for ourselves. Taken further, it can deepen the love we have for those that surround us, especially our children.

Following the ending of a six-year relationship that resulted in a broken engagement, a few broken promises on my part, and some broken hearts in the process, my former fiancée moved to LA to pursue her acting and writing dreams, and I continued working at my nonprofit gig in the Bronx, performing as one of the lead emcees in a band I was in, and moved back into the bedroom I had grown up in since I was in sixth grade. Humbled was putting it modestly. Breaking up with the love of my life at the time felt like a death sentence. I was a man-child—reluctant to grow as an individual but ready to saddle myself to someone, the dead weight of my lack of financial support and my meager artistic career weighing us both down. At the time of the breakup, I had felt assured that I would be the very cool and hip uncle at the family functions who loved babies and was great with kids but would not have any. My former partner and I had talked about it. We talked about a lot of things. I was just never ready. It wasn't that having children wasn't a want or a need, but it wasn't a priority. A luxury I realized I could not afford. Patriarchy allows us as men to not have to wonder timelines and the internal clock of childbearing that society forces upon women. But I vowed, if and when I ever decided to have children, I would be married to my partner forever. We'd share the same bed and home, we'd eat at the dinner table together, we'd argue at IKEA . . . normal stuff. My partner would feel safe and loved, and our children would grow up in a two-parent household. However, things rarely ever end up how we plan them: fast-forward a few years after the breakup. I was still in that same bedroom, still in the band, still trying to get my life in order—and I was going to be a father. Lilah's mother and I had dated on and off for several months before she was pregnant. When I listen to the song "Hash Browns" from my 2015 project, *songs for charles*, that served as an open letter to my then-living father, Charles, I come back to the lyric I rapped that feels prophetic more than anything else:

I wanna be a father
Wanna raise a daughter.

The song was recorded at the tail end of 2014, with no knowledge or thought of a child even in the periphery. We found out we were having a child in March 2015. And I remember because her mother's blood pressure grew. And I ran downstairs and got coffee for the family. And because the hospital chairs are never comfortable. And afterward, I was still in the bedroom at my mama's home. And I was still in the band performing for pennies and living like I had all the time in the world for my dream to come true. And I was still at the job paying me very little, paying me enough to feed myself and myself alone. And I was still feeling less than a man at thirty-two years of age. I was ashamed, embarrassed, and, at times, suicidal. What was I doing? Where did I go wrong? On top of that, because Lilah's mother and I weren't together but making a real attempt at co-parenting, there was none of the physical intimacy that two people who are in love share when they are expecting: no listening to her belly to feel our daughter kick; no trying to hear her heartbeat. I'd rub her feet and her back when it hurt. I'd run to the 7-Eleven when it was still open on Eastchester Road and get her a beef pattie and ice cream. But those things needed to be done. They were a responsibility but were all void of the deeper sense of being that connects lovers to each other. We were both robbed of that experience, unfortunately. And for me, because I couldn't share in that physically, I returned to the source, to the one thing that I had seen had the power to ground me and potentially connect me to my unborn child in a way that felt both supernatural and real, something that could feel not only organic and honest but also rooted in something bigger than me. I started talking to trees.

I saw Q do it first. We were barefoot. Well, as I remember it, she was barefoot first. Chelsea Piers in the first days of summer can feel magical in the nighttime; the air tender but crisp enough to feel like frolicking is appropriate. Early love can feel that soft, intoxicating even. You drink up the other person, and there almost always feels like there isn't enough. We talked about hopes and dreams. We talked until the crunch of the turf under our toes mixed with the belated dew and dove headfirst into whatever we were going to be. It was around that time, feet indulging in artificial grass, that she hugged a tree. And when she did it, I didn't necessarily poke fun at it, but I did the thing we do as Black folks when somebody does something around us that we haven't seen in our own lives: I maybe poked fun at it a little bit. Carefree Blackness in the wild is an uncontrollable substance that can be neither commodified nor homogenized, no matter how much white America tries to repackage it and sell it to us as our own. We see it on packages for period products, alcohol brands selling us culture and coolness, and smiling dark skin as the emblem for a newfound joy that has moved from the appendix to a sharper, jagged little edge of an intro to what our lives can look like if we just drink a little more, diet the right way, stream the right album. But at that moment, what Q was doing was revolutionary: she was connecting back to the source, to the root if you will. The rules of nature are so much bigger than any of us. And to reimagine what love can look like, what life can look like, going back to nature may be the detour we need to reexamine community; reimagine what it means to collaborate with the seasons of our existence, rather than fight them with a closed, balled-up, recycled fist. We're all just recycled versions of the genes of our ghosts, no? We are breathing the cycle. And so what Q gave me was a regrounding, a practice I could implement so profoundly that I wouldn't be able to truly acknowledge it until the seeds of nature birthed something so real and so pure for me, it would take me tapping into the source to find my way again. At that moment, I was able to take a step back and reflect on how trees have played a central, significant role in how I engage with the world.

During my lunch break, I'd lock the door to the office. I'd leave the building and step into the air of the South Bronx: cuchifritos, methadone maintenance clinics, and halfway houses; job programs and dollar stores; furniture spots and loosie connects; police-infested train stations and bodega bachata. I'd walk through ambulance siren noise, the waft of halal warming nostrils. Mott Haven's energy hits different. Everything is loud. Everything is aggressive. But you're also in the heartbeat of culture. People sleep on the Bronx. But there is too much history here. Too many Young Lords and Crazy Leg stories. Too many Slik and Kool Herc Stories. Too many pinstripes, too many house parties, and Afrika Bambaataa. And so, when I'd walk to St. Mary's Park to get my steps in after the tacos de pollo y arroz con frijoles settled, I'd stop by the two trees I nicknamed Ben and Jerry not too far from the entrance of the park and, with my left hand on the trunk and my right hand over my heart, I'd talk to Lilah while she was still growing, learning, and listening in her mother's womb. I'd lay my palm on the bark, sweaty and thirsty for love, and I'd close my eyes and I'd try to see her with all of my senses. I'd slow my breathing just enough to see if I could hear her in the pauses—each breath in and out a silent prayer. I couldn't feel her kick, but something told me she could feel my voice echoing through the fibers of my fingers into the rings of the tree I was connecting to her through. The interaction was never timed. I wanted to wait to hear my daughter's voice, to feel her talking to me through the roots, within the hunkering heights of a trunk. The tree was my portal to her. It was my gateway back to finding what had felt lost and distant—the love for what is here and what is yet to be. This was my organic attempt at getting right what I felt I had mishandled so terribly, to find what I was losing by reconnecting to the sacredness of nature, exploring how we travel with energy to the people and places we hold dear to our hearts. Sometimes I'd cry. More often though, I'd smile.

Lilah Josie Daniels was born on November 15, 2014. Lilah has never known a home with both of her parents living together under one roof. Her mother and I were never married. Up until then, my mother didn't even know she existed. We tried. My brother D would tell me after Lilah's mother gave birth and we spent time together as a family, I'd feel different. And I knew he was wrong but I listened because that's what a good younger brother should do. And we were still learning ourselves as parents: parenting styles, our past trauma as children resurfacing, each of us trying to navigate this new terrain almost as strangers. Sleepless, tired, hurt strangers. And so, when all else seemed to fail and crumble, I pushed. I had finally left the social service space and ventured into digital marketing and advertising, using my newfound Twitter growth on the platform along with growth as a rapper-turned-essayist to leverage a role as a community manager at a start-up. I left the band and continued working on a plan to ensure both my future and Lilah's would be bright ones while trying to repair a co-parenting relationship that needed time and nurturing to heal. This involved a lot of reading, self-talk, and real accountability—something that early on in the dynamic I hadn't been great at. I dated while Lilah's mom was pregnant. I didn't communicate enough. I didn't set clear expectations or boundaries for myself, which caused undue harm and stress in the partnership. I had to take a really hard look in the mirror and decide if I wanted to lead with love or disharmony. Because I said I wanted the former, but my actions were screaming for the latter. Part of the new narrative I needed to create would be to lean into love and treat all of it like a social experiment. Capricorn shit. I told myself I would pour all the love I knew could exist into my child and see what would happen. And I told myself I would pull from whatever well of patience and understanding I could find for her mother because none of this was easy on her either. All of us, trying to find a new way to forge a path of love that we hadn't seen reflected in our own experiences.

I never wanted the stigma or label of being what some thought was the stereotypical Black father—absentee, confrontational, noncommunicative, not present. It took a lot of work, time, and effort to finally realize that, for us, maybe the commitment we made as parents didn't need to involve wedding bells and a shared household. Maybe for us, co-parenting lay not only in the layered nuances of our partnership but also within the capacity of our hearts to tend to another human that we had created . . . together. It would include love, a nurturing environment, and space for us to show up in ways that would feed Lilah long after we left this earth. We had to reshape our vision of what parenting was, to what we knew in our hearts what our relationship could be. Fast-forward, and Lilah is now four years old: she's in pre-K, loves gummies, and says things like "my heart is filled with love." She's the most loving, kind, and empathetic human being I know.

This is co-parenting. And because of this, Lilah's amazing mother was able to get her bachelor's degree in international business at Baruch College. Six to seven days out of the week, while she studied nightly and went to work, I stayed with Lilah. I don't deserve a medal for this. This is co-parenting. And in an ideal world, my mother would have had a co-parent, too; she would have had a break, and time off. In an ideal world, every parent is a co-parent. I dream of this world every day when I see the disparity in wages between mothers and fathers—according to the National Women's Law Center, women are paid eighty cents for every dollar paid to their male counterparts, with mothers earning sixty-nine cents compared to fathers. Co-parenting translates into opportunity—if one parent has to turn down growth in their career or industry because there is no balance in the household, everyone suffers: the family grows weary from the weight and pressure, businesses bear the burden of a lack of diverse leadership, which essentially hurts our economy.

In an ideal world, both parents share the weight and brunt of the work appropriately. Lilah's mother and I have a schedule—I have Lilah some nights and pick her up from school, and some I don't. Lilah's mother gets to go rock climbing or study for the

LSAT, and I get to have coffee with friends or go talk to a room full of inspiring, bold, and dynamic women about dad stuff. It is work, beautifully hard work, dismantling the systems that would have us believe a mother's role is in the kitchen tending to all things domestic, while the hapless dad fumbles over himself whenever he has to spend a weekend alone with the kids. It is work that needs to happen. Right now.

Far too often, it seems like when both parents work, one person is primarily tasked with organizing the household, and keeping the home in order. That person is typically a mom or someone who identifies as such. Far too often, those who identify as women have had to sacrifice their dreams because motherhood takes precedence over all else. I'm not here to say it doesn't, but what I am here to say is that, as equal partners and parents, we have to create safe spaces where the pursuit of our partner's passions doesn't need to take a back seat just because we're too self-absorbed to show up as allies. Co-parenting can make this space possible, for everyone.

As a co-parent, I have gotten to share and spend time with Lilah in ways I would have never imagined. The alone time I get with Lilah is time I cherish, time that has personally allowed me the opportunity to be fully present for my child, moving away from the notion that the emotional labor required to raise a child is a woman's work. As a co-parent, Lilah and I have gone to museums, and art exhibits, and had dance parties; she's sat with me while I've led workshops at Columbia University about the intersections of poetry, theater, and hip-hop. We get to have conversations about her feelings and her emotions because we have exclusive time together. Lilah can tell me when she has questions about her body parts, about her gender, about building LEGO houses and about friends she misses, having changed schools at least three times over the two to three years she spent going from New York to Houston back to New York during the early onset years of the pandemic starting in 2020. We talk about her intentions that she chooses to set for the day. We talk about the friends I haven't met yet. At seven years old, she is as smart and as loving a child as I could hope and pray for. It is planned time, organized around not just my schedule, but also her mother's. Both of us, as co-parents, have unique parenting styles. And while we may not always agree, we have a shared understanding of what it takes to raise a human . . . our human.

The moment Lilah's mother decided to return to Houston *with Lilah* to be closer to her mother and immediate family, my world shattered in what felt like an instant. Couple that with the birth of my second daughter, West, with my current partner and love, Bria, and things began to spiral. This moment was cause for celebration, and then everything shut down. There was a disconnect between West and me. By March, I was working from home with a newborn in my arms and my then four-year-old daughter roughly 1,600 miles away, with no clear timeline of when I would physically see her. While my partner slept, I lamented having to care for a child that felt as if she didn't love me and wouldn't love me as much as my first child. I wasn't diagnosed, but in those moments, I'd frantically search chat rooms at 2:00 A.M., looking for fathers who, too, may have been suffering from postpartum depression. I was angry, I was sad, I was frustrated. I felt like a failure as a father, partner, and co-parent: if I would have been able to do more they would have stayed in New York; maybe West knew I was struggling with becoming a new father from the womb. Missing my firstborn, the stress of being in the house with a lack of sleep, and dealing with an infant was feeling like too much for me. I needed a lifeline.

Their departure signaled growth and change—my daughter, Lilah, and her mother and I had finally gotten to what is now a strong, open, kind, loving, and supportive co-parenting relationship—her mother reclaiming her love for Jesus and me reclaiming my voice and patience. The departure for Lilah's mother was a sensible one: she had a larger network of family in Houston compared to New York. She would have more space and freedom to pursue law school, a dream of hers that she was determined to see through. I was reluctant and combative upon hearing the news but eventually let go, understanding that co-parenting is a marathon. It is a journey in which we ride the ebbs and flows, highs and lows, all while keeping our focus on the thing that matters most—the love and safety of our child.

Technology saved my life. With a lack of a regular structure, I had to develop new routines while honoring my relationship with Lilah. I was so used to picking her up from school, getting her dinner and school clothes ready, bathing her before bed . . . reading her bedtime stories. While some of those things I had grown to cherish and love with Lilah couldn't be transferred over to a phone screen—those moments that we shared face-to-face—the one thing we could always rely on was the love. We had been here before. The early days of fatherhood were hard, and dangerous, for myself and Lilah's mother. We hurt each other in ways we both regret. What kept us from teetering over the edge was our shared love for our daughter. In those days, when I questioned if I was good enough to be her father, her smile was my North Star. Now, even over FaceTime, that smile is still the beacon guiding me home. I read her stories over the phone; I watched her eat dinner. Her little sister only gets excited when Lilah's face is on the other side of the screen. They finally met in person in November of last year, and it was magic. Watching my two little girls love and learn the language of each other is something I wouldn't trade for the world. Despite how much COVID has taken from so many of us, technology afforded us as a family the opportunity to lean on what now we all do so well: love each other, no matter the distance.

No one understands the weight and responsibility of a parent until you are one. That sense of weight is heightened when you are a co-parent. Add to that being a co-parent away from your child while in the middle of a pandemic and you have a recipe for disaster. A few hours after I flew back to New York from a visit to Houston, Lilah FaceTimed me. She was all smiles following church, ready to scarf down pancakes from their favorite barbecue place in Houston. The ice had melted in the city and some places had opened their outdoor seating. She was radiant in the dress her grandmother bought her, which I saw in the video her grandmother sent me of Lilah as she sang quietly onstage next to the pastor at the end of service, like she always does, proving to me she is quite unlike her rapping daddy as I watched her mouth mumble too close to the microphone. As we FaceTimed from her grandmother's phone, we laughed and threatened each other with punches to the nose and maple syrup to the face.

I have never and will never experience holding a child in my body for nine months. I will never know the trials and tribulations of breastfeeding; the full physical, emotional, and chemical toll carrying a child has on the female body; the potential for postpartum depression. What co-parenting does is hold each of us, as parents, accountable for creating a more balanced home and work life for all involved. Co-parenting says that, while parenting may involve sacrifices, the weight of that sacrifice does not solely rest on one parent only. No matter your relational dynamic, no matter how you identify as a human—he, she, they, zee—co-parenting creates space for better communication and empathy: I hear you, I see you, how can I show up for you in a way that benefits our family? And even now, as West grows and her gap-toothed smile mirrors mine and she picks her lip like her daddy does and mimics her sister's every move because her sister is in Bed-Stuy with myself and Bria under one roof, I am met with a reminder of how precious life truly is. Every day I walk outside, trees are reminders that life is so very precious. So that when Lilah touches a tree or talks about them, I know for certain she heard me all those years ago. And when West reaches for a branch, she, too, is an extension of that life force that feeds us all. Every moment of the breaths we take is governed by a life force that reaches beyond a sky we can touch, even on the tallest of days, ankles expanding and reaching above to a cloud too far from reach but close enough to feel through a branch or shadow sliver of shade forming the bulk of a trunk. Trees give us that. Trees gave me that. They gave me life. They are the original co-parents in every sense of the word.

I want all fathers to embrace co-parenting as a way to create a better today for ourselves and our parenting partners. I want more fathers talking about fatherhood. I want more people to know that Black fathers, in particular, are more than just child support or the court system. Our value as fathers and co-parents is not in the number of zeros at the ends of our checks, but in the content and quality of the time spent and shared. Being a parent, and being a father, is not only a responsibility but an opportunity.

Nothing stays as is. Everything is changing, some things more rapidly than others. Life is dying all around us. Even trees. They will outlive us. They always do. One of my followers on Instagram, Nickie Sloan, told me under one of my posts that redwoods have to be burned alive to produce a new redwood. Imagine that. Every day, each of us is dying tiny new deaths. We were all young once, even the redwoods. Fancy, sprouting from the ground up with our noses to the sun, careless and frivolous with our time, and sometimes with nature. We'd eat our honey buns, and if the trash can was too full the wrapper would wind up somewhere carried by the wind onto the curb and the street sweepers would have their way with it. Sometimes we'd miss the trash can completely because we were aiming for a Jordan number in the fourth, trying to go pro with a spin of the wrist, still holding a Capri Sun or quarter water or nut buster in the other hand, the trees watching us disheartened. We were wasteful. The trees I prayed with were not—not an ounce of anything is not being used for something, fulfilling its rightful place in the ecosystem. I say that to say this—we think we have time, but we do not. The leaves are changing all around us; they are falling, and the branches are parting ways with each other like lovers bidding adieu before one last ceremonious breakup. I thought Lilah would be gone forever to Houston but she wasn't. It felt like I would be sixteen forever, then thirty-two forever. But I wasn't.

And now, in my forties, I see how much the trees are teaching us time and time again—there is death and then there is life over and over. The cycle repeats because everything is new and yet everything is the same as it ever was. Nature is teaching us everything we will ever need: one parenting tree at a time.

My name is Joél , and I'm a co-parent.

A Conversation on Afro-Normalism

Walking Dilla, our bulldog, is boring. I like it. If you listen intently while walking on the block, you'll hear the chirping and nesting in one of the many trees lining the curb. The NYC Open Data website has a community-created hyperlink that drives to a listing of the trees in Bed-Stuy, sorted by name, trunk, diameter, root, and a whole host of other descriptors. I'm not a tree expert so I wouldn't be able to give you any real specific details to help you know which trees live on my block, but it seems like the most popular can be found in the *Tilia*, *Quercus*, or *Acer* genus, or the zelkova family. So, while I walk Dilla, I'm watching the trees. Or being mesmerized by brownstones. Rows and rows of them. On any given day, Sly, my neighbor, will be parked outside his home, smoking a cigarette and drinking a Coors. Or helping Manuel bring groceries into the bodega. Walking Dilla recently, Sly recommended changing the dog's diet because his pee was a little brownish. When we got Dilla from Kansas City, the breeder told my partner to keep Dilla on the same diet until he turned at least a year old. His veterinarian agreed. Sly didn't. "I've been raised around dogs all my life," he said boldly.

I had just come back from my trip to Marrakech, bags just brought upstairs, still feeling high from a business class seat ticket from the layover in Madrid that brought me back to Brooklyn safely and at peace with whatever I wasn't before my trip. "Don't listen to damn vets. My brother did. Guess what happened? His dog got cancer and died." Sly, who also believed that monkeypox was herpes, is usually not the person I listen to for sage advice. But I appreciated his wanting to help.

I kept walking Dilla—we named him because who doesn't want to name their dog after J Dilla, the greatest rapper/producer in the history of music? I like walking Dilla in the early morning. Right around 6:00 A.M.–ish, when the sun hasn't peaked beyond the sky because the winter still owns the dusk. The block is quiet outside, besides the cars going home, going to work, going to school, going going going. In the stillness of the morning of New York City, there is also the quiet of life, still breathing, the low humming happening in spurts. Stores still closed, many eyes still shut, many cars are still parked. Nothing is happening here yet. And yet, the nothing is also an invitation for everything to exist—the babies cooing, the doors unlocking, the graffiti-laced gates of Manny's to be lifted by the chain links; the grandma telling her grandson to pull his mask up as they head to the crosswalk. So much happening, with so little needing to be done.

We keep waiting for something extraordinary to happen. And the extraordinary is right here, waiting for us to accept it. If you're Black, being with what is can also feel like a form of self-inflicted torture. We can look at the world that surrounds us, look at the systems that have created the world around us, and wonder if what's here is even worth being present for. But, if we're able to breathe, even for just a second, then maybe there's an opportunity to take a step back and see that no one is coming here to save us. I don't want us reaching for some metaphysical, spaceship delusion that has Black folks not looking at the reality of our greatness here on earth in both the past and present tense. Afrofuturism, while beautiful and expansive, also feels limiting. Like a form of escapism. Like "if we not gonna make it here we gonna make it somewhere else." We do so much looking into the future for a reprieve. Anything to relieve us of the stress that comes from the need to achieve the things that have seemed to be outside of the means the media has taught us we are supposed to deserve—a world where we accept the bare minimum because our ancestors had to. We expend so much time and energy looking into the past for answers, searching the tombs of our history, that we often leave little to no room to reexamine and reimagine what the current gets to be. And to do so we need to also pressure test the narrative we've created around who we are and what we get to be in this era of existing.

"Slow down" is a refrain I share with my daughter Lilah at least once a day. She is newly seven, forever expressive and emotive gently and beautifully. And she is constantly in motion. Running from our dog Dilla, running to her sister West. Running to the kitchen, jogging to the bathroom. Having fun is extremely urgent to her. As if there is a quota she has to meet, her gleefully rushing to her books or Nintendo Switch or iPhone 12 mini to text her mom in Houston or create new memojis or play with the translation app to practice on the little Spanish she seems so often to forget, her Dominican ancestors surely cursing her out from under the seas near the island. Because in the slowness is god. The beats per minute are intermittent, and if we can get smitten about the space in between them, I want to tell her, that is the secret to the heaven her grandmother prays for her to reach, just in the way I am sure she lovingly prays for her hair to be anything but the texture her Blackness allots. Slowing down feels too small for her. It feels like too tall of an ask. But I think her moving in a way that doesn't make way for the ease that can come with the undoing involved in slowing down the pace of life is the kind of run-of-the-mill commonplace existence I pray for her.

What I want for her is to find comfort in the routine, in the ritualistic habits she is so accustomed to that they are like a second breath to her, a new but forgotten lung that is consistently there. It is also a reminder for me to sit with the same idea: things can be boring and don't need to be anything other than what they are. And *that* ideology historically is different for Blackness than for anyone else, a people who, not by their own will and cognition, have made hustle and labor a staple of how to get ahead. Capitalism and consumerism got us in a trance, hyperfixated on doing more to accumulate more, a dance that continues to take us away from a life that is truly connected to what is present, real, and true. The homie Ramon reminded me over coffee on a brisk Friday afternoon that so many of his memories growing up in Cleveland were of his *abuela* cleaning the crib, mopping up the floors and their memories along with it. I could hear the mop plopping down and the Fabulosa scenting the room as he spoke—every Sunday like clockwork his grandmother would begin her routine of resetting their home by cleaning it, music blaring. This was her routine. Simple. And normal.

What is normal? And then what is a Black normal? I wonder if there is a difference. We can look at the griots, the greats of before who came forward with a set of ideas and ideals as templates for what a life of ease can be. So much of our experience is wrapped in the container of hardship. There is a belief that things need to be hard. It is supposed to be hard. When I ask my mother about how she's doing, more often than not I'm met with this energy connected to an idea of work, of challenges, of hardship. Lately, I have been reevaluating my stance and feelings on work and what work means. Our language surrounding work generally is seen through a Westernized, capitalistic, patriarchal lens, with hierarchies remaining supreme and us as humanity serving as cogs in the machine here to fulfill an agenda, a majority of which has been uniformly decided for us since the advent of the industrial revolution of the 1940s here in the United States. How we view work is directly tied to tangible outcomes: money, advancement, promotions, and praise. And that requires motion and constant activity, none of which has anything to do with mindfulness. Which for me has become not only a practice but also a way of life. A way of living that is directly correlated to how I view art and our existence as a community. An existence that can allow us to see the mundane and simple practice of showing up as we are, with just being as a state of being, as a way to define a new way of being normal for us. I think a lot about how Christine Platt, author of *The Afrominimalist's Guide to Living with Less*, has chosen how to show up in the world and how that living is a blueprint for how to not only embrace a life where we condense intentionally, but also live simply. And for me, there is nothing more beautiful, and boring, than that. The boring is what we need more of.

> **Afro-normalism** (ahf-roe nörm/a-leišm): the art of capturing, depicting, and celebrating Black people doing things that are considered mundane and ordinary to the

general public. E.g.—Black people fishing; Black people making tea; Black people reading comics; Black people living.

Justine Allenette Ross's work is a portrait of the lives of Blackness that live outside the conversation surrounding Black excellence—the idea that being extraordinary is a means of celebration. Hailing from Detroit, Justine incorporates shades of Blackness and bits of the future while honoring the normal and mundane moments of our living. Christmas shopping, waiting room chatter, jaywalkers. Her art lives in a world where existing as a Black person is neither wrapped in the trauma of media headlines nor warped by the triggers that have become a part of social sound bites. Her art lives and breathes in the mundane moments of how we as Black people venture out into the world: in our homes, resting in a bath; dining at a restaurant, head tilted back; camping or fishing, tents waiting for us to return to a burning campfire. Seeing her art made me think about how so little attention is paid to the Black experience outside of us being excellent at everything or dying for nothing. Seeing Justine's art reminded me of how easily white people get to slip into a scene and become background noise, and how Black people want so desperately to not have to be the featured product without our bodies getting in the way, our skin getting in the way—of a bullet, of a funeral, of a cop car. Our normalcy is usually replaced and turned over by something tragic, something that assaults our present moment, interrupting our day, and our lives. We want to blend in. We want to be regular. We are regular. That is what makes us beautiful. Afro-normalism is what springs forth from that beauty. And so much of that beauty can be found in

the examples of art and the Black artists who engage in the space
and have redefined, reshaped, and helped mold what a sense of
normalcy can look like for a Black body. *Negroes at Home Mind-
ing Their Business Pt. 3* does a phenomenal job of capturing a
moment that represents Black joy that feels familiar to any and
all, no matter where you land on the spectrum of your identity.
In it, three characters: An unidentified Black man, lounging in
a love seat. Across from him, another Black body leaning in. In
between them both, a Black woman, potentially their mother or
aunt or even family friend. The home is pleasantly decorated,
moderate and sleek. The man is fashionable and comfortable, the
adult Black woman casual and cute. We see conservation happen in unison, an old-school rotary phone. This could be your
grandmother's home. This could be a Sunday after church. It
could be a regular Saturday. The days roll into the next one, each
feeding a simplicity that we say we crave, but more often than
not we are looking toward the next thing, the new future we
are hoping to have a stake in. The details in the image are easy
to overlook because they are so synonymous with how we live
and breathe our daily lives sans the chronic scrolling and hustle
we are told will get us free. In Justine's artwork, we see a long-
standing tradition of honoring the moment, of grabbing hold of
what is immediately present and knowing that is enough. Being
Black in any moment will always be enough. *Brunching Negroes
Pt. 2* could be a moment between myself and my nephew Justin,
or my brothers, or any one of the homies I'm in community or
fellowship with. Empty plates, a fly Black woman as a fly on the
diner wall, intercepting the conversation and the bill, perhaps.
Us going nowhere or anywhere the day will allow. We chide
each other over southern biscuits, over pancakes and waffles

and dad life and what dating is like now for us as Black men, knives speckled with the ketchup and the hash browns on the side. The image is still, yet there is so much motion. And even in that motion, everything is as it should be. Everything feels normal and ideal because our natural state as humans is being. What Justine does is take Afro-normalism and cue it up for the viewing audience. Everything is intentional, a secret and silent screen grab for us to indulge in. It is the quietness of all the Black noise that surround sounds the imagery that makes it sweet and grand.

So much of artist Henry Taylor's work captures the majesty of Blackness in its essence: stillness. The portraits are an homage to his past and also reminiscent of the moments of Blackness that don't require us to travel to a dystopian existence in the Octavia Butler vein but in the dynamism of your little cousin cutting up after a UNO game, or your mother cutting down the greens to soak before the big dinner tomorrow. It is less about the activity and the action than the energy behind it. His portraits range from a Kendrick as an Egyptian pharaoh standing beside a humbled Nipsey to the capture of a Black man lounging, fully dressed, on a beach chair. It is this mix of ordinary and a reimagined decolonized past that paints the future that speaks to the crux of what Afro-normalism is to me—we don't need to be anything but Black. Henry paints other races and ethnicities, and in that way, he makes us even more normal. Because we are so special and yet, not. Because the current narratives spin a Blackness weaved in, mired in, a certain kind of magic that keeps us from our humanity.

To be Black is to be in motion: dancing, on a slave ship, at a retail job on the sales floor, working with people you cannot stand; in a cubicle typing a life away; on a football field waiting for a body to drop or a heart to stop. Diddy made "Can't stop, won't stop" scripture, with each of us finding new ways to adopt the slogan as principle, as a means by which to revel in the sacred art of doing. Being is only in service when we are being great, or being something other than just the state of stillness. For some that can be scary. It can also be freeing—unattached to an idea of how and what we should be to progress, to liberate ourselves from the daily oppressive forces that force us to change how we choose to show up. So we do and do and then do some more.

The Black experience as a whole is usually fetishized, metamorphosed into superhuman capabilities, or reduced to criminality. Our range is depicted in meaty love stories with multiple love triangles happening at once, or the stories of fallen martyrs or enslaved peoples nearing the end of their runaway status. We're not afforded the luxury of being seen as something that isn't meant to be worked, to be harmed, to be athletic, to be soulful. Seldom are we allowed to be ordinary. So much is asked of us—in our homes, in our workplaces, in our bedrooms. Afro-normalism speaks to our being as enough. There is so much pressure to go above and beyond, to be more than you were yesterday. But our days are not made up of miraculous feats. We wake up, we call our lovers, we text our parents; we commute from one place to the next, breathing and yawning and stretching like everyone else. Some would argue us being alive is miraculous enough. Some days we are barely making it out of bed. A lack of a PhD or MBA, the inability to start that LLC or to have 100K followers across social channels does not speak to your value or merit. We have been programmed to believe that our excellence and magic are rooted in what we contribute to the world. But this is unequivocally false. As we look at the wide range and breadth of our experiences as a community, we begin to see that true art lies in the mundane, and exists in the space of being.

But Afro-normalism speaks to the beauty of our beings, to the art that is our lived-in experience as a people, all moving and seeking and searching, all failing and floundering, all glowing and growing and grieving. Our lives are a mishmash of stars, orbits, gaps and snores, drools and kisses; we are made up of delayed trains and teakettles kettling and laundry being sorted and sneaking kisses before the alarm goes off. We get to sit in the joy of streaming *Snowfall*, of wiping away tears and the last crumbs of a Wingstop order. It is trivial and heartbreaking, the lives we lead, but they are ours. And they are unalike yet so similar to everything else that lives, loves, and breathes under the sun. We don't have to look to some dystopian future or Wakanda-type entity to take us away from what is here. The action is here, the freedom is here; the fight for abolition and restorative justice is here on this soil, on this land, in both our hearts and hands.

Blackness operates in circles I imagine. I like to think we are reciprocally shaped, each of us eating circles of light, spinning in our aura, basking in the glory of our complete spheres. We are the earth, we are the same. We run circles around each other, too. Playing off the cycles of our living, passing the bayonet from one open hand to the next, rounding out the cipher all the way home. Because of this, I am thinking about legacy more, now that I am forty, thinking about it in a bit more of a masculine way than I have been accustomed to. A lot has to do with the passing of my father. Mainly because I am seeing the world through the eyes of someone who can no longer see for himself. It feels like I am bearing witness to two souls now instead of one. I am ever more cognizant of the kind of world I want to shape for my two little girls and the kind of world I would want them to inhabit when I am gone, primarily because I don't think anyone was doing that for my father. I am living all of my father's lives I think. In that living is also the cognizance that is attempting to will anything to be anything other than what already is, that what is here is itself a form of suffering.

I am forcing myself to write about uninteresting things because our trauma has not allowed us the space to be with anything but. Everything must be excellent, must excel, must be an example, must be an exit strategy from whiteness; must push the envelope, push the bounds, stay out of bounds, to exist and push outside of the margins. We are being told to think critically about our marginalized reality. But Black existence is already a consortium bound to critiques—of both the world and each other. Walk into any hair salon, any barbershop. Whether we agree or disagree with the discourse, folks are bringing a critical eye to the topics of the day because Blackness doesn't make any room for anything other than looking at the world through a lens that is diligent in its approach to navigating the world, primarily because nothing about our lives invites in anything but a close cross-examination of everything we engage with. And so, when my man Fred and I are having a conversation over the phone that starts with sharing our thoughts about Popeyes' new mac and cheese recipe, which then turns into a conversation on Twitter about the Popeyes new mac and cheese recipe, it is with the pretext of the Popeyes historically bad mac and cheese, our community's and Popeyes' relationship to that knowing, and Fred's and my ability to see the mundane humanity in the conversation, to begin with; the ability to remove the need for it to be anything but itself, without overintellectualizing or codifying the experience to meet the demand of an audience who wants nothing more but for Blackness to perform at an elite level. Because that is the only level we are allowed to play on, play in, and play with. If you type in *boredom* and any of your favorite white-leaning publications, chances are you'll pull up several articles that speak to boredom as the entry point to some kind of inspirational breakthrough. Boredom in this way gets to be the anecdotal remedy to what ails us as a community that lacks creativity and imagination when it comes to the more disheartening issues of the world today. It also gets to be transcendental in the same way the Buddhist tradition of mindfulness is. The approaches of its more prominent teachers—Sharon Salzberg, Ram Dass, Michael Beckwith, and Tara Brach—to mindfulness serve as a more enlightened gateway to the ever-evolving expressions of humanity. And yet, what starts to bubble to the surface is also how boredom is in large part a byproduct of privilege and access. Black bodies cannot be bored. We have bills and rent and children and institutional and systemic racism and police-sanctioned violence and a crumbling healthcare and education system and generational trauma and microaggressions and the general day-to-day oppression we have to deal with in the workplace and almost any place where we choose to show up. Boredom is a luxury, a classist delicacy that a select few can access and have available as part of their practice.

When Tyron and I would go to White Castle, our conversations would range from the politics of dating to the politics of 1990s cartoons and indie films. The range was wide, varying, and vast. And to the outside world, it would just look like two average Black niggas shooting the shit over crinkly fries and square burgers. But the intimacy at play was and is revolutionary as fuck. And the context of us in any sort of restaurant having stimulating yet, for all intents and purposes, boring-as-hell dialogue exchanges is not lost on me. So many Black bodies were lost defending the right for us to live very normal lives in an America that lynched, spat, and shot at us, subjecting us to an onslaught of violence and in many cases, death. All because we wanted to be Black and normal. There was a time when even being Black and normal could get you killed. It can still get you killed, but the frequency has shifted somewhat, and now the killing may happen over cigarillos; the killing may involve Skittles. Maybe the killing happens while you are running too fast too soon. Being bored while Black is an option for those of us who cultivated a life that provides the kind of comfort where boredom gets to be a choice rather than a happenstance allotted when white supremacy pretends to be on vacation. The mere existence of choice, of autonomy within the framing of a Black body that is not in need of being in motion, in labor, by definition is in direct contrast to what we know to be normal. If the still-very-ongoing pandemic has taught us anything, it is that there is a sharp dissonance between those with the ability to work from home in a flexible environment at a moment's notice where an imagination actually can find some room to roam and those whose livelihoods are steeped in a stolen agency of sorts, where alternatives to anything other than the capitalist function of commodity and cattle for a machine's sake is not even optional. Boredom is anti-capitalist. And in a culture where hustle is rewarded by offering up more opportunities to hustle more, boredom gets to be the antihero to the narrative.

Blackness, our day-to-day existence, is normal. Black people, we look at rainbows. We ride trains and buses to work. We make love, we steal sandwiches from the work refrigerator. Black people read books. We drink coffee and learn the names of our professors; we show up late to class. We go shopping for water filters and shop at IKEA like everyone else. Far too often, our art and representations of us in the media don't get to depict this. We don't get to be normalized. We don't get to be human. What we deem to be banal is also subjective. But my interest in what is boring has as much to do with the act of being as a form of rebellion and resistance as it does with the idea that we don't need an idea of what a state of being is to just *be* in the first place. Pardon the opaqueness and metalanguage here. Black gets to lay, gets to play in the snow, and have it be art or just have it be anything we tell our aunt about over a Martha's Vineyard summer because it is the first time we are swimming with our cousins without thinking about dying. My Blackness is recording my daughters wearing their Halloween costumes in 2022 and in the house in the late spring of 2023, dancing and yelling in tandem like two little Black girls who have not a care or worry in the world. I watch them and see all the joy they have and how that joy gets to fill me, and that in and of itself is amazing and holy and beautiful in the ways prayer is. Or watching a Knicks game when they actually make the playoffs. My brother D and I watched Knicks games religiously growing up, him making me a fan by default. That is Black and as joyful and as normal as it can get. Our rituals, our habits of leaving stove lights on, of flicking the kitchen lights on to keep the roaches at bay; the hood that colors our walls and drapes our ceilings. It is the collection of the moment-to-moment existing that is the bed frame for how we find rest, how we renegotiate the terms and conditions for how we approach being in this world of chaos. Afro-normalism is really about the middle ground, the things and love we partake in. Playing punch buggy. Yelling "UNO OUT." Stopping to do the electric slide in midconversation at a moment's notice, no matter where you are or what you're doing. Our Blackness gets to be about walking your dog while listening to the Black Men United song "U Will Know" from the *Jason's Lyric* soundtrack one evening as you cry over Cameron Gunter dying of heart failure. When I was crying, I had to pause to scoop Dilla's poop. I cried again after. Because there is something very sad about a thirty-one-year-old Black man not living long enough to see marriage or children, or just him taking more pictures, taking more trips. Or doing more boring things like leading work meetings, or watching the 76ers on his couch. Or reading a book on a Sunday, like I get to do now, children in different rooms around the apartment, Dilla asleep in his crate, Bria using the headphones that were mine that are now hers. The calm in that is not miraculous by nature, and by description is not something to particularly write home about. But that is life and that is living and that is beautiful. It is stillness. It is quiet and quite boring. I like it.

Death by Visibility

Feat. Kanye West, Rodney King

When someone comes up and says something like, "I am a god," everybody says "Who does he think he is?" I just told you who I thought I was. A god. I just told you. That's who I think I am.

—KANYE WEST

I love watching how little white boys play outside. There's so much freedom in them. So much glee. A carefree, almost reckless abandon that seemingly is carried nonchalantly, boldly, proudly. A true lack of inhibition. In their smiles—a mischievous nature and quality in how they interact with the world. Imaginations run amok. I can tell very quickly, whether by watching them or interacting with them, that they are not thinking about dying. Death is not in their mouth, not on the tongue; not sitting idly, waiting beside the bedside of the next breath, seeking the next body to destroy. Some may say that children should not be thinking of death. I disagree. Death is both natural and nature. Because it is everywhere. In our food, the plants, in the textbooks . . . even the banned ones. But death is different for little white boys. Death for them is cyborgs blown up by rich white men in ironclad suits. It is a half-man, half-robot character proclaiming he will be back thirty different times in thirty different movies, where he indeed does come back over and over, shooting up all the bad guys. It is an imaginary white man who is hung on a cross, only to be resurrected on the third day. And to celebrate, we gather together and hunt eggs. All of the white men die and come back, and in different ways. The boys know that they will not die. They will survive on the strength of their faux bootstraps. So much imagination in them. And frankly, that is exactly as it should be. Our children should feel invincible. They should all want to feel as if they should be the teapot standing center stage, tipping their arms to raucous applause from adoring parents cheering them on from their auditorium seats, elementary school sweat and under-the-seat popcorn cooling the air. All children should feel that confident. They should feel safe enough to be visible; to be seen and loved and nurtured and not have that confidence be questioned or, worse, get the shit hung out of them for being too loud or brazen or bold enough to stand tall in your skin. Being Black and loud can make you invisible.

The cute, innocent white boys I see in Brooklyn streets range from two years of age to the nimble character that lives in an eight-year-old. I can see that they live without question or worry, except if their best friend will share with them a juice box or lollipop or toy figurine. I can also see in the glimmer in their eyes they live in a world that does not question their right to exist in the first place. Little white boys go unchecked, unfettered, and unbothered by the world around them: playing with dandelions in the garden and crushing them with bare hands and feet. And we laugh and laugh and imagine what stocks they will have or what public office they will control and we hope and pray they will be leaders of whatever the free world will look like with them in charge of it.

They are living in a world that does not question their color, their education, their acute ability to obtain and retain knowledge, their potential, their SAT scores, their ability to be prone to violence or acts of rage. They are already debt-free, both from an economic standpoint and also from the standpoint of something that is not owed to the world merely by their breathing. This is not a privilege, no, this is something more abstract in nature: it is the idea that their aliveness is inherently deserved. They do not have to earn "being." It simply just is, and they simply just are. I am jealous. I am envious of their freedom—how apparent it is. It feels unattainable. I think about who they will grow up to be, and the choices and the say they have in that matter.

To be Black is to be seen by everyone and no one at all; to be at once coveted and loathed; to be both heard and misunderstood— both herd and cattle, martyr and savior. They, are always wanting, always asking more, demanding you give, what you offer. They, want you to pretend to be invisible, wanting your chic, your cacao.

To be Black, and to not also be crazy, is a miracle, a mystery, a modern marvel of science; to be Black, to not reach for a trigger or a hammer because a rope may be far too triggering; looking to blow brains away, yours and cohorts alike, is a phenomenon. As phenomenal as a solar eclipse, as a man walking on the moon, as the grassy knoll. To carry the history of a people in your marrow—while simultaneously bearing the brunt and weight of the brutality laid across your feet daily, that daily dalliance done with death, it is dancing, diving onto grave and tombstone—is a modern-day mystery.

To live this life, a Black life, is to be too tired always, is to be tried more often than you would like, than would be counted; is to be the fly on the wall everywhere, to be sensitive to all sights and sounds and touches and avoidance of such—to see people pivot their bodies, alter their speech, hide perishables, keeping all things holy out of plain view.

If your dreams are not scary as shit, if the life laid out for you is not you gambling for the bigness in the stars and your heart, then you are to be told you are missing out on your grandness. It is a fairy tale, a mythological fable passed from American schoolchild to American schoolchild, the cleaned-up, idealized, bastard version of opportunity. You are told that if it speaks to you, if they speak to you, follow that, listen to that—heed whatever beckons and calls to your bones, to the marrow in you. And while this is inherently true, true if you believe in a power higher than heaven, in universal law and karmic cycles and spirits and Yoruba guidance and such, its application across the board for all of those who are walking the path of living, seems to be partial to a select, cherry-picked few, with the marginalized many scratching the bottom of the barrel for the remaining scraps.

One of my best friends, the pianist and songwriter Arthur Lewis, had a show, after a somewhat lengthy hiatus from the stage, at the top of 2023 at Rockwood Music Hall in the Lower East Side. The pandemic changed a lot of how performances happened for us. Before the pandemic, we had sold-out consecutive shows on the smaller stage and proceeded to pack the house in their larger room. Several years prior to that, Arthur and I were part of a ragtag crew of phenomenal bandmates called the Melting Pot. I joined the Melting Pot in the summer of 2007 with the LP of the band's frontman and Lilah's godfather, Jon Braman. After the band broke up—schedules, parenthood, the normal rock star problems—Arthur and I joined forces for a smaller iteration of the band featuring our friends Bobby and Sonny. We downsized considerably and kept it to a duo, primarily for the convenience. Arthur and I had a sort of synchronicity that is hard to match or duplicate. Arthur is structured whereas I tend to be more behind the beat and loose. It is also a reflection of our kinship in some ways. Our dynamic was a far cry from the clubs I performed in with a CD and instrumental tracks featuring my prerecorded hooks. In those leaner years, me working a social services job during the day while killing mics at night, the dream was to be signed to Roc-a-Fella Records. My reoccurring dream saw me signing a contract under some diluted light in a dank and dark basement, with Jay-Z and Dame Dash looking over my shoulder, a diamond-encrusted Roc-A-Fella chain in tow. When I fast-forward to the moment in January of 2023 with myself and Arthur onstage, what I realized then and what I sit with now is how much the urge to be front and center pales in sharp comparison to the need and want to be surrounded by community. The need to be seen had been replaced by the need to have others seen through the lens of togetherness. I had always felt my art to be a conduit for that. But as I've aged—a girl dad with two daughters, a steady income, a home for my family I am proud of—I realized all of the wants I carried in my earlier years were about reaching the heights of success that would keep myself and the ones I loved safe. And I realize now that the barometer for that success could only be measured by that. So even as my profile grows, the need to be seen as successful by others has dwindled dramatically. Hip-hop not only thrives on its competitive nature. It also thrives by our willingness to go above and beyond for an audience; to bleed and suffer and put ourselves out in front of fans or haters or empty clubs and barrooms day in and day out, the seat treading itself against our pores while we watch and dance and spit and split ourselves up for money and applause and plaques we will never receive and mansions we will never own and whiteness we will never have.

When whiteness wants you invisible, the price tag can be phenomenal. It may also come with a toe tag—albeit not in the physical realm, if at times that seems resoundingly to be the case, but at the very least a more personal one. In May of 2023, a viral video showed a Bellevue Hospital nurse in New York City arguing with a group of young Black teens over a Citibike. In the video, the white woman, wearing her hospital scrubs, can be heard yelling "Please help me!" Repeatedly. She removes her hospital badge, grabs one of the teens' phones, and tells one of the other teens that they're hurting her fetus. Another hospital staff member approaches the woman, and this is when the cloak of invisibility rears its head. Because in that moment, she chose the emotional dog whistle of a white woman's faux tears to create an environment that she knew, whether subconsciously or not, would level the odds in her favor. The weaponizing of white tears is a sort of explicit violence that looks to make those on their end participatory ghosts in the never-ending saga of racism. In this way, we see the cloak of invisibility as a dagger by proxy—a weapon used to mute the voices of those who would rather speak to truth than remain silent while the injustices and microaggressions of this world brutalize us to sleep. And those weapons play themselves out in any environment where a Black body chooses resistance over compliance—from the streets of Joburg, to the blocks of the Bronx, to the projects on the South Side of Chicago.

> *It was a strike against me that I didn't wear baggy jeans and jerseys and that I never hustled, never sold drugs.*
>
> —KANYE WEST, *Time* MAGAZINE

In the late summer of August 1998, I may have been in the crib enjoying Rap City. My moms would have cooked something like some spaghetti and beef with Ragu sauce. I'd be sitting with legs crossed, window screens in the room with the ceiling fan on, and Kool-Aid Kiwi Lime in my favorite glass. And then, a voice: "Laaaaaaaaaaawd . . . lawd have mercy . . ." Yasiin Bey, the artist formerly known as Mos Def, and Talib Kweli came together to form Black Star and released the single "Definition" along with the video. The song and video helped usher in a new era of hip-hop, a direct contrast to Puff and Bad Boy's "No Way Out" and Juvenile's "400 Degreez." Both the single and album harkened back to an era where A Tribe Called Quest, De La Soul, the Jungle Brothers, and the rest of the Native Tongue movement, along with groups like Brand Nubian and Poor Righteous Teachers were leading the pro-African, pro-consciousness era of the music to something that was less commercially viable but successful in its own right. Interestingly enough, what was thought to be ATCQ's last studio album, *The Love Movement*, was released the same year as Black Star's *Mos Def and Talib Kweli Are Black Star* album, a subliminal passing of the torch if you will. Black Star's debut wasn't mainstream—it was underground. It also helped usher in the backpack movement. At any cipher in any of the boroughs, you'd see a flame-carrying rapper with a book bag holding their notebooks of rhymes, maybe some acrylics for bombing all inside. The backpack symbolized struggle, symbolized "I don't need capitalism to run my life." It became the archetype for Jeru the Damaja–type cats—heavy on the Five Percenter, Black-man-is god, true and living rhetoric that was inherited from Afrika Bambaataa and others in the 1980s and '90s. Rawkus Records, Fat Beats, Stones Throw, and Rhymesayers defined that era of music. Black Star's debut album would usher in another monument carried over from the likes of *In Living Color*: the hip-hop-centered skit show.

Predating *Wild 'N Out* and pulling from Prince Paul and De La's skit-laden LPs in the early days, all the way back to Flip Wilson's Black-centric comedic work, MTV's *The Lyricist Lounge Show* in 2000 also reintroduced us to Mos Def, to Wordsworth, and to a young Tracee Ellis Ross. The show aired until 2001, but its impact was resonant, as it pulled so much from the genre—the show itself was based on the heralded New York City show of the same name, a hip-hop musical showcase that eventually spawned a record deal and a few compilation CDs. Blending hip-hop and theater, the show also served as a precursor to MTVs foray into original films with *Carmen: A Hip Hopera* (starring Beyoncé and also featuring Yasiin Bey, then Mos Def). *The Lyricist Lounge Show* existed in the shadow of the wildly successful TRL era and made its entry at the same time as TRL's competitor, BET's *106 & Park*. But it would be the year 2003 that would make way for two projects that would heighten the sense of what Blackness could look and feel like: Little Brother's *The Listening* and Dave Chappelle's *The Chappelle Show*.

If you were a real hip-hop head, *The Listening* was the litmus test. Emcees Phonte, Rapper Big Pooh, and producer 9th Wonder captured the energy where Black Star left off. Drake would say in interviews Phonte inspired him. Little Brother, along with their crew, The Justus League, while never asking for the crown of the backpack, certainly became the darlings of the genre. If you haven't listened to "The Yo-Yo," "Shorty on the Lookout," or "Whatever You Say," you are missing a lot of the context that emcees who now rap for the blue-collar fan frame their work around. "So Fabulous" would see Phonte taking on the character of other rap legends in flow and verse before Black Thought would do the same on "Boom!" As underground sensations, the groups set a gold standard for the everyman rapper, who felt relatable in a world where a visible Black presence could mean that maybe they went to the club like you, went to college like you, or dropped out of college like you, too. This same year, Dave Chappelle's hip-hop-inspired and game-changing show, *The Chappelle Show*, combined music and skits, carrying on the tradition of so many before him: *The Richard Pryor Show, The Chris Rock Show, In Living Color, The Flip Wilson Show*. But this was different: Chappelle was tapping into the sticky, jagged, and pointed sides of Blackness. It was smarter than anything on TV. Mos Def and Talib Kweli would return to perform on the show, along with performing for Dave Chappelle's *Block Party*, where the neo-soul and backpack movements would converge for a summer day full of music and comedy that would prove to be a foundation for the Roots Picnic and Budweiser Made in America Festival (both, notwithstanding, were influenced by the then still ultra-Black Afropunk). The projects were shifting their respective genres of art in new, fresh, creative, and interesting ways.

So much so that, if you happened to be watching broadcast TV in 2004 like I was, you might have been met with a commercial that featured a beat-making rapper wearing a Louis Vuitton backpack while he also wore a bear costume that resembled an ensemble a school's mascot would wear; it was hard not to watch. He made you watch. He was a Black man turned visible in the most relatable way. Kanye is so Kanye that you can only refer to him as you would refer to Oprah—by his first name. Kanye. In 2004, I was a college dropout, too. I was having my studio time for recording my rap songs funded by my brother Dwain and our pseudo management slash party promoting team, Hipnotiq Entertainment. We made poorly designed T-shirts, sold tickets to parties at Mars 2112, didn't make a lot of money, and were very bad at financing. But we loved each other. And when I was invited to Buckwild's studio due to his connection to our around-the-way homie Sam also known as deejay SupaSam, and I saw the plaque for Biggie's "I Got a Story to Tell," a song that Buckwild produced, he sat me down and told me I reminded him of "Kanye West, but street." I cried on the inside because that's what I wanted. I wanted to be visible like Kanye was. His freshman debut, *The College Dropout*, changed my life. It changed a lot of lives. When cats like Fresh Daily, Skyzoo, and Torae; like Emilio Rojas and Chaundon; like 6th Sense and Wildabeast and cats like Oddisee and Kev Brown and the Low Budget Crew; when Pac Div and J. Cole; when Lupe Fiasco and Tanya Morgan and Blu and Mickey Factz were vying for the hearts and minds and streams and write-ups from the fans and rap blogs, we were standing in the shadow of Kanye. Kanye made it culturally acceptable to be Black and proud and capitalist. Kanye would perform at Def Poetry Jam and within the same breath be front row during *Vogue* fashion week next to Anna Wintour. He straddled the two worlds mercilessly and beautifully.

I saw myself in Kanye—or at least the self I wanted to be. He made being yourself seem effortless. In a world that cloaked us in darkness, that wanted our light so dimmed, so narrowed and pigeonholed, Kanye made it okay to be open and honest about your greatness, and your desires, along with the bumps, bruises, and pitfalls suffered along the way to get there. He was Posdnuos but cooler, Yasiin but a tad more commercial and acceptable, Common but less poetic, flashier in a way that bridged Puff and the Last Poets together for a rendezvous chat.

When I was still performing at underground rap shows in Midtown at 2:00 A.M. to an audience of maybe my brother D and two of the other acts on the bill that night, Kanye was crashing industry parties, standing on tables, and yelling at the crowd to say "I'm going to be the greatest rapper ever!" Which would normally be met with laughs and guffaws. What Kanye was saying was "see me." Make me visible. See me in all my talented glory. Kanye was raised by his educated Black mother, Donda, on the South Side of Chicago. The year Kanye was born, 1977, the Index Crime Rates had Chicago ranked fifth in the nation. The legendary house music club, Warehouse, also opened its doors. The 192-home-run-hitting Chicago White Sox, better known as the South Side Hitmen, took Major League Baseball and the whole city by storm. The Black P. Stone Nation, the notorious South Side gang, were engaged in an internal turf war, as the El Rukn faction, led by their chief, Eugene Hairston, fought for dominance. According to the website ChicagoGangHistory, Mickey Cogwell was shot in front of his house. The murder would move the formerly Mickey-led Cobrastones to leave Black P. Stone Nation and become the Mickey Cobras that same year. By the time Kanye's parents separated and moved from Atlanta, Georgia, where Kanye was born, to Chicago in 1980, a census included in "A Special Report: Race and Poverty in Chicago in 1983" stated that "one in five of Chicago's residents lived below the poverty line, an increase of 24 percent since 1970." In Coodie and Chike's *jeen-yuhs* Netflix documentary, we see a young Kanye making his way in and around the city, trying to make a name for himself both as a rapper and a producer, being rejected, talked down to, and disregarded. Folks wanted his beats. No one wanted Kanye the rapper.

> *My mama ain't here. My mama was sacrificed.*
>
> —KANYE WEST, INTERVIEW, NOVEMBER 11, 2022

What Kanye wanted, more than to be seen, was to make his mama proud. And by virtue, being seen was his strategy to do that. Black mamas are not only the magicians of the world, they are also the bearers of the hopes and dreams aspiring artists and athletes pin their ambitions to. I had a phone call with Mary Pryor, my good friend and cannabis activist, where we discussed Black men's need to avoid obscurity at any and all costs. And some of that pressure comes from the patriarchal need to take care of a household and be responsible for those who were responsible for you. And so, Donda retired from her role as English professor and chair of the Department of English, Communications, Media, and Theater at Chicago State University, moved to California, and became Kanye's full-time manager. And what we see in those early years is Kanye in a flight to become invincible by building a catalog and brand so fiercely tied to art, culture, and capitalism, his growth was matched only by his irrefutable ego. An ego that would be kept somewhat at bay by the love and direction of his mother. "There is no room for shyness." This would be Donda's response when talking about Kanye. As a child, Donda and her father took part in the Katz Drug Store sit-in in Oklahoma City, one of the first sit-ins of the civil rights movement. Donda knew what invisibility to a Black man could look like, could feel like. It was as lived-in for her as the protests she took part in. So when, on November 10, 2007, Donda died at age fifty-eight from what the January 2008 coroner report described as "coronary artery disease and multiple postoperative factors from cosmetic surgery," what we were witnessing was a mother's need to be seen as beautiful, as desirable, as wanted and valuable. Right alongside her son. Donda's real cause of death was visibility. Kanye has been slowly dying ever since.

Visibility is a Black man's defense mechanism actualized. It is our shield. It is our comfort. The visibility checklist is as follows:

- ☑ chains showing
- ☑ skin glowing
- ☑ new kicks
- ☑ fresh fit
- ☑ pockets swole
- ☑ new job role
- ☑ trips overseas

- ☑ baddies on IG
- ☑ look at my watch
- ☑ middle fingers to cops
- ☑ pose for the flick
- ☑ rap, ball, or swish
- ☑ everybody, look at me
- ☑ alive, no jail time, an LLC
- ☑ look at me, please

We are told early, normally around the same time when we are made to believe, and also when we are too young to question the likelihood and validity of receiving money from fairies for fallen teeth, or mystical fat men flinging themselves down chimneys, that if we only work hard, if we only meditate on the goodness of the world and the people and dreams in it, if we only go the extra mile and place our best shackled, mangled foot forward, or bow our heads in the most uncomfortable of positions for the most exalted of gods using the most holy of prayers, that we, too, can have our slight slice of Americana, of the American dream. Which is interesting—to grow up in an apartment building where hallways were littered with Budweiser beer cans after late-night house parties and stairwells carried scattered used condoms and their affiliate wrappers strewn about, having to rationalize why Saint Nicholas aka Santa Claus only came down chimneys and did not climb through windows using fire escapes as leverage, in the stories shared in classrooms. We wrote letters to him each year, and each year I would receive none of the things I asked for. (Jesus and Santa seem to hold similar spaces in my heart in that way.) But this is the rapturous tale that is weaved by the fairest of skins for the most disadvantaged, disenfranchised, colored, and unsaved miscreants of the world. We are told at youth that we are to gobble up these old wives' fictions of racial harmony, the fiction once conceived by the Founding Fathers, these men who owned other men, who used race as a blowtorch to ignite bias and prejudice, inciting hate as a means of justifying the perfunctory methods government has used to pillage communities of color. We are told to place our faith in the future of our nation on the shoulders of these men, these patriots of our bigoted past.

To be born as a Black man is to be born believing your life is truncated upon birth, and that everything to follow forth is all but farce, a mere stage play, with your livelihood as the punch line. America is the greatest of performers ever; we are all bearing witness to the fruits of our magical labor. Can you see it? "It" is the Starbucks attendant on West Forty-Third Street staring blankly through big windows, perhaps he is six foot one, he is brown and he is waiting for you, you and your latte leaving, to see him human; or the woman sitting on the D train at the far end corner, earphones in with no music, holding tears like infants; perhaps the construction site crew member just home from Riker's, still Cripping, but still trying—it is all of them and none of them, all of us and none of us, all waiting to be visible.

We are more visible now than we ever have been—body cams have helped dramatically. Every day, we now get to tune in to our demise live on candid camera. Tyre Nichols's murder was prime-time television. Rave reviews apparently from the Memphis Police Department. The lead-up to and hype of the video's release was something of Hype Williams in his heyday kinds-of-epic. Pay-per-view death match for the world to see, no subscription or payment needed—Black death comes free of charge. George Floyd's murder was must-see TV, no closed captions needed. Both men cried for their mothers before their last breaths. Kanye calls for his mother in every episode. We keep tuning in. We keep watching. We kept watching Muhammad Ali fight to stay seen, even when he could no longer see the damage boxing was doing to his body. There is shit we do as Black men to stay heard, to stay hot, to stay relevant; to not fade away into obscure, pixelated dust forever gone into the disappearing. We watched Damar Hamlin's heart stop on a football field and look! look at the cute remembrances on jerseys, cleats, helmets, and hats. We watched Damar watch the Bills from his hospital room with family and friends surrounding him, him out of his coma, only for him to ask who won the game. We watch Black men fling themselves into recording studios, into boxing rings, onto football fields and basketball courts to razzle and dazzle and amaze and entertain us, to do a thing they were born to do, that they love to do and are extremely passionate about, risking life and limb. Jim Jones told us being a rapper is more dangerous than being a cop. If you don't believe him, ask Tupac. Ask Biggie. Ask Mac Dre. Ask Nipsey. Ask Takeoff. Ask Big L. Ask Jam Master Jay. Ask anybody in YSL. Ask Bobby Schmurda. Ask Kanye. And ask, Is it the love or the visibility? Yes, I wanted to rap but I also wanted what the rappers had—money, fame, clothes, invitations to the places I was never invited to, being in videos with women who wouldn't love me for me but love me for what I could offer. Yes, I wanted to rap, but I would have gladly taken all the other things that came with rap, even if it meant dying to do so. We're dying every day anyway, right? Why not make some scratch from it: buy your mama a home, your lady a Benz; post it all on IG for you and your friends to like and comment and share and hashtag goals in the Stories for all the followers to see. Death is inevitable for all of us. But it is a different kind of dying we do that stretches beyond what is seen as reasonable for Black men and boys.

> *I'm living three dreams:*
> *Biggie Smalls', Dr. King, Rodney King's*

—KANYE WEST, "NEW GOD FLOW"

Kanye was speaking to the three dreams still un-lived. They beat Rodney King to death. He did not die necessarily on the night of March 3, 1991, San Fernando Valley adjacent, 1987 Hyundai Excel, parked beside the Hansen Dam Recreation Area. On that night he would die a different death, and we would all watch it and die a bit, too, because somehow, we thought seeing it would be enough, seeing him would be enough. Rodney was beaten to near-physical dying, a dying that would force him to see himself in many different ways: victim, martyr, comic relief. King would continue to fight to be seen after his first death. Here, a timeline of visibility:

☑   In 1991, King would sue the City of Los Angeles and win a $3.8 million settlement. He would invest some of the winnings into a record label, Straight Alta-Pazz Records, looking to employ minority employees. It soon went out of business.

☑   In May 1991, he was arrested on suspicion of having tried to run down an undercover vice officer in Hollywood, but no charges were filed.

☑   In 1992, he was arrested for injuring his then wife,

Crystal King. On August 21, 1993, he crashed his car into a block wall in downtown Los Angeles. He would be convicted of driving under the influence of alcohol and placed on probation.

☑ In July 1995, he was arrested after hitting Crystal King with his car and knocking her to the ground during a fight. He was sentenced to ninety days in jail.

☑ On August 27, 2003, King was arrested again for speeding and running a red light while under the influence of alcohol. He slammed his vehicle into a house, breaking his pelvis.

☑ On November 29, 2007, while riding home on his bicycle, King was shot in the face, arms, and back with pellets from a shotgun.

☑ In October 2008, King joined the cast of season 2 of *Celebrity Rehab with Dr. Drew.*

☑ King also appeared on *Sober House,* a *Celebrity Rehab* spin-off focusing on a sober living environment.

☑ The site of the 1991 beating is now Discovery Cube Los Angeles.

☑ On September 11, 2009, King won a celebrity boxing match against police officer Simon Aouad, at the Ramada Philadelphia Airport.

☑ On March 3, 2011, the twentieth anniversary of the beating, the LAPD stopped King for driving erratically and issued him a citation for driving with an expired license.

☑ On Father's Day, June 17, 2012, King's partner, Cynthia Kelley, found King dead underwater at the bottom of his swimming pool. King died twenty-eight years to the day after his father, Ronald King, was found dead in his bathtub in 1984.

☑ On August 23, 2012, King's autopsy results revealed he died of accidental drowning. The combination of alcohol, cocaine, and PCP found in his system were contributing factors, as were cardiomegaly and focal myocardial fibrosis. The report's conclusion stated, very matter-of-factly: "The effects of the drugs and alcohol, combined with the subject's heart condition, probably precipitated a cardiac arrhythmia, and the subject, incapacitated in the water, was unable to save himself." King's last death—a broken heart.

If I have learned anything being compressed in this skin, it is that self-love can save your soul, Frankie Beverly's voice can bend metal, and every day is a blessed one; I have learned that James Baldwin knew everything, that a heart can keloid, that memories can steal themselves from the vacant lonely buried in loins. I do not know what holding back means; I have no use for it—I will live and die with a heart of water, fluid until the dam breaks (or cartilage, from carrying the struggles of other blacks, something America will force you to do whether you are strong enough or not). It is this love that allows me to tolerate and deal with both the macro- and microaggressions that have presented themselves since birth to my doorstep—comfortably arranged and ordered to solicit rage at the slightest occurrence of disrespect—an ill-timed side-eye, a scuffed Jordan, a perceived scoff digested as an insult. I know of no big lives, full lives led, being driven by the spirit of one who plays it "safe," not here, not in this country. Safety is for NRA conference conversation, for airplane flight attendants, safety is a luxury, is a Lexus or Acura—it is not for those seeking to peel back the layers of resistance; all who I admire the most have pushed themselves to the edge, seeking that which is unidentifiable; searching for a purpose bigger than self. That self, this purpose, is tied defiantly to a cause if you are born Black. This is not by choice, this cause has been bred in you, branded onto you.

We, Black men, are still here. We are trying to be. We are loving ourselves through muck and high water, arms flailing, mothers calmly wailing for us to find a shore. Tides bearing pregnant feet and lost tribes tossed to the seas, now fodder for sharks, the memories of the drowning embedded in the DNA. We are waiting for a miracle to come and save us. And I wonder if we know we are the miracle. Do we know we are the seeds? We are still the unmet dreams of Dr. King, promised land be damned. Even still, we stand amongst mountains, tall as Olympus's nightstand, making room for it all. Trying desperately to stay alive. Trying our damndest to be heard and seen.

Survivor's Guilt

I come from a long line of people who tell stories. And in those stories you have to listen and listen some more. And wait for the punch lines and the climax. I am good at storytelling because of the stories that have been told to me by those who are here and those who I wish still were. And my ability to tell stories made me a good liar. I would lie for small infractions. Big infractions. Infractions and their scale are all very subjective. But they almost always took the form of "I didn't know," "I didn't mean to," "I won't do it again," "I didn't mean for this to happen," "I forgot," "I was scared." The general, garden variety of lies. And almost always there was a fear of having to go back home—to a lover, to a sibling, to a parent, to a friend. Lying was easier than honesty because honesty would require accountability. And accountability comes with guilt. The guilt of being ashamed, of being wrong, and of being caught in a story that is not real. I won't lie anymore—not to my daughters, my mama, my partner. Lying is expensively tiring. Cheating because you don't want to get caught, fibbing because you would rather be nice than be honest, stretching the truth because you would rather be seen as cool than actually being it. The guilt that comes from that also has a home. It, too, has come from something. The guilt is an effort to have us confront something we don't want to see. That is guilt's origin story. Because everything has a home—a base of sorts.

We all come from something—a person, a body, a place. We can point to the fingernails, to the adjusted screws and peeling lead and dried paint, to the handprints staining the suburban walls of a yesteryear we are removed from. We can point to a bodega, stoop, or enclave of block and residence and say, "I remember when so and so hopped such and such a fence and ran from such and such a person or people." We can walk an old avenue or street, named after someone who left too soon, who left a legacy that makes sure family and councilpersons create a forever namesake in the form of renaming a corner after them, a corner a transient resident may not care to acknowledge. In contrast, others who were born and raised when the avenue and street were changed can point to the slaying that happened, the work that was done, the energy that was spent, on the corner that now shares a namesake with a ghost. In that way, those people and places become *our* people and places. We take ownership, we claim residence, we take all the parts and sketch and draw them into our memory, jogging them into place until they become one with how we see the world, making something that once felt dissonant and disconnected into something more accurate, more true, like a Rembrandt up close. We can point to a legacy, a remembrance of what once was and has now gone but is not forgotten because whether we are aware or not we are the embodied remnants of said legacies, living and dying daily in our cells. And so it goes that the once *was* lives on as *is*, the "as is" being us, living as a testament to a thing that no longer exists. It lives in a past life, a thing that may seem dormant at first glance but is still very much alive as a spark of something very real and very true.

I remember Boyz II Men's first single, "Motownphilly," yes for its melodic groove and yes for Michael Bivins's first foray into management after leading what once was the original boy band of the century with New Edition. I also remember it more fondly because of the video. And not because the video itself was all that impressive but because, if you were watching the video when it first dropped on Ralph McDaniels's legendary East Coast staple music show *Video Music Box*, a small ticker would appear at the bottom of your TV screens that mentioned Alexander's. Alexander's was a chain of retail stores that were widely popular in New York City, following in the same vein as Woolworth, JCPenney, Macy's, and Sears. Alexander's offered discount wear and clothing. The Alexander's on Fordham Road and the Grand Concourse was built in 1933. By the time the "Motownphilly" single was released in 1991, I was in third grade and Alexander's had lost upward of $20 million in revenue, with closings of the Eatontown location in 1983, the Westchester store in 1986, and the Edison, White Plains, and Milford outlets by the end of the 1980s preceding bankruptcy and a purchase of 20 percent of the company by a real estate heir named Donald Trump (who would later return his holdings in the company to the guarantor in 1991). But in 1991, eight-year-old me just knew Alexander's as the place my mom would go to for any and all things domestic, to glitter and glam her closet and wardrobe. And when it wasn't Alexander's it would be Conway. And when it wasn't Conway it would be Mandee, Bon Bini, or Strawberry. And so the ticker at the bottom of the Boyz II Men video was a reminder of where I was—not just through the lens of the urban landscape in which I heard and saw the world but through the words coming out of those televised boxes and rectangular boom systems, through the wheelings and dealings of the people who made and played the music and the places they played it in. The video was always a reminder that I was always home. And walking past Alexander's would also be a reminder of where I was: it was the Alexander's that was stationed not too far from the army recruitment center that I walked into right before graduating high school when I was almost dumb enough to think I wanted to risk the chance to die for a country that would never love me so I would have something to live for and maybe pay for college in the process. The same Alexander's that would be replaced by a Caldor and an Apple Bank; the same Alexander's that was not too far from the Petland that is now a floral shop that is owned by the Mexican man and his family who, before they owned the shop, sold flowers at a small stand that stood right in front of the Fordham Road D train station and near the watch repair shop where, for five dollars they would replace your battery and maybe even adjust the screws on your glasses; the same Alexander's that was also not too many blocks away from the pizza shop on the corner of Creston Avenue and 188th Street that used to carry arcade machines inside the shop and gave out ice and pizza during the blackout in the 2000s; the same Alexander's that was not too far from the bootleg man that sold all the mixtapes or the bootleg man that sold Dwain the Black Bart Simpson shirt we had to run with because the cops were coming; the same Alexander's that was not too far from the toys, furniture, and baby supply store where I would buy G.I.

Joes. Being born and raised in New York City, being born and raised and proud to be from the Bronx, you see so many haunts change and leave, come and go: Loews Theatres. Music Factory. Sammy's. Buster Brown. Lionel Kiddie City. Nobody Beats the Wiz. Caldor. Sam Goody. Circuit City. Woolworth. The pizza shop with the arcade machines. The Blimpie. The fried chicken and seafood place is still standing but under new management. All of them are remnants of the past long forgotten, a past new-comers won't ever know existed. I remember these places nos-talgically while sitting in the guest room of our three-bedroom apartment in Bed-Stuy, feeling glimmers of shame for leaving home. I left the Bronx first for college, attending Temple Univer-sity. Leaving LaGuardia High School of Music, Art, and the Per-forming Arts with slips of paper in an envelope, containing the names of agencies, agents, and their phone numbers, all of whom had seen me perform in the senior showcase and wanted to hold further conversations with me, sent me into a panic. So did the idea of auditioning for the Juilliard conservatory. So did leaving NYC and my family and friends to study theater in Moscow. So I did what any other sane child would do: I waited until the very last minute to apply to schools and applied to the same school that Bill Cosby and Daryl Hall and John Oates graduated from. After failing to apply for financial aid in time and failing to file for my student loans, I left Temple after my sophomore year and returned home. And then I left home again . . . for love. I found myself in Lakeland, Florida, as a roofing technician and then in Atlanta, Georgia, as an unemployed boyfriend. And then I came back home. And then home for my partner and me became Park Slope. It became the Upper East Side. And then we broke off our engagement. And I came home again. And I would be home until the birth of my second child, raising my first child while still holding court in the same bedroom I sat in watching old music videos, bags from the pizza shop with the arcade machines, bags of greasy sandwiches from the fried chicken and seafood place. Many of the old haunts still remain. I know this because I still go home though nothing looks or feels the same. And I get to judge and point and ridicule and reminisce about the days of old from the spare room I can afford that I know my mother never could or my father never could or his father never could or my brothers never could. This is my survivor's guilt.

It starts when you least expect it. Your cupboards are full of the foods you want. The refrigerator and the freezer are stocked, full of items from a grocery list. You still have money to spare. You walk around your expansive apartment like you own it. You don't but it feels like you do. Your dog, your daughters, your partner—you walk up and down the halls, cleaning and dusting and vacuuming and laughing. Sometimes you yell and sound like your mother, except when telling your girls to quiet down, it is merely a response to your own childhood rearing its head from under the covers, reminding you that noise of any kind is disruptive. You sound like your mother except you don't hear the stirring of mice or the downstairs neighbor banging on their ceiling because you are being too loud. You buy the expensive lotion you tried at the expensive Austin hotel you were staying at while recording a project in an expensive studio with expensive friends, and you decide you need the lotion because you can afford the lotion and it feels good and you realize that even just a little bit more money than the money you had the day before actually can bring you happiness. Rich be lyin'. They be lying because they don't want you to have as much money as them, so far removed from not having any of it they can easily forget what having it can actually do for you.

More money meant moving out of my partner's rent-stabilized one bedroom in Bed-Stuy to our three-bedroom apartment in Bed-Stuy, which also meant me getting the papers delivered to our door every weekend because I could afford it and meant getting the record player I really wanted because I could afford it, and Biggs moved to Monroe and Dwain moved to Monroe and Boola not too far from Monroe and Elvis left and Buc never got the chance to. But we were all migrating for what seemed to be greener pastures. Some of our ancestors did the same, leaving their homes in the South to make the big move to the northern cities. Except when they left, they left on the Atlantic Coast train, the Illinois Central, and the Southern Pacific Railroad, bringing their stories, their history, their families, their memories, their hurts, their lessons, their traditions, their recipes, and their fried chicken wrapped in tinfoil along with them.

In *The Warmth of Other Suns*, Isabel Wilkerson describes with beautiful, detailed, soul-stirring precision the Great Migration, the period of time between 1910 and 1970 that saw many Blacks leaving their homes in the South for the urban cities of the North and the West Coast, heading to places like Chicago, like New York, like Los Angeles. By weaving the stories of those risking their lives and safety to start over and start anew, Wilkerson also captured the spirit of Blackness, from being stolen from our original homes to being beaten and enslaved in our new ones, to defiantly challenging the systems and leaving everything behind to find home again. We are a people born to remix, born to not only survive but to take the leavings and leftovers and to leave those things while bringing parts and pieces of those things with us over and over again. And in that leaving, in that changing and rearranging the lens of our departures, oh the guilt in knowing not everyone comes with you. They shared letters and postcards filled with love and pictures: new jobs and romances and babies and friends and neighbors. And in the letters, in the cards and love notes, were also the gaps, the unsaid things: how they missed the home cooking, how isolated they felt, how racism was still a thing no matter where they went or where they moved or who they fucked or who they worked for because their Blackness migrated with them—the one thing they could never leave behind even if they wanted to. The hidden hate that came in the checkout lines, in the sporting events, in the everybody-fend-for-yourself-ness that could occur in those pockets of communities outside of anything above or west of the Mason-Dixon Line. All of it called attention to the guilt of knowing that being Black and southern meant being closer to the root while being closer to the death that would surround it during the years when so many Blacks were looking for opportunities that existed outside of their home states. Having access to and securing the means to leave whatever home you left would take diligence, great timing, and at times take great luck and great pains to make happen. To be the one to "make it out" if you will, is like a badge of honor. It is a decree you shout from the mountaintops, breath full of air, out of exasperated lungs, "Look I made it out! I did it!" It is an accomplishment. It is seen as any way to leave your hood to grow from the concrete a fully bloomed rose that gets to explore the world and your role in it by any means necessary. Those means may require you to obtain work or some kind of financial status that will allow and afford you and your family the opportunity to move and migrate. When I think of the Great Migration, I also think of all the lives and loves altered, all the stories born in new places. It also begs the question of those "left" behind. Is staying just as hard as going?

My mother didn't stay in Dominica, a Dominica rich with resources and home to a family rich in love . . . and land. To let my mother tell it, in the village of Calibishie our family lived like kings. Grandpa was the most loving man you would ever meet, Mom would tell anyone willing to listen, over a pot of rice and peas or plated hors d'oeuvres of pigs in a blanket, cheese and crackers, and mini egg rolls. Goats, cows, pigs, fruit, vegetables, a restaurant . . . Grandpa would feed the family and the village. He was an owner and a businessman. Grandma tended to the household, ruling with a firm but loving fist. So when my mother got pregnant at nineteen and left the only home she knew with my eldest brother for the harsh winters of Boston, Massachusetts, to clean the floors of a white woman in order to gain her visa, it was in pursuit of an American dream she had heard of and sung about alongside Elvis Presley and other crooners whose songs told her about a kind of love and romance that only existed in the arms of slenderly built, well-dressed white men. She would come to know and cherish these songs she heard from her next-door neighbor playing the Top 40 on the radio not far from her own window, the same songs she still plays in her living room in the Bronx today. But my mom did not only leave for a dollar and a dream, she left for adventure. My mom gets that adventure on Fordham Road. Her bones and limbs may ache, her kidneys and glaucoma taking their toll, but my mother will still peruse Marshalls and the discount stores that stand now that Alexander's and Woolworth and Caldor are long gone, looking for random knickknacks to add to the collection she continues to house in her forever home. My mom has no guilt or shame about leaving Dominica. And my mom will never leave the Bronx, will never leave apartment 2C, no matter how much she eyes the co-op apartment on Mitchell Avenue. Years ago, my mother and Auntie KK would walk up and down the hills of Fordham Road, Auntie KK wanting to stop at every store on every block, gathering items for herself, for her children. And for the barrel or two she would be shipping back home. The barrel would take up space in our kitchen, week by week getting fuller and fuller until it was time to be picked up. I don't know if Aunty KK felt guilt about making the same kind of move my mother made, the same kind of move many made during the Great Migration—being the first settler of your community to start sending for others. My mother would house and feed my uncle Vincent, would house and feed Aunty KK and my cousins, would house and feed Aunty Rhona before she would move to Baton Rouge, Louisiana. She sent for my brother Kelvin first. Whatever guilt my mother, aunts, and uncles may have felt may have been washed away with the yearly visits back to the island. After their childhood home was accidentally burned down, my mother wanted no real part of the island. Home for her wasn't the island but the physical house built on it.

My father left home, too. He left Pensacola, Florida, his first home, to fight in the Vietnam War. I cannot ask him why he never returned to Pensacola, Florida, because my father is not alive to answer that question. My father would return to Pensacola after he and my mother divorced, but our kind of communication was the kind where a multitude of words were almost always left unspoken. I do know my father, along with his siblings, suffered abuse at the hands of my grandfather. It leads me to believe that my father enlisted because he needed to leave home, that he needed to find another means of shelter. Or maybe he just wanted to see the world. Maybe he really did think the Vietnamese were the enemy. I do know my father came home and suffered from night sweats and from post-traumatic stress disorder and would tell my mother after feverish nightmare upon feverish nightmare that he wasn't sure if he had murdered any children or not. But even if my father was alive and had the words needed to voice what made him leave his version of home, I doubt the words would have been many—my father's primary choice of language usually revolved around a cigar, a beer, or a hand. My father would sometimes write us letters when he was still living with Grandma in those years after he and Mom divorced, before he started splitting more and more of his time between Aunt Caroline's in the Bronx and the local bar around the way that he would frequent whenever his SSI check came or when he'd found an odd job to work or enough bottles and cans to gather together to deposit for recycling to gather some pocket change. In those letters, he would include a dollar and a message like, "Don't do drugs." The PSA was a warning my father was providing that at its core was him using as effective means as he had at his disposal to keep his children safe. I can say that now as an adult and a father who has more language than my deceased dad. But younger me would chuckle, slight disdain on my lips, guffawing at the thought that my almost always inebriated father felt like he had some sort of wisdom or knowledge he could bestow upon me that would be helpful. A part of me is mad I no longer have those letters. Or maybe I do have the letters and haven't looked hard enough, haven't trudged through the boxes upon boxes of essays, songs, poems, and journal entry notebooks sitting inside of my old bedroom in my old closet that my mom asks me to go through at least once a month. The funny thing about leaving where you came from is looking back at what and where you left and not remembering what parts of you or things of yours you left along with it.

My daughter had tears streaming down her face the night she walked into the guest room/office of her home with the big windows and large plants and told me she did not want to choose which home to live in—her home here in Brooklyn and her other home with her mother in Houston. I told her she did not need to choose, offering the same refrain I have offered her during the past four years since she transitioned from the Bronx to Houston and back to Brooklyn. I tell her she has love everywhere, homes everywhere: home with parents, grandparents, and cousins. I tell her this plenty. I am a good liar. Because we are asking her to choose every day. Every day as a long-distance co-parent, whether you are the one long distancing or dealing with the one who is, juggling the financial and emotional strain of managing a child and their expectations and their mighty heart with their mighty questions and their giant curiosity is undoubtedly asking said child to choose you, to choose a home. And to ask her to leave behind people and places each time there's a vacation, a school switch, or when a friend moves or a grandparent dies. Or a school shooting happens. Or she reads about slavery. Or learns why we're on Lenape land and asks why we have never seen any Lenape in Brooklyn. My daughter feels torn and I understand. Her homes are not about the physical places and spaces but about the people who inhabit them: her parents.

We all leave somewhere. We are all surviving something—a

loss, a broken thing needing to be amended; a grief so earth-
shattering the seismic rupture it causes in the body is enough
to bring in all the floods you forgot you kept: a broken promise,
a broken relationship, a broken home. We are all surviving for
something, for someone. We are all mourning a thing that is no
longer, a place we have left, even if that place is not a physical
place but merely an existential thing to be admired and fawned
over again and again in class photos and construction sites where
the last pieces of the awning, the last annals of the interior brick
walls are being demolished for a Starbucks or a wave of gentrifiers surfing along the coast of your corner, begging the bodega
to get rid of the beloved bodega cat because of allergies or gluten
intolerance or whatever else gentrifiers use to avoid the rash that
comes with sharing survivor blood with colonizers. The shame
we feel when we leave is forced upon us, the guilt a cape we are
given by those left behind—a fictional "those," a dead "those," a
still living in the moment and place you escaped "those." But their
shame is not wrong. When I go back to the Bronx, back to Fordham Road, my breath feels stiff, stifled by the food deserts, the
overwhelming police patrols and assaults, the thickness of the air
filled with the lack of resources and support, the lack of consid-
eration local and state government have for the needs and wants
of the people, and how it has always felt and remained so, that
is until white students at Fordham University began frequenting
the neighborhoods of the Bronx more often. The Fordham Plaza
I grew up around was a hub for all things healthcare related,
with a Sears rounding out the dental and medical offices that surrounded the first floor of the building. Now the plaza, along with
the town square that houses the Metro-North Railroad that lives
alongside it, offers up a TJ Maxx, a Starbucks, a Chipotle, movie

nights, and flea/food markets over summer weekends. To see my Bronx now is to see it with new eyes, but this could be easily compared to those who have left Bedford-Stuyvesant to come back to see ramen shops and French cuisine, smoothie shops, and artisan coffee, a far cry from the Bed-Stuy neighborhood Biggie rapped about on his albums. The displacement is real, the gentrification is high and mighty. Am I a gentrifier? As a born and raised New Yorker, I'd argue no. Some would say otherwise because of my tax bracket. I'm not sure of the right or wrong answer. There is nuance around every corner. But I do know that the guilt that comes with knowing others I grew up with who are not in the same position to leave as I am hurts. I also know the guilt of those who I maybe did not grow up with but who are in the same position to leave and haven't, also hurts. So I shop local as often and as much as possible. I talk to all my neighbors, in ways I was never allowed to as a young adult in the Bronx because we were too busy moving to the next store, the next job, and the next thing to keep us from remembering that we were being left behind. And then I left them behind too . . . maybe? I go back every couple of months and that is good I will tell myself. My kids are hard to travel with, I will tell myself. The train ride is too long I will tell myself. Again, I am still a good liar. The reality is every time I step off of the D train at Fordham Road, or the 4 train at Fordham Road, or the 2 train or B train or 5 train or 6 train or 13 bus or 1 bus or 2 bus or 36 bus or the 12 bus, I am reminded of all the ways I feel like I have let my borough down. So I scream it from the rooftops on every call, in every guest appearance on a stage or in a book, at every conference and every event, proudly stating I was born and raised in the Bronx and the Bronx is as much a part of my story as my mother and father, brothers and sister are.

But all of this is impermanent. This life is short, this living not as long as we wish or intend to be. It is impractical, it is unruly, and it is far from linear. Everything is changing, almost always at the same time—each breath, each step, each movement of the hand is simply us leaving one moment and heading into another. And in that impermanence maybe there is a semblance of peace, of hope. The idea is that we all change, will change, and the places we love change along with us. The change happens so gradually, though it may feel sudden. The wrinkles, the creases, the cracks in our bones, and the cracks in the concrete are synonymous with the ways everything here is moving, leaving and transitioning in some way, shape, or form. The truth is there should be no guilt in surviving. Because if we are truly surviving in the ways our elders and their parents and their ghosts may have wanted us to, we are carrying them with us. They come along with us in the wallet-size photos that nest beside our IDs; they sit in the email folders and boxes with the saved letters from jail stints; our people come with us everywhere we go even when we are not where they are, even when they are not here with us in the physical. The guilt is still heavy now, but not as weighted, not as strong. And this, too, I can wear like a badge, knowing that the Bronx walks with me everywhere I go, no matter how far that going may take me.

The Eulogy of Charles Lorenzo

Feat. Charles Lorenzo

I am not exactly sure what you are supposed to do when your father dies, especially if and when he dies like you expected him to. I suppose one talks to siblings. I left a voicemail for my sister. Her sweet southern-sounding voice makes everything sound like it is dipped twice in a something I know I am supposed to be fond of. At the moment I wrote that, I was still waiting to talk to her. I know I went about ignoring voicemails. Condolences make me tired, to be honest. It is the thing we are supposed to offer when we cannot deliver a pie or cake or dessert-type item to someone's door. I talked to my brother D about Charles this morning, and I could hear the faint distilling of trauma, of unhealed things peeking from out of our audio; he bear-hugs his weight, succumbs, and suffocates it well beyond its years—his poise under pressure is both familiar and unnerving. There are all these things that rattle unsaid when death arrives. I think about all the moments as brothers we shared fending off the demons we were too afraid to acknowledge to each other out loud. Dwain would build us forts for our bunk beds and hide under the blankets, lights off, us determined to find love in our sibling laughter. Even now I am waiting for his spine to burst and for me to hold him and those pieces together with my open hands and arms. He has seen sides of my father I knew both in theory and in reality . . . the parts that only the eldest son could love and loathe with equal measure.

Grieving in limbo is an interesting place—on one end you grieve what you never knew. You hanker and hunger, the want gnawing, a cantankerous affair in which you reimagine scenes with a father who couldn't daddy you the ways you probably wanted. But these scenarios generally don't play themselves out until I see Black men gush about their living fathers, or at least at the minimum, share photos with them as adults, a reconciled sort of love that I could never quite understand.

I felt it in my body, first. Deaths and births are somatic by nature—they are all about our bodies coming and going, for both the ones passing or entering and for the ones in charge of guiding them through both. Charles has always been a phantom limb to me—existing always but never present in a tangible way. Interestingly, I am closer to my father in death than I ever was. He is easier to love. I am kinder to him in spirit. Now we can talk. I tell him about my goals and dreams and don't have to wait for a reply. Me loving my father has always been a nonnegotiable. I loved him dearly. I loved my father like someone who loves a fictional character they see on their screens, or read about in their comic books. Not because my father was a superhero, but because he was unreal. What was open for discussion was how much I loved my father, and how much could that love exponentially expand if allowed the time and space to do so. Through that question, I was also able to see how I loved other Black men in my life. My relationship with my father was probably the best form of therapy I never knew I would need. To examine, to really examine the empty is an act of courage, and love in and of itself. We are most curious about the times in the world that have a chance to show us something new that exists within us. And that, to me, is love. And so even now when I think of my father I think of love. When D and I talk about Dad, when we do talk about Dad, it is no longer about the trauma, but what could have been and the moments that weren't suffocating our childhoods, but were hugging them, tirelessly. My father worked. His hands showed it. So did his feet. The wear and tear of the world wore mercilessly on his clothes, in his face. And it has nothing to do with scouring the family archives, talking to relatives to glean what else I can about my father's past and who he was. Because none of that matters without hearing it from him, in his voice. All of our lives in death are colored by the experiences of others, how others experienced us in the times they knew us. My father was not distant in the ways we think of distance to be, especially masculine distance—a cold affront meant to hide all the years of insufferable torment that comes from never truly being able to be free without the threatening gaze of another man trying to define manhood for you, or beat it into you or out of you, their own trauma a closed fist waiting to be undone. My father's stance was not for effect or raucous applause to be taped live in front of a studio audience. My father was bipolar. My father battled bouts of schizophrenia, returning to Vietnam or childhood in ways that would make him forcibly violent. I would tell my older sister, Tanja, a devout Christian, strong runner, and even stronger southerner, years after we had met and I became a father and adult in a way that humbles the candor you get to share with older siblings, that she spent a lifetime running to find our father while us Daniels boys spent our lives trying to run from him. Even when my father played monster in the house, it always felt real. Not in the ways I imagine my daughters run from me—with glee on their faces; a sacred kind of chase that happens when your children feel safe enough to both cry and laugh in your arms. I ran from my father because I never knew what kind of monster would be waiting on the other side if he caught me. Because of this, my big brother D and I learned so many things on our own. Our eldest brother, Skee, never knew his father. So here we are, lost boys floating upstream.

Who am I but my father's son? The things I loved most about myself lived in my father. The things I feared most, ran from and avoided, ducked and dodged and drank my way in and out of, I found them in my father, too. Looking like Charles Lorenzo is inescapable. I am fortunate that my mother harbors nothing but love and genuine care for the man whose jawbone and cheeks and face bear the striking resemblance to my own. Everything I do has a little bit of my father in it: the way I wear my hats, the way I walk. The fact that I walk everywhere, the fact that I read everything. As a child, I would go to underline information in our encyclopedias only to find my father had beat me to it. And if there was pain, then our father would beat us through it until it was time to find a bar or something to smoke, or something or someone to hold on to that would make him feel whole again, like a man, like a human not void of feeling. My father was adept at swinging a sword/taking a swig, a practice I would hone, too, but with a pen instead. Black men use their dicks as armor. My father has died, and I don't know if I should sing or sink slowly into a wormhole; if I should sling crack or sling dick in his honor. The first time I learned what a blow job was, my father told D

and me outright after a visit, and while D laughed, I thought
my father was telling me at the age of eight that he was going
to work for a company that makes ceiling fans like the one we
had in our living room at the time. My father burned down the
home on Bronxwood Avenue that D, Skee, and my mama had
lived in, and for years my mom would retell the story, sharing how my father burned it down because he thought it was
an enemy bunker. Another part of the story: the Rod Stewart
"Do Ya Think I'm Sexy?" record that was lost in the fire along
with D's Spider-Man record player. Years would go by before D
would mention staying in the shelter and feeling sad to leave
the friends he had made there. Recently, a colleague of mine told
me about a stat she overheard: we are made up of 40 percent of
our parents' genetics, we just don't know which parent. I think
D and my father are similar in their 40 percent when it comes
to the pain hidden just below the surface, the unearthed trauma
sitting at the top of the chest, volcano-like, the molten lava alive
and bubbling, unspoken and hot to the brim of its core. Such an
interesting way to live.

You think everybody else is dying but your daddy. You
think everyone else is vacating but him. Mom tells the tale of
Dad's feet and how worn they were—he wore his combat boots
and still had some even after Vietnam. I still have his army bag
in her closet. I lost his leather jacket after I used it as a rehearsal
piece for scene study in high school. I was so negligent with
his things—his clothes, his story, his feelings. I was so angry
at him for making me visit his crackhead girlfriend in Pensacola. I knew she was a crackhead because he prefaced it before
I met her. At fourteen, all I could do was sigh and silently judge
him. My father recorded a song on tape about a friend of his

who died due to AIDS-related symptoms. The song was titled "Crying About You." I remember because my cousin and I had to fight back our laughter. I look back now and I cringe because I can see how much my father was reaching for me in the only ways he knew how, and how unreceptive I was to it all.

When D, Tanja, and I went to see my father in 2017, he was a ward of the state of Florida. One of my uncles, also suffering some type of mental health disorder, missed payments on their home in Pensacola. The house was soon to be foreclosed, forcing Mama D, my grandmother and the cornerstone of the Daniels family, to vacate. My father needed a village to take care of him, and with that village spread out and dispersed, the state of Florida became his legal guardian. By that point, my father was suffering from dementia. I lost my phone—while we walked during the early hours of the evening, I dropped it on the beach and it was washed away by the ocean. The day my father passed, I dropped my phone, the screen broken beyond repair. My MacBook's battery completely died. So many things meet their end energetically whenever I am dealing with my father. I think about a lot of the moments I never shared with my father and how I had more language to at least uncover what I didn't know, the language to ask the questions that would more than likely lead to more questions. Language gives us permission. And there was a language my father spoke, a language of trauma that was weathered and worn and had been mastered and undone at the same juncture. It is a language I am still learning today. Language that my father never got the chance to sift through or be held by. Now, I speak freely in podcasts and interviews about the idea of breaking binaries, of removing ourselves from this unhealthy attachment to what gender roles are to look like. My father fought in Vietnam to get away from his father I imagine. It also allowed him to run from the demons that chased him until his dying day.

You don't wake up on a Monday morning expecting to hear that your father is dying. But I already knew I wouldn't be going to Florida for his funeral. I said this after I downed half a liter of raspberry ginger ale in less than a day, nonchalantly ignoring Dr. Kim's prediabetes warning issued to me in his whiter-than-white office over the summer. After this, I kill the army of ants that have decided to move into our kitchen in Bed-Stuy to taunt and test my once-declared Buddhist mission to avoid harming creatures. I am talking and sending voice notes and hearing what sounded like sobbing behind messages, and drowning a little bit, too. I was drowning listening to my mother tell me how tired she was and what she had to do for us to save a little bit of herself before my father would swallow it up along with us, too. D and I sent each other photos the day of our daddy's funeral—we were both wearing Chuck Taylors in honor of him—D's were black and mine were yellow. D was in Florida and I was in New York at Rockwood Music Hall, performing with one of my best friends, Arthur Lewis. We had booked the gig several months in advance before my father had fallen in his nursing home. The date of his funeral and the date of my show felt like a strange kind of alignment that I wanted to trust. I got to honor my father with friends and strangers, evoking his name in between songs, a prayer to be shared.

My father didn't talk. And even now that I am thinking of him, I wish I would have kept somewhere the letters he had sent us. But my father and I were never close enough for me to see sentiment in those things. My oldest daughter, Lilah, has her folder in our home of the pictures she's drawn that we've saved. I want her to remember that I remembered her always. My father's disability didn't leave him room for such eccentricities. I remember one Christmas being excited about an SSI check my father would be getting that would help to afford me the Power Rangers set I had been dreaming of. And secretly I hoped my father would give me the money and allow my mother and me to shop on our own or, even better, me going to one of the toy stores on Fordham Road and getting it on my own. When the amount my father promised me was smaller than expected, it was a reminder to never expect too much from him. But even in that memory, I am also forced to reckon with the idea that maybe I misheard my father. Or maybe it didn't matter at all. I would soon receive an SSI check each month until I was eighteen because of my father's service in the military.

I hear other Black men share stories of their fathers: redemptive stories, cautionary tales, episodic adventures, and humorous recalls that are pulled from loving and kind memories. Everything that is the relationship between my father and me is me filling in the gaps and spaces with what I wish was there, the holes as empty as the beer glasses he drank from. All the periods and commas in his slurred, drunken speech or his sober silence are all me insinuating what lay between them or what is to follow.

Sloppy. I remember that the most; the moistness of it, how the saliva would stick to my forehead long after it landed, the wet becoming dry, and the nagging fear that would make itself present when the thought crossed my mind to take the back of my hand to wipe it away. He would kiss my forehead and the saliva would smell like Philly blunt wrap and Budweiser beer cans; no beard, all mustache. His feet—jagged little claws, combat boot heavy, the Vietnam stuck in his gums, hands; a receding hairline and a memory of hand slaps. For a second you forget a hand can feel like water, like breakfast. Or that you hate cashews because your father hated them. Maybe you ask why you hate the things he loved, loathe the things he craved. Charles loved sugar water, and Hershey's with almonds. Even now typing, writing, and thinking about all of these things connects all the dots for me. Before my father passed, the last time I saw him at home was in 2008, after he hitchhiked to the Bronx from Manhattan to see my mother. My mother, knowing my father was having a mental health episode. It was in the Bronx Veterans Hospital in the psych ward that I would see him. The last time I could remember seeing my dad's face was in the mug shot of him, arrested after burning down an abandoned home in Florida. I kept the newspaper clipping with his picture taped to the inside of my closet door for years. In the psych ward, I would be searched. I brought my father quarters for the pay phone on his floor, a cherry Coke, and a Hershey's bar with almonds. My father was on medications. My father did not like being on medications. And I could tell—he was quiet, reserved. Whatever version of self my father was, this was not that. The Charles I remembered would fart and laugh, would drink sugar water, would buy and bring me an extra cheese pizza with sausage every Friday, right before *Super Mario Brothers* on Fox 5 would start at 4:30 P.M., when he got his SSI check. The same Charles who my mother would recall would pull flowers from gardens to bring to my mother when he didn't have money; the same Charles who would bring me random trinkets like Spalding tennis balls whenever he would pick cans in the neighborhood for money. The same Charles who was also known as deejay Dapper Dan spun records on the local radio station in his heyday. Staring at this man dressed in all white, in an all-white room, him smelling like Ivory soap, all the while hearing the screams and yelling of patients, was a spectacle I couldn't prepare for. My mother was used to these trips, visiting my father, with my brother D straddling her hip, to either get him out or to visit him. If I would have known that then, maybe I would have treated the visit differently. Maybe not. I don't have the language for that, even now.

The day Lilah started kindergarten in August 2021 was the same day I found out my father would be transitioning. But to be honest, my father has always been transitioning . . . we all are. It almost feels as if my father has always been dying, though. I have been preparing for my father's death for years. While trauma and suffering are relative, my father suffered more than most. And the suffering was worn like a badge, like a medal, like a prosthetic limb to be carried and held. At times quiet and loud, boisterous and dangerous, loving and brave, my father also was a homemade bomb waiting to happen. Drafted to the U.S. Army in 1968, he was a decorated Vietnam veteran who earned a Bronze Star and was honorably discharged in 1970. He would often reminisce to my mother that he was never sure if he murdered any children while on active duty. At seventy-two, he died of natural causes, but I would argue Charles Lorenzo Daniels died because of a broken heart. My father suffered from dementia, bipolar II disorder, and post-traumatic stress disorder, effects not only from the war but also from his childhood, growing up in a still very segregated Pensacola, Florida, community as a Black man in the fifties and sixties. I would argue Charles died because he was tired of living; died because a system meant to provide and serve him neglected him from the moment he was born. I'd argue he died because as a Black man in America, he was long taught to prepare for his death long before it happened.

When Virgil Abloh passed, I thought of my father. I think many of us did. I think many of us, as a Black community and especially as Black men, thought of all the other Black men we know and love—our friends, fathers, our brothers, and ourselves. Because to know Blackness is to know death, as close to us as breath is to being. Virgil, a fashion designer and icon, died at forty-one from cardiac angiosarcoma, a rare type of cancer. For two years Virgil hid his diagnosis from the public, a story far too similar to that of actor Chadwick Boseman, who died from colon cancer in 2020, following his diagnosis in 2016. Their silence about their struggles, a shattering kind of quiet. My father does not have a Wikipedia page, but his story, too, would read in a similar way—not because of the cause of death, but due to the silence that permeates and stalks the rooms and communities of those who share air, space, and lifetimes with the Black men we have lost too soon.

What exactly is premature death? How do we conclude that life has left before its time? What is the time frame in which a life is considered to be too short to be considered worthy of remembrance? No one knows when they are going to die. But as Black men, we do know we will die sooner than most, our dying being a direct result of the many factors that play a role in us leaving this planet earlier than expected. According to the Brookings Institution, Black men die four years earlier than white men. There is no crystal ball, no soothsayer, no psychic hotline, no palm reading or tarot card, that can absolve us from the unknown that awaits on the other side of this living. But as

Black men, we are not only prone to be scared of death but are also literally scared *to* death, a life that is constantly in peril, being in the presence of trauma, realizing the dangers of our existence. We see ourselves played out in every hospital visit, every eerie emergency room stay, every deathbed, every encounter with law enforcement or too long of a stare; every media camera rolling the final credits of our last breaths.

What was it like to be Virgil, in those two years? Was he counting the clock, the minute hand meeting glorious, terrifying hours like my father did? Like I do from time to time. A study by JAMA Network reports Black males had the highest increase in suicide attempts compared to any other race, increasing nearly 80 percent. I've struggled not only with suicidal ideations but also with an undying fear unlike that of my own imminent death. This is the fear of not being enough or too much or the even scarier unknown in between that exists between Black life and the death that we as Black men see and feel peeking around the proverbial corner in our day-to-day lives. Because Blackness itself is a condition of the heart when living in a world that is slowly trying to kill you in as many ways as humanly possible. The National Library of Medicine found that everyday and perceived racism along with internalized masculinity norms influenced Black men's reluctance to seek medical help. It's also why on average, depressed African American men are significantly less likely to seek help compared with depressed white men. Our masculinity, and the fragility surrounding the ego it upholds, keeps us from asking for and receiving the help we need.

In 2017, the CDC reported the top four leading causes of death for Black men were: heart disease, cancer, unintentional injuries, and homicide. In the summer of 2021, I finally went to see my doctor. Maybe I wanted to eliminate any of the four. Maybe I just knew it was time, because it was the first time I had gone to see a primary care physician in over twenty years—I'm currently thirty-eight. After Chadwick Boseman died in 2020, understanding that African Americans are about 20 percent more likely to get colorectal cancer and about 40 percent more likely to die from it than most other groups, I sifted through tweets of other Black men, seeking others who were feeling their own pending mortality like I was. My good friend, acclaimed author Frederick Joseph, shared a tweet where he describes a conversation he had with Boseman. In that tweet, I first learned my friend was dealing with multiple sclerosis. It is in this chasm of both enduring strength and the impending danger ever present in our lives that I also see a common thread: silence. We grieve and at times even die, in silence.

Did DMX feel death biting at his neck while talking to his daughter on the roller coaster? The audio of his soothing her cries while they're being thrown round and about on a theme park ride was later used by Kanye West for his *Donda* album, dedicated to the mother he, too, lost prematurely. That roller coaster that rapper Earl Simmons was on can be seen as a metaphor for the ride that the Black male body is constantly sitting on—forever being thrown about by law enforcement, by school systems that label us before our mouths are open; by healthcare systems that refuse to see us beyond our Blackness. In findings from a 1998 Aspen Institute research paper, of the African American men in some poor urban areas, two-thirds of fifteen-year-old Black males cannot expect to survive to age sixty-five. This number is representative of less than half the probability of survival to age sixty-five of white males nationwide. The deaths of actor Michael K. Williams, rapper Nipsey Hussle, and, recently, slain rapper Young Dolph, paint a clear picture of Black male death in the ways that live outside of terminal illness unless we consider socioeconomic discrepancies such as suffering school systems, lack of quality access to affordable mental health and medical care, as terminal. There are many causes of death for us, for to be a Black man in a Black man's body is to be subjected to an everyday violence that exists when your mere presence enables fear in the lives of others.

My sister, Tanja, said talking about mortality—about our daddy—would bring "peace, real peace, not perfumed over." Death and our grief over it have a way of stealing the taste of the world from us, clouding and crowding the senses we hold dear. I wonder if every Black man who dies in the public eye will make me think of my father. It probably will. I think about my father now more than I ever did while he was alive. That may sound cold to some. But for me, it's freeing to know that my father is free now, too. I hope that those thoughts will not linger in silence but will instead be as audible and as loud as my father's cries for help that went unheard. Will be shrill shrieks that awaken us all, that make us pay attention to the Black men who never had enough time, but should have.

Charles Lorenzo Daniels was my daddy, and I loved him in the ways I knew how. I like to believe he loved me the same. Love is complicated. Life and love are, too. I am everything and nothing like my father. It took me years to become okay with that. I am thinking about legacy more, now that I am turning forty soon, thinking about it in a bit more of a masculine way than I have been accustomed to. A lot has to do with the passing of my father. Mainly because I am seeing the world through the eyes of someone who can no longer see for himself. It feels like I am bearing witness to two souls now instead of one. And because of that, I am ever more cognizant of the kind of world I want to shape for my two little girls and the kind of world I would want them to inhabit when I am gone, primarily because I don't think anyone was doing that for my father. I am living all of my father's lives, I think. I write for him, his ghost. Sometimes we think our daughter West sees my father in the house. I like to think that's true in some way. That with each chill in a room, with each victory lap, his spirit is somewhere beside me dancing. I often say I put my foot on the neck of America for my father. I say his name in interviews, invoking him, calling him, and forcing others to call him out, too. I want everyone to grieve for him. In that grief, there is room for joy, for celebration, too. My father is finally free. And so am I.

Our Poetry Will Save the World

Everything in the world feels like it is burning. This is not Burning Man, a new TV show, a diet infomercial—we are all in this boat we had no plan to be in, watching the shore and wondering . . . what next? The questions we ask, all clinging to answers tied to science, rooted in vaccinations, in GoFundMes and donation pledges. Our faith has left office and now sits with R&B singers and Hollywood power couples.

We are dancing for salvation, painting for salvation. We are performing and doing acrobatics in our living rooms, holding handstands. We are in our churches, masks over our noses, praying for a Bible to come from the front row with a benediction, thinking it will rain on us; an offering at our feet so thick, so deep in pedagogy, that it will misdirect whatever is falling from the sky. In all of this, we can see the religion beautifully encrusted in the hands of the artist, the ones who are alive when things like government, like AIDS, like COVID, like atom bombs and Jim Crow and internment camps, tell us to stay home. When concentration camps and bickering between parties become podcast press. In these times, art has been the beacon. Right there, lying on the surface of it all, is a poem. There is a poem in everything.

I have seen it happen often—the scattering of words that happens when we have been afforded the time to be amongst all of the dreary. The days get to bend with poems, they get to take shape in our hands, into specially crafted molds that take everything we find insufferable and put it into a language, into a context we get to understand on our own terms and embrace.

This is where the poem ends and we begin.

I have read poems about suffrage, about Pokémon, poke bowls, about bowel movements, about hand sanitizer and couch cushions, about being comfy and being a cougar, about being a coon, about being negligent, about rape, about race, about radical love—all those poems have a reason to live, to exist.

When the world became cold, poems and their affable words still resonated. Still pictures of us borderline everything on the *DSM* scale, but making it poetry. People are dying. They are hurting while worried about their futures, about their pensions and the pennies never saved, the voice notes never sent . . . How can they reconcile that? We all are wrought, all ducking the drowning that happens when the drought is over, and the overboard becomes as heavy and weighty as the idea of floating away. It is then that we can pick up the dusty pen and notepads and search for the meaning behind whatever is shaking us down.

Because we are all poets; we are all alchemists; we all have a poem lingering, wistful and watery, buoying us through the tough and tranquil; through the trough and trials of being a martyr and just a speck of matter on a glass. Every poem I have loved started in a person first, and that has made me want to see the world differently. This has made me want to hold my daughters higher than the sky could ever permit. Poems allow us the luxury to do that.

When I was poor, poems made me feel as if I didn't have to *be*. That having no money would never matter, because of my voice; my voice with its rhyme, reason, and color. All of the joy that truly binds us together is gently being seen in the margins of the poem. We can look at the dust on the blinds, the curtain drapes, and the luster that happens when the sun comes in just before your afternoon drip coffee runs.

I've seen poems happen—in elevators when no one thought anyone was looking; poems scribbled in bold on the tongues of strangers; in headphones inaudible. Poems dragged to the front of the bookshelf by the back of their hardcover spines. The prettiest of pretty poems I saw in high school in English class. The first time I heard *pixie* and *fairy* used in anything but a Disney show was out the mouth of a white girl named Anastasia—her language was Dylan and Fiona and grunge; it was dirt under nails and the balls of her feet and sweet clementine on the palate.

The first time I heard Carlos Gómez talk about words as weapons, as Gaza, as Palestine, as borders, I knew flesh was incomparable to script. Saul Williams made me want to slam everything—my notebook, my job, my father, my abuser, my exes, presidents, city council persons. Nikki Giovanni made me want to call my mother, to fuck everything, to be a Black man like the ones I saw in Jim Brown's pupils. Sonia Sanchez wanted me to make love, to make planets, to make my bed, but with ginger instead of blankets. Jack Kerouac made me want to learn American. Allen Ginsberg made me want to be un-American. Common told me rap is a chapbook. All the poems were all different—as different as my classmates, as my bullies, as the gang colors we memorized in the backs of our composition notebooks, the ones with the multiplication tables, by the metrics.

We would mutilate ourselves with poems. We would remember our slave masters with poems. We would cry to R&B songs, talk to hummingbirds, travel to palm trees, rub palm oil on everything with poems. Poems taught us how to talk to girls, how to talk nonbinary, how to bring someone to your mother; how to learn the way your mother crocheted her way through life; made a machete out of all the moons they could. All of these poems mattered to me. They matter to us, now more than ever.

Every poem is an opportunity to reexamine what we are pulled toward, what we are trained to see, what triggers them to shoot at us first and read rights later. All poems—tiny poems about humans, about ponies, peonies; things hinged on what we will opine about later. Ugly poems, bright poems, big poems, small poems . . . all confronting problems, as contorted as those problems may be, and holding them up to the light. Poems have pierced our ears, have nursed our parents. When I wanted to die, I wrote a poem. Then I wrote more poems. Then I read poetry. And even the things that didn't make sense, reset themselves. Poetry has saved my life, has saved many lives. That has not changed and will not change.

Please. Write all the poems now. And often. Break them open with your teeth, with a pen. Take them from the pit of the stomach and shout them out, make them loud. Poetry will be our greatest soundtrack, our ears to the streets; soapboxes replete with box sets of the latest and greatest from street corner church revivers, from porno turned photo all-stars, from those that study genetics and the laws of tea and pottery.

Poets grow stems, do STEM research, make masks, wear masks for safety, for optical illusions; do makeup tutorials; get titty lifts; deadlift essays; and shine shoes. Poets will clean from windows, practice hang-time, hang themselves from balconies, from branches, will hang their art on their cars, on their graves, on their teacher's tombstone. A poem is a dancer, a seed in a pomegranate, the eruptions in Pompeii. Poems, they are pompous, derivative of the bourgeoisie and the burdened. Poems are about pussy, about politics, about anonymous people and the private parts they love. The world is changing. Poems are not. Poems, still deified, still dying, still dripping in the sweat of ancestors.

Poems are slaying dragons. They are saving us, even still. Our poetry will save the world.

Acknowledgments

When I was a kid, one of my favorite parts of listening to an album was taking out the CD booklet and reading the thank-yous. It's where I learned the names of artists, of producers; the names had meaning, added context and weight to the music. So you would listen to a B.I.G. verse and he would mention C-Gutta and you would see the name in the thank-yous, and in those notes a reference would be made to the depths of their relationship. The thank-yous connected the dots. They told me I had like three to four pages so I was like fuck it, we gonna keep this real hip-hop and I'ma just thank everybody who has loved me, guided me, taught me, comforted me, and made me feel safe and seen. Because you only get one first book. And who knows what happens after this, but I know that I'm pretty damn proud of me, word to Uncle Snoop.

So, thank you to the ones who paved the way—Heavy D, Kid 'n Play, MC Hammer, Busta Rhymes, Das EFX, Poor Righteous Teachers, Biz Markie, Black Rob, G. Dep, Trouble T Roy, Tupac, MC Breed, Bönz Malone, Michael Eric Dyson, Amiri Baraka, David Foster Wallace, Charles Bukowski, Ta-Nehisi Coates, Cheo

Hodari Coker, Selwyn Seyfu Hinds, Danyel Smith, Mimi Valdez, Kim Osorio. Shout-out to the *Source*, *XXL*, *Slam*, *Ego Trip*, *Scratch*, *Right On!*, *Jet*, *Ebony*, *Video Soul*, *Rap City*, MTV Jams, *TRL*, *Video Music Box* . . . all the media I took in that taught me everything about hip-hop and my place in the world. Scott La Rock, KRS-One, Grandmaster Caz, Fat Joe, Kool Herc, Big Daddy Kane, Rakim, bell hooks, Audre Lorde, Sonia Sanchez, Nikki Giovanni, D'Angelo, André 3000, Yasiin Bey, De La Soul, LL Cool J, Biggie, Diddy, Nelson George, Greg Tate, James Baldwin, Kiese Laymon, Eve Ewing, Allen Ginsberg, Jack Kerouac, Miles Davis, John Coltrane, Frank Ocean, Jay-Z, Kool G Rap, Scarface, Nipsey Hussle, Kanye West, Sugar Hill Gang, Sylvia Rhone, Roxanne Shante, MC Lyte, Lauryn Hill, Queen Latifah, Tweet, Common, ATCQ, Stretch Armstrong, Bobbito, Kid Capri, Droop, Ron G, Supa Sam, Dirty Harry, Ralph McDaniels, Chuck Chillout, Crazy Sam, N.O.R.E., Big Pun, Young Thug, Snoop Dogg, Dr. Dre, Warren G., Nate Dogg, E-40, Mobb Deep, Little Brother, Jazmine Sullivan, Aretha Franklin, Donny Hathaway, Al Green, Michael Jackson, Otis Redding, Beyoncé, Usher, Big L, Buckwild.

Shout-out to my New York City public school education and the teachers who guided my footsteps: Ms. Chow, Ms. Miller, Ms. Weinberg, Ms. Robinson, Ms. Piotrowski (without you I don't audition for LaGuardia. I don't trust my acting ability. I owe you so much), Ms. DeMarco, Ms. Eisner, Mr. Kurtz, Ms. Ruiz, Mr. Plaustino, Mr. Yusim (you gave me tools for acting I still carry with me), Ms. Nagel, Mr. Shifman, Mr. Moody (you asked us, "What did you learn today?" And I ask my daughters the same question now. You were the first Black man I saw on TV who I also saw in real life), Ms. Pearce, Mr. L, Ms. Winnick (you were a life vest when I needed it), Carla Stockton (I am so blessed to have you as a guide).

Shout-out to the ones who were in some way, shape, or form a part of the journey: Torae, Skyzoo, Vega Benetton, Kil Ripkin, Stephen Joseph (my first studio engineer), Chaundon, Kenn Starr, Emilio Rojas, E$$O, Oddisee, Tanya Morgan, 6th Sense, Wildabeast, Elisabet Velasquez, Carlos Gomez, Jeary Selves, Tre DeJean, Archie Green, Kevin Nottingham, T. Hemingway, Albert Rivera, Cory and Christian, David G, Franchesca HoSang, Jessica Ortiz, Jennifer Drayer, Dee, Tristan, Garnett, Dar, Quincy, Kimberly Bowser. To Dari, thank you for being a teacher. We created Lilah together and I am forever grateful to you for such a gift. RIP Cameron Gunther—you left here and it was sad but every time I see the sun I think of you. RIP Michael Latt. There was so much we were supposed to do and never got to. I thought we had time. Silly me. I'ma see you on the other side. Until then, I'ma keep honoring your name through the art, I promise.

Thank you to the Creston crew and beyond: Biggs, Boola, Ed, Jay, Mike Boogs. Elvis, Travis, Trevor, Tony, Tee Tee, Rich, Selwyn, Pookie, Ratchet. And thank you Buc—I take you with me everywhere I go. You never got to leave Creston, bro. But this book will be everywhere. So you'll be everywhere, too. I miss you, fam.

Shout-out to the Black men who I get to navigate life with: Michell Clark; Rob Hill Sr.; Kyle Jones; Tre DeJean; Jeary Selves; Eric Mosley; Frederick Joseph; Robert Jones Jr.; Tareq; my nephew Justin Daniels; my nephews Isaiah, Sean Jr., Tomas, and Isaac; Archie Green; Cyrus Aaron; Marc Lamont Hill; Jeff Johnson; Michael Hugh Tonge; Joshua Kissi; Anthony Demby; Bobby Rogers; LeMar McClean; DeSean McClinton; and so many more. Thank you all for being in community with me.

Thank you to Black women. To the Black women who have loved me, who have allowed me to love them. More importantly, thank you to the Black women who carved out a space for me, held me, and listened and loved me when I didn't have the language yet to better love myself: Mahogany Browne, EbonyJanice, Rachel Cargle, Sade Ayodele (for always being the bravest Black woman in the room), Drew Dixon, Tanisha Sykes, Aunty KK (RIP), Hyacinth aka Woodsie (RIP), April Reign, Angela Nissel, Cali Green, God-Is Rivera, Christine Platt, Chrissy King. Thank you Kirstyn Nimmo for all those talks. Thank you to Tia Mowry, to Jamira Burley, to Kimberlé Crenshaw, to Derecka Purnell, to Julie Wenah; to Rachel Ricketts, to Michelle Saahene, to Tarana Burke, to the countless Black women and femmes who have shaped, formed and informed my thoughts and theories on Black love and Black liberation.

Thank you to Ashley Simpo, my favorite writer. Thank you to Zola Ellen, my favorite abolitionist. Thank you to Qimmah Saafir, my favorite creative. Thank you to Tyron Perryman, my favorite Black man and friend. Thank you to Tiffany Rose, my favorite alchemist. Thank you to Jon Braman, my favorite white friend (lol). Thank you to Arthur Lewis, my favorite voice. Thank you Karlie Hustle, my favorite cancer survivor (who is WAY more than a cancer survivor). Thank you, Geneva, my favorite director. And thank you Kerry and Grace and the Faherty team for seeing my magic. Thank you, Brianna Bishop, for taking a chance. Thank you, Sean Zepps, for taking a chance. Thank you, Ian Schafer, for taking a chance. Thank you to Tony Signore for taking a chance, and for showing up in love for me and the fam like you have over the years. Thank you, Kristen Rock, for taking a chance. Thank you, Sharon Salzberg, for being my spiritual teacher when I didn't know I needed one. Thank you to Craig at Bottlecap Press—the first publisher to see the vision and support it. Major thank you to Felicia Megan Gordon and *Those People*—the first place I really started to hone in on the language that would show itself in this book. Thank you, Felicia, for seeing in me what I wanted so many to see, too.

Thank you, Dwain, for the lessons, for the love, for the studio time you paid for, for the nights you shared your food when there wasn't any, for taking me to Nathan's to play arcade games, for teaching me how to dress for the first day of school, for playing all the songs that would shape my future—this book doesn't happen without you, D. To Skee, I'm so proud of you. The game didn't take you out. The system tried to. But you're still here. Look at how far you've come. Thank you for the White Castle late nights. Thank you Justin, for being a nephew but also a younger brother and like my right arm. Thank you, Tanja, for providing me wisdom, love, and guidance when I was still learning myself.

To my team at Folio Literary and Henry Holt: Katherine and Sonali—thank you for believing in the work, guiding the work, and trusting the work and my voice. Let's write all the books and tell all the stories. Thank, you Retha Powers—from the moment we hopped on Zoom to talk about the book I knew it would be you to help bring this book into the world. Thank you for seeing the vision. Thank you to Leela Gebo, thank you to Shelly Perron. Thank you to the design and marketing team at Holt.

To my mama, Linda T., I learned love from you, first. Before bell hooks, before any poem or poet or song or hymn or verse, it was you, Ma. Always you. I pay my debt back in how I try to spread the message of love you taught me so effortlessly to others. To my two fires: to Lilah, my firstborn, you taught me love in the purest sense of the word. My journey to understanding myself started with you. This book does not happen without you. My TED

Talk doesn't happen without you. My first book through Bottlecap Press doesn't happen without you. Your gifts are immeasurable. To West, potentially my greatest teacher. Thank you for teaching me patience. Thank you for your curiosity, for pushing me to be a better father, a better human, a better Buddhist. Thank you for refining me over and over again. Thank you for choosing me to shepherd you on your journey. I cannot wait to see who you choose to be.

And to Bria, my love. Thank you for choosing me, for choosing us, over and over again. If this book is a labor of love, your labor and heart is a part of this story. Our chapter is my favorite. I want you to soar. You still are the freest Black woman I know. I am lucky to love you. I am blessed to love you. Thank you for teaching me liberation in the most spirited sense possible and imaginable. We are untraditional in every sense and I would not want it any other way. I never needed a ride or die. We are riding, flying, gliding toward whatever the next thing may be on this journey. As a mother, as a partner, as a co-parent and friend, you are the prototype.

And to you, the reader, if you've gotten this far, thank you. Do remember, Black masculinity gets to be all-encompassing—firm, soft, vulnerable, present. And we get to affirm each other in all the ways humanity has afforded us. To deny any parts of the human experience for Black men also denies us the opportunity to be fully human. I've waited a lifetime for this. I hope this offering serves as a reminder that you can be all the things you desperately want to be. I love you.